Johann Hermann Heinrich Schmidt, John Williams White

An Introduction to the Rhythmic and Metric of the Classical Languages

To which are added the lyric parts of the Medea of Euripides and the Antigone of Sophocles, with rhythmical schemes and commentary

Johann Hermann Heinrich Schmidt, John Williams White

An Introduction to the Rhythmic and Metric of the Classical Languages
To which are added the lyric parts of the Medea of Euripides and the Antigone of Sophocles, with rhythmical schemes and commentary

ISBN/EAN: 9783744797603

Printed in Europe, USA, Canada, Australia, Japan

Cover: Foto ©Thomas Meinert / pixelio.de

More available books at **www.hansebooks.com**

AN

INTRODUCTION

TO THE

RHYTHMIC AND METRIC

OF THE

CLASSICAL LANGUAGES.

TO WHICH ARE ADDED

THE LYRIC PARTS OF THE MEDEA OF EURIPIDES AND THE
ANTIGONE OF SOPHOCLES, WITH RHYTHMICAL
SCHEMES AND COMMENTARY.

BY

DR. J. H. HEINRICH SCHMIDT.

TRANSLATED FROM THE GERMAN, WITH THE AUTHOR'S SANCTION,

BY

JOHN WILLIAMS WHITE, Ph. D.,
ASSISTANT PROFESSOR OF GREEK IN HARVARD UNIVERSITY.

BOSTON:
PUBLISHED BY GINN, HEATH, & CO.
1883.

PREFACE.

Dr. Schmidt's "Leitfaden in der Rhythmik und Metrik der Classischen Sprachen," of which this book is a translation, was issued in 1869 from the press of F. C. W. Vogel at Leipzig. It is a compendious statement for the use of schools of the principles established in his larger work, " Die Kunstformen der Griechischen Poesie und ihre Bedeutung," the first volume of which had already been published when the "Leitfaden" appeared. The four volumes of the larger work are the following : —

"Die Eurhythmie in den Chorgesängen der Griechen. Allgemeine Gesetze zur Fortführung und Berichtigung der Rossbach-Westphalschen Annahmen. Text und Schemata sämmtlicher Chorika des Aeschylus. Schemata sämmtlicher Pindarischer Epinikien." Leipzig. F. C. W. Vogel. 1868. Pages xxiv, 429. Large 8vo.

"Die antike Compositionslehre, aus den Meisterwerken der griechischen Dichtkunst erschlossen. Text und Schemata der lyrischen Partien bei Sophokles und Aristophanes." Leipzig. F. C. W. Vogel. 1869. Pages xx, 532, CCCLXXV. Large 8vo.

"Die Monodien und Wechselgesänge der attischen Tragödie. Text und Schemata der lyrischen Partien bei Euripides." Leipzig. F. C. W. Vogel. 1871. Pages xxx, 170, DXXXVII. Large 8vo.

"Griechische Metrik." Leipzig. F. C. W. Vogel. 1872. Pages xxii, 680. Large 8vo.

Dr. Schmidt, now Oberlehrer in the gymnasium at Wismar, Mecklenburg, began to study in a special way the subject so fully presented in the volumes just named in 1866. He had previously undertaken the study of Greek "Synonymik" and "Tropologie," but found it impossible to proceed without first making a careful investigation of Greek Rhythmic and Metric. The results of that investigation are the four volumes of the "Kunstformen," and the "Leitfaden." He then gave in two gymnasium programmes, the one of Husum and the other of Wismar, specimens of what he proposed to do in "Synonymik" and "Tropologie," and has since published the following:—

"Synonymik der griechischen Sprache." Vol. I. Leipzig. Teubner. 1876. Pages xvi, 663. Large 8vo.

"Synonymik der griechischen Sprache." Vol. II. Leipzig. Teubner. 1878. Pages xvi, 648. Large 8vo.

Dr. Schmidt's investigations in Rhythmic and Metric have caused much discussion. From the first he has had the support of Professor K. Lehrs, of Königsberg, and he has besides many warm adherents, whose number is constantly increasing. There is much in which he agrees with Rossbach and Westphal, not a little in which he departs from their conclusions. Acknowledging the great work which they had done in their study of the ancient writers on Rhythmic and Metric, he proceeded, using these results, to establish a system founded mainly upon the actual study of the Greek poets themselves. In pursuance of this he worked through Pindar ten times, and then as many times through the choruses of Aeschylus, Sophocles, Euripides, and Aristophanes. Not until then did he begin to formulate the principles which he found to prevail in the composition of these great works of art. Such a method must recommend itself to honest investigators.

It would not be proper to make a special argument here in support of Dr. Schmidt's system. The most satisfactory test of his theories will be to apply them. Then it will be seen how clear he has made much that has heretofore been uncertain. All who have laboriously read Rossbach and Westphal will be grateful that he has brought a difficult subject down from the clouds and made it easily comprehensible even by beginners.

This translation was made in 1874 conjointly by Professor Dr. Karl Riemenschneider, of German Wallace College, and myself. Dr. Riemenschneider, whose rare scholarship is equalled only by his modesty, refuses to let his name be put upon the title-page, because he has done so little in the general undertaking. But those days when we were at work together are pleasant days to me to look back upon, and I am much more confident that this is a good translation than I should be if he had not helped me make it. The manuscript was afterwards revised by Dr. Schmidt himself, who made some changes and a number of additions. Since then it has been twice revised by myself and finally sent to press. The proofs have been read by Professor W. W. Goodwin and Professor J. B. Greenough of this University, and by Professor F. D. Allen of the University of Cincinnati, to each of whom I am greatly indebted for valuable suggestions.

So far as I am aware, no elementary book in English on the Rhythmic and Metric of the Classical Languages has appeared since Rossbach and Westphal began their studies. Such a book, however, is certainly needed. A strong persuasion of this has led me to publish this translation not only here but also in England, where Dr. Schmidt is likely to have had a fairer hearing than in his own country. I hope that the three indexes that have been added to the translation and the table of contents will make the book an easy one to use. Specific directions seem unnecessary. Teachers will probably differ in opinion in regard to the extent to which such a book as this should be used in school and college instruction. But certainly no teacher can afford to ignore the subject of which it treats. We may doubt whether our pupils had better learn to chant Homer as did the rhapsodist, but we can scarcely do less than teach them to give the quantity and mark the ictus as they read. The melody and dance of the Greek chorus may be gone forever, but it is hardly less than a breach of trust for the teacher not to unfold the theory of its composition, and give to those under his instruction a glimpse at least at the high art of the poet who was not only poet but also musician and master of orchestics.

JOHN WILLIAMS WHITE.

HARVARD UNIVERSITY, CAMBRIDGE,
July 12, 1878.

CONTENTS.

FIRST BOOK: Phonology.

	PAGE
§ 1. Introductory Remarks	3
2. Vowel-Articulation	3
3. Quantity	7
4. Intonation	11
5. Accentuation	15

SECOND BOOK: Metric.

6. Origin of the Forms of Poetry and Music	19
7. Preliminary Statements concerning the Measures	22
8. Fundamental Forms of the Measures	25
9. Shortened Final Measures	27
10. Examples of Verses in the different Kinds of Measure	28
11. Prolongation of Long Syllables (τονή)	34
12. Doric Melodies	41
13. Logaoedics	43
14. Further use of the "Two-timed Trochee"	48
15. Sixteenth Notes	49
16. Recitative Chorees	50
17. Metrical Correspondence	52

THIRD BOOK: Rhythmic.

18. The Rhythmical Sentence (κῶλον)	55
19. Close of Sentences	57
20. Intonation of Sentences	61
21. Length of Sentences	63
22. Sentences Occurring Most Frequently	67
23. Interchange of Measures	73
24. The Rhythmical Period	79

CONTENTS.

FOURTH BOOK: Typology.

	Page
§ 25. Introductory	60
26. The Recitative Type	83
27. The Lyric Type.	
I. Free Metrical Forms	89
28. II. The Epodes (οἱ ἐπῳδοί)	93
29. III. Four-lined Groups	96
30. IV. Lyric Systems	105
31. The March Type	113
32. The Choric Type	116
33. Choric Strophes	120

FIFTH BOOK: Eurhythmy.

34. The Periods according to their Grouping	124
35. Preludes and Postludes	134
36. Position of the Verse-Pauses	136
37. Metrical Agreement of the Corresponding Members	144

The Lyric Parts of the Medea	154
The Lyric Parts of the Antigone	170
Index of Metrical and Musical Characters	191
Index to the Metres of Horace	192
General Index	194

First Book.
PHONOLOGY.

§ 1. Introductory Remarks.

RHYTHMIC (ἡ ῥυθμική, sc. τέχνη) treats of the general principles of rhythm (measured movement) which underlie poetry and music, and essentially distinguish poetry from prose.

METRIC (ἡ μετρική, sc. τέχνη) shows how the materials of language are used to produce rhythm. Metric, therefore, differs in different languages, while their rhythm can remain the same; yet the rhythm of each language also is more or less perfectly developed, in proportion as the organization of the language renders it possible.

A more exact definition of rhythmic and metric than this cannot at present be given, because the confusion of terms that prevails in the grammars necessarily makes any concise definition obscure. A number of topics, therefore, which properly belong to grammar must first be considered; not until this has been done, and the necessary terms have been distinctly defined, will it be possible to discuss the main subjects without danger of misunderstanding.

§ 2. Vowel-Articulation.

1. Every vowel in Greek and Latin is pronounced either with a *protracted* (*gedehnt*) or *sharp* (*geschärft*) sound. To indicate *protraction* of a vowel the sign (‒) is drawn just under it; to mark its *sharp* sound the sign (∪) is used in the same position. For example, compare

§ 2. VOWEL-ARTICULATION.

α in κρᾶσις = *a* in *ah*, with
α in κράτος = *a* in the first syllable of *papa*.
η in μῆτις = *e* in the French word *fête*, with
ε in μένω = *e* in *met*.
ι in ἶσος = *i* in *pique*, with
ι in ἵνα = *i* in *pin*.
ω in σκῦμμα = *o* in *mote*, with
ο in σκότος = *o* in *intonation*.

The diphthongs are regarded as protracted vowels.

2. The various means found in some modern languages for indicating the protraction and sharpening of the vowels, as in English the doubling of an *e* or *o*, or the addition of a silent *e* (cf. *pin* with *pine*, *not* with *note*), to mark protracted sounds, or the doubling of a consonant to show the sharpening of the preceding vowel, do not exist in Greek and Latin. In these languages the doubling of the consonant has nothing to do with the protraction or sharpening of the vowel. E. g. we find in Greek both γλῶσσα and Ἄτοσσα, both πρήσσω (Att. πράσσω) and ἐρέσσω. In Greek, further, the two sounds of *e* and *o* are respectively designated by different letters, ε and ο when sharp, η and ω when protracted.

3. The accents in Greek do not serve to distinguish the above-mentioned protraction and sharpening. E. g. the protracted o (ω) can
    1) be without accent, as in ἄνθρωπος, ἥρως;
    2) have the acute, as in ἀνθρώπου, λιμώττειν;
    3) have the grave, as in τὼ ἄνδρε;
    4) have the circumflex, as in τιμῶ, γλῶσσα.
So the sharp o can
    1) be without accent, as in ὁ, ἵππος;
    2) have the acute, as in ὅδε, υἱός;
    3) have the grave, as in θεὸς ἔφη.

The circumflex is the only accent which cannot be used on sharp vowels, but for a different reason. For this, see § 5, 4.

4. It is absolutely necessary to pronounce the sharp vowels in Greek as really sharp, and to do it without doubling the following consonant, e. g. neither τῶπος nor τόππος, but τό-πος.

§ 2. VOWEL-ARTICULATION.

In the case of the vowels *a, ι, v*, where each letter has but a single character for both its sounds, reference must be made to a good lexicon to determine in the different cases whether the vowel is sharp or protracted.

It is well to practise on words like περιεγένετο, i. e. *pe-ri-e-ge-ne-to*. Whoever fails to articulate the vowels properly will never understand the metric of the classical languages, and his notions of their rhythmic, i. e. in other words, their poetic forms, will be forced and unnatural. In Latin also the sounds of the vowels must be carefully distinguished. E. g. *homines* always *ho-mi-nes* (ὄμινης), never, as is often done, *ho-mi-nes* (ὤμινες), where every syllable is mispronounced. The ablative *mensa* was perfectly distinguished in pronunciation from the nominative of the same orthography; and so in all like cases.

Pronounce *bene*, βένε;
" *rete*, ρήτε;
" *monere*, μονήρε.

5. When in Latin poetry one word ends and the next begins with a vowel, the first vowel, as is known, is elided. E. g. the hexameter

O felix una ante alias Priameïa virgo, Aen. III. 321,

is pronounced thus:

O felix un' ant' alias Priameïa virgo,

or

O felix unantalias Priameïa virgo.

Both ways, however, are wrong, though the latter is the better. For in such a combination as *sacra in urbe*, for example, it is clearly impossible to pronounce *sacr* by itself; it must be pronounced in two syllables with a half-sounded *e* at the end, so *sacrᵉ* or *saker*. Final syllables in *-m* also, it should be remarked, are treated as if ending in a vowel, since the *m* only gives a slight nasal sound to the preceding vowel; e. g. *eam* must be pronounced as *éam* and *éan* are in French. That in no case, however, the final vowel is to be completely suppressed, can easily be shown. Who, for example, would understand sentences like the following from Terence?

Romna principi audies.
Auscultaudivi jomni. Anne tomnia?
Filiut darin seditionatquincertas nuptias.

I. e. *rem omnem a principio audies. — ausculta. audivi jam omnia. anne tu omnia? — filiam ut darem in seditionem, atque incertas nuptias.*

§ 2. VOWEL-ARTICULATION.

How these are to be pronounced is shown by words in English poetry containing a syncopated *e*, such as "quiv'ring," "glitt'ring," i. e. "*quiv'ring*," "*glitt'ring*"; or, better still, verses in which *to* or *the* appears to have its vowel elided, as in the following:

"I must confess, that I have heard so much,
And with Demetrius thought *to* have spoke thereof."
Midsummer Night's Dream, I. 1.

"Truth crushed to earth shall rise again:
The eternal years of God are hers."
BRYANT, *The Battlefield*.

No one will read here, though the rhythm seems to require it, *thave* or *tave*, and *theternal*, but rather *t°have* and *th°eternal*.

The poets often indicate by an apostrophe that this half-suppressed vowel is not to give rise to a new syllable, as:

"On Lemnos, *th*' Aegean isle: thus they relate,
Erring; for he with this rebellious rout
Fell long before; nor aught avail'd him now
T' have built in Heav'n high tow'rs; nor did he 'scape
By all his engines."
MILTON, *Paradise Lost*, I. 746–749.

Still we say *th°Aegean* and *t°have*, not *thaegean* and *thave* (tave). The same is the case with *heav'n* (pronounce *heav°n*), and *tow'rs* and *'scape* (pronounce *°scape*), but not in "avail'd," where we say simply *availd*. That the apostrophe in this case signifies the partial suppression, and not the omission of the vowel, should be carefully noted.

Hence the above sentences from Terence should obviously be pronounced thus:

R̄omn̄°a princ̄ip̄i °aud̆ĭes. Ausc̄ult°ă aud̄ivi j°omni. anne t°omnia? — Fīl˘ĭ°ŭt dar°in sedition° atqu° incertas nuptias.

If the same vowel follows, the first can be completely suppressed, as *j°omni. anne = jam omnia. anne.*

If Latin poetry is not read in the manner explained, then by full pronunciation of the final vowels on the one hand, with hiatus, it becomes pure prose; on the other hand, the complete suppression of the final vowels makes what is read unintelligible.

§ 3. Quantity.

1. By *quantity* is understood the time that passes in pronouncing a syllable. Syllables are distinguished as *long* and *short*.

Syllables which end in a sharp vowel in particular can be pronounced rapidly. All syllables, on the contrary, which end either in a protracted vowel (or diphthong) or a consonant, require a longer time for their pronunciation. E. g. the following syllables can be hurried over very rapidly:

tra la la la la la la la, etc.,

while the word "woe" repeated just as often, as

woe woe woe woe woe woe woe woe, etc.,

cannot by any means be given with equal rapidity.

How rich the Greek language is in short syllables is seen in words like περιεγένετο, already cited.

Long syllables are marked by this sign (—) drawn over them, short ones are marked by this sign (⌣) in the same position.

2. That quantity is independent of vowel-articulation, and that consequently syllables as *long* and *short* are not to be confounded with syllables as *protracted* and *sharp*, and that, therefore, they are not to be marked by the same signs, can be seen at once from the following considerations:

I. Sharp syllables are always long when they end in a consonant, as in στέρ-γειν, στορ-γή.

II. But the syllable also that ends in a sharp vowel can be pronounced, as well as sung, *very* long. In the refrain *tra la la* all the syllables are sharp, but the second *la* is usually made long, and there is no reason why the voice should not dwell on it, not only in singing, but also in speaking, until it is made equal in time even to three or more other syllables. This syllable is then pronounced *lā* (not *lă*).

In Greek the exclamation of pain ἒ ἒ seems often to have been made very long, though the vowels remained sharp. Further Homer, *Il.* XII. 208, has ὄφιν, which certainly was not pronounced ὄφφιν. The same occurs in a fragment of Hipponax (*Fr.* 49, Bergk): ἢν αὐτὸν ὄφις τῶν-τικνήμιον δάκνῃ.

III. Protracted vowels are regarded as short in Greek, when they end a word and the next begins with a vowel. The same is true of diphthongs. The very first verse of the *Odyssey* furnishes an example:

Ἄνδρα μοι ἔννεπε, Μοῦσα, πολύτροπον, ὃς μάλα πολλά.

In the tragic poets this occurs sometimes also in the middle of a word, particularly when the protracted vowel or diphthong precedes a long vowel or diphthong, e. g. δειλαία, πατρῴους (Attica correptio).

3. Syllables with a protracted vowel are called *natura longae*; those with a sharp vowel, but ending in a consonant, *positione longae*. So φύσει or θέσει μακραί (sc. συλλαβαί).

But the first of two consonants does not always belong to the preceding syllable, and consequently does not always make "position." In Greek the following rules in general hold good:

I. Position is always caused by the doubling of a consonant, by λ μ ν ρ σ with following mute, by the concurrence of two mutes, by ξ ψ ζ (= κs, ps, ds), and finally by all other consonants with following σ:

τἄλλω, πέσσω; — βέλτιστος, λάμπω, σπένδω, τέταρτος, μασχάλη; — ἔλεγχος, τυγχάνω; — ὀξύς, τύψω, ῥέζω; — ἅλς, ἕλμινς.

II. The quantity is doubtful before two *liquids*, yet a short syllable occurs very seldom here (ὕμνος, very rarely ῠ-μνος). The quantity is doubtful also when *muta cum liquida* follows the vowel, e. g. τέκνον (i. e. *tek-non*) or τέκνον (i. e. *te-knon*), ἔπραξα (i. e. *ἐπ-ραξυ*) or ἔπραξα (i. e. *ἔ-πραξα*). The Attic writers were very strongly inclined to draw both consonants over to the following syllable.

But in the case of compound words where the first consonant belongs to the first part of the word, position always results, e. g. ἐκλείπω, not ἐκλείπω, since we naturally pronounce *ek-lei-po*, not *e-klei-po*.

4. The Greek language, on account of its many short syllables, could be pronounced with great rapidity and ease. This is seen also from the fact that the pause between the single words was very short and that consequently an entire sentence sounded, in comparison with an English sentence, almost like a single word. This appears from various facts, of which the following are of importance in metric:

I. The shortening of protracted vowels and of diphthongs at the end of a word, when the next word begins with a vowel:

Ἄνδρα μοι ἔννεπε, κ. τ. λ.

§ 3. QUANTITY. 9

II. "Synizesis" of final and beginning vowels:

πλάγχθη ἐπεὶ Τροίης, κ. τ. λ.

This could indeed be read also:

πλάγχθη ἐπεὶ Τροίης;

but this pronunciation is impossible in those cases where (the verse being hexameter, e. g.) neither a dactyl nor spondee would result, as in this verse:

ἦ εἰπέμεναι δμωῇσιν Ὀδυσσῆος θείοιο, Od. IV. 682.

Here it is not allowed to read ἦ εἰπέμεναι, since a measure like $\cup\_\cup\cup$ is impossible. But, on the other hand, the example above from the *Odyssey* could not be pronounced ἄνδρα μοι ἔννεπε, since then the hexameter would begin with a trochee, which is equally impossible. Exceptions are only apparent.

III. Two consonants which begin a word make position with the final vowel of the preceding word, e. g. ἀνὰ σκήπτρῳ; even single consonants are sometimes doubled in this case, especially the liquids:

αἰεὶ δὲ μαλακοῖσι καὶ αἱμυλίοισι λόγοισι, Od. I. 56, i. e. δεμμαλακοῖσι.

It is, however, to be observed, that there are peculiar reasons in Homer for the apparent doubling of the initial consonants λ μ ν ρ, which occur frequently. It is in the highest degree probable that there was originally still another consonant before these consonants, which was afterwards no longer pronounced and, therefore, was also not written. The digamma (F) fell away frequently before ρ. Before λ, χ may often have fallen away (cf. χλιαρός and λιαρός); before μ and ν, σ was probably often dropped (cf. σμικρός and μικρός, σμύρνα and μύρρα, etc.). Od. IV. 430, e. g. is to be read:

δὴ τότε κοιμήθημεν ἐπὶ Ϝρηγμῖνι θαλάσσης.

The above statement, therefore, that single consonants, especially liquids, are sometimes doubled, refers only to the pronunciation which the Athenians employed in the poems of Homer, and which was imitated by the later Epic writers. Cf. more at length on the point in question, Schmidt, *Metrik*, § 5. A similar falling away of initial consonants before other consonants in the same word is very common in English, except that the consonant is still written though no longer pronounced. This is especially frequent in the case of *k* before *n* and *p* before *s*, as e. g. in *knight, knave, knife, psalm*.

§ 3. QUANTITY.

It is to be noted that position is made much less often by two consonants at the beginning, than by the same combination in the middle of a word.

IV. A word with a short vowel in its final syllable, and ending in a consonant, has this last syllable long only when the following word begins with a consonant, not when it begins with a vowel. E. g.

on the other hand:
$$\overline{ὃς} \ μάλα \ πολλὰ, \ Od. \ I. \ 1;$$
$$Μῆν\breve{ιν} \ ἄειδε, \ Il. \ I. \ 1.$$

In the latter case the consonant was drawn over to the following syllable, and the words were pronounced = *me-ni-n'a-ei-de*.

Apparent exceptions occur in the case of words which have a digamma, which, as is known, was not in later times pronounced, and so also was not written:

$$ἀρνύμενος \ ἥν \ τε \ ψυχὴν \ καὶ \ νόστον \ ἑταίρων, =$$
$$ἀρνύμενος \ Fήν \ τε \ ψυχήν, \ κ. \ τ. \ λ., \ Od. \ I. \ 5,$$

pronounced:

ar-ny-me-nos-ven-tep-sy-chen-kai-nos-to-ne-tai-ron.

5. Not only should an accurate pronunciation according to the above principles be acquired, a pronunciation which is indispensable in order to understand and also to feel the ancient rhythm, but the false pronunciation of some of the consonants and their combinations should also be carefully guarded against; as e. g. in Latin *c* and *t* should always be pronounced hard like *c* in *cat*, and *t* in *time*.

A correct vowel-articulation (which term it must be remembered does not refer to the quantity of the vowels) is not intrinsically difficult; it must, however, be acquired early. Then the proper pronunciation becomes *far easier* than the careless one in vogue, since it remarkably facilitates the reading of verse, and thereby becomes more firmly fixed in mind.

6. In Greek poetry it is a fundamental principle that *a long syllable has twice the time of a short one.*

Since English poetry is composed on the basis of accent and not quantity, an Englishman is inclined, when reading Greek and Latin poetry, to give the syllables the same length and distinguish them only by accent, which is an error that must be corrected at once. This can be done only by beating or counting the measure. Since now hexameter verse, e. g., is composed of light and heavy dactyls (cf. § 10), i. e. of

§ 4. INTONATION.

♩♪♪ | ♩ ♪♪ | etc., or ♩♩ | ♩♩ |, that occur interchangeably in all the measures except the last which is always a heavy dactyl, each of these measures has four beats, two for each long syllable, one for each short one, e. g.

Ἄν-δρα μοι | ἔν-νε-πε | Μοῦ-σαπο | -λύτ-ρο-πο | -νὸς μά-λα | πολ-λὰ.
1.2. 3.   4.   1.2. 3. 4.   1.2. 3. 4.   1.2. 3. 4.   1.2. 3. 4.   1.2. 3.4.

At the close of a verse a syllable otherwise short can be regarded long, and conversely: *syllaba anceps*, συλλαβὴ ἀδιάφορος.

7. The accents in Greek cannot be regarded as marking the quantity, for

I. Long syllables can have any one of the accents or none at all:

στέργω, τοὺς, τοῦ, τιμῶ.

II. Short syllables, likewise, can have any one of the accents or none at all:

λόγος. τόν, τοῦ ἀνδρός (cf. § 3, 4, I.), ἐγώ.

8. From this it is clear that "accent" and "quantity" are not terms that can be used interchangeably. The true theory of the Greek accents and the correct definition of the word "prosody" (also sometimes confused with the term "quantity") will be given in § 5.

§ 4. Intonation.

1. The syllables of a language are tones, in considering which the three same principles appear which are found in music. These are: *duration of tone* (quantity), *strength of tone* (intonation), *elevation of tone* (accentuation).

The second of these (intonation) will be discussed in this section.

The different syllables of a word are not pronounced with the same force, but rather in every word one syllable has most weight, and to this the chief ictus is given. This ictus will be indicated best by a dot (˙) set over the syllable on which it falls. In music this mark (>) has been employed, but it is not expressed at the beginning of a measure, — for every measure begins with a tone more strongly pronounced or sung.

In accordance with this the following words have these ictus-relations:

manly ♩ ♩ or ˊ ˋ

report ♩ ♩ or ˋ ˊ

§ 4. INTONATION.

And in the first verse of the *Odyssey*:

ἄνδρα   ♩ ♪   or −́ ⏑

ἔννεπε   ♩ ♪ ♪   or −́ ⏑ ⏑

πολύτροπον ♪ ♩ ♪ ♪   or ⏑ −́ ⏑ ⏑

πολλά   ♩ ♩   or −́ −

In longer words there can be more than one ictus. These are then of different strength, and are distinguished by the number of dots set over the syllables on which they fall. E. g.

universe ⸱́ − ⸱
householder ⸱́ ⸱ −
agriculturist ⸱́ − ⸱ − ⸱
instrumentality ⸱́ − − ⸱ − ⸱
incomprehensibility − ⸱ − ⸱ − ⸱́ − ⸱

In no word can there be more than one chief ictus, but more than one of the second or third grade may occur.

2. This word-ictus is subordinate to the ictus of the sentence. Every simple sentence sounds to the ear like a unit from being controlled by a single chief ictus, just as a word appears as a unit through its single chief ictus.

The words of course are separated from one another by short pauses (in Greek by *very* short ones), the sentences by longer ones (indicated by the marks of punctuation).

It is by these ictuses and the pauses between the words that have just been mentioned that sentences like the following are distinguished:

I bought iron, tools, and wagons, i. e.

− − ⸱́ −, ⸱́, − ⸱́ −

and

I bought iron tools and wagons,

− − ⸱ − − − ⸱́ −

Further, the sentence "Our soul waiteth for the Lord" has with reference to the ictuses the notation:

− ⸱ ⸱́ − − − ⸱́

Here the first syllable of *waiteth* has only a secondary ictus in the sentence, though it is the primary ictus-syllable in the word itself.

§ 4. INTONATION.

3. On the other hand, compound sentences have no single chief ictus, but each member has its own.

The various involutions, incorporations, ellipses, and so on, which arise when sentences are grouped together in a period, render the relations of the different ictuses difficult to understand. A scientific investigation of these relations is not now necessary.

4. Intonation is not indicated in Greek by the accents any more than vowel-articulation and quantity. That this is so in poetry is to be seen with the utmost certainty from the first verse of the *Iliad:*

$$\text{Μῆνιν ἄειδε, θεὰ, Πηληϊάδεω Ἀχιλῆος.}$$

The six ictuses fall upon:

$$\mu\hat{\eta}\text{-, -ει-, -ὰ, -λη-, -δεω, -λῆ-.}$$

Of these, three are accented syllables, two with the circumflex, one with the grave; the remaining three have no accent. The syllables without an ictus are: -νι νᾰ-, -δε, θε-, Πη-, -ϊά-, Ἀχι-, -ος, of which two are accented with the acute, and the rest are without accent. The same is true not only of all hexameters, but of all other verses. The rhythmical ictuses have nothing to do with the accents, but fall arbitrarily on syllables with circumflex, acute, or grave, or without accent. So also syllables with these accents can be without rhythmical ictuses.

It is to be noticed, however, that the accents are not entirely without influence in those cases where many short syllables come together without mixture of longs, or longs without mixture of shorts. See more at length Schmidt, *Metrik*, § 10.

The question arises: "Where then did these ictuses of the words and sentences fall in Greek prose?" It is necessary to answer the first part of the question only; since as soon as the word-ictuses are known the sentence-ictuses are also known: for the chief ictus of the sentence coincides with the chief ictus of that word on which the main weight of the sentence rests.

Unfortunately this question cannot be answered with certainty. The old grammarians have left no information in regard to the ictuses in prose, and in writing Greek no marks were used to indicate them. But from certain facts in the language itself it may be concluded:

1) That the ictuses originally fell on the root-syllables of the words. Old alliterating formulae, especially in Hesiod's *Works and Days*, prove this, e. g. V. 235:

$$\text{τίκτουσιν δὲ γυναῖκες ἐοικότα τέκνα γονεῦσιν.}$$

§ 4. INTONATION.

The alliteration here is unmistakable and, as in many other places, *not* the result of chance. It determines the prose ictuses to have been as follows:

τίκτουσιν δὲ γυναῖκες ἐοικότα τέκνα γονεῦσιν.

The ictuses fall on root-syllables only. This position of the ictus is natural, and historically probable, since the same rule holds in the other Indo-European languages.

2) Soon, however, the Greek language tended towards putting the ictuses on the long syllables, without reference to the root-syllables as such. Had not this early been the case, how could it be explained that in poetry the long syllables in particular, at first exclusively (in hexameter, trochaic tetrameter, etc.), had the ictuses? It is impossible that the same word could have had one ictus in poetry and another in prose. This would have been contrary to nature.

3) But early there began a further change, namely, that the accented syllables more and more received the ictus. This is shown not only by the fact that sometimes words like ὄφις (cf. § 3, 2, II.) could have the ictus on the first syllable, just as if this syllable were long, but particularly by the influence of the accent upon the protraction and consequently upon the quantity of the vowels and their syllables. The ending -a in words of the first declension, e. g., as we see from comparative grammar, was originally always protracted. It lost the protraction, however, in many words where it did not have the accent, as in γλῶττα, μέμμα; but this protraction remained intact without exception where the final syllable was accented, as in φθορά, φορά, etc.

At a later date the Greek language probably came to the practice of nearly all modern languages, that of making ictus and accent always coincide.

The position of the ictus in Greek words, therefore, suffered the greatest changes, and was perhaps at no time completely fixed. The new principles of art, consequently, developed at a later day, allowed the ictus in poetry to be placed somewhat arbitrarily as compared with its position in prose.

5. That expressions like "accenting," "accentuation," etc. cannot be used with reference to strength of tone, will be made clear in § 5. The best term to use is " intone," "intonation."

§ 5. Accentuation.

1. Not only in singing, but also in common speech, syllables receive tones of different pitch (τόνοι, *toni*). But in prose, as in recited (but not sung) poetry, the intervals between these tones are variable, not regulated with strict mathematical accuracy as in music. In ordinary discourse five of these tones are distinguished, which will best be understood by illustrations from English.

This "singing" in common speech becomes most noticeable when persons are heard to converse in a foreign language. The Englishman is astonished at the wonderful singing in the language of the German, the German at the same thing in the language of the Englishman. That he himself sings neither observes, until a foreigner makes him conscious of it by exaggerated imitation.

It is also the case that within the bounds of the same language this difference of "modulation" is sometimes very noticeable.

2. I. The greater number of syllables is pronounced in about the same tone, which can be called the *middle tone*.

II. The syllables with the chief ictus in English words have generally the *high tone*, as the syllable *good-* in *goodness*, *-treat* in *retreat*.

If the middle tone be indicated by a note between two lines, and the high tone by a note upon the upper of these lines, the tone-relations of the syllables in these two words will be as follows:

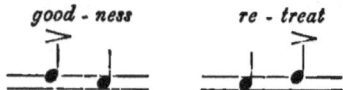

III. However, if in an interrogative sentence other syllables follow that which has the chief ictus, this is given a much lower tone, which consequently has the name of *low tone*. So in the following sentence these tones occur:

(The low tone is to be designated by a note on the lower line.) Or, further, the syllable following the low tone has the high tone, and is then without ictus:

§ 5. ACCENTUATION.

IV. In monosyllabic exclamations of surprise, especially when spoken in a tone of derision, the word is begun with the high tone, which then passes in the same syllable into the middle tone. This may be called the *falling tone*, and is to be designated as follows:

V. Finally, if a question closes with a monosyllabic word which has the chief ictus, the middle tone follows in this the low tone. This may, therefore, appropriately be called the *rising tone*, and is to be designated as follows:

3. The syllables of Greek words had the first four of these tones; the rising tone was either unknown to them, or else so seldom used that it had no special mark to distinguish it. Still, some of the grammarians are said to have observed the rising tone in words like τιμώμεθα, where the second of the contracted syllables had the accent.

Since these tones are much more apparent in singing, it is with reference to this that they received their names, and so too the signs used to designate them. These are the accents, *accentus* from *accinere*, προσῳδίαι, from πρός and ᾠδή, i. e. *marks for singing*, or, marks used to indicate tones of the voice and *not* the ictus.

The middle tone had no special mark. The acute, προσῳδία ὀξεῖα, stands for the high tone; the grave, προσῳδία βαρεῖα, for the low tone, which may often have nearly coincided with the middle tone; the circumflex, προσῳδία περισπωμένη, for the falling tone. All these terms were borrowed from music, where high tones were called τόνοι ὀξεῖς, etc.

It has been shown above that in English the ictus does not necessarily fall upon a syllable that has the high tone, but may fall, e. g., upon one with the low tone. From this it is easy to see that a Greek verse can and must be pronounced throughout with the prose accents, and that this can be done without any conflict arising between the prose accents and the quantity of the syllables and their ictuses in poetry.

The following verse must, therefore, be read:

§ 5. ACCENTUATION.

Here, *as it happens*, the high tone and the ictus coincide in the first measures, but not in the fifth and sixth.

But in English, as before remarked, the high tone is almost always joined to the ictus; for the exceptions in the case of interrogative sentences and in some other instances are of no great importance. To illustrate, the following verse is accented in reading as follows:

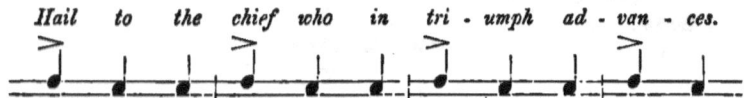

In this way there arises a regularity in the succession of the high and low tones which very closely resembles singing. Yet this is not perceived in one's vernacular, while on the other hand a reading of ancient verse in which the accents are observed, as given above, appears much more like singing. Further, the quantity is neglected, and consequently the above hexameter in the mouth of an Englishman is:

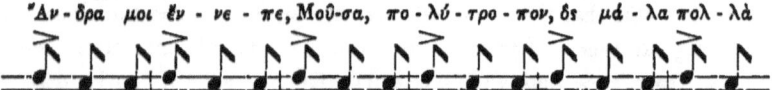

This reading, to be sure, is not to be entirely condemned, since the ancients themselves, while their poetry was still sung or chanted, employed other notes than those used in prose. But it is as certainly not to be recommended in verses which are recited without the accompaniment of musical instruments. Most of all should false quantities be guarded against.

4. That the explanation of the accents here given is the true one is proved not only by their names and the testimony of antiquity, but also various facts in the language itself can be explained only on this supposition. The circumflex, the mark of the falling tone, stands, e. g., with few exceptions which arise from a blunt sense of language or by analogy, only on those contracted syllables which before contraction also had the same succession of tones. E. g.

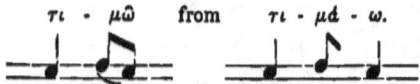

§ 5. ACCENTUATION.

Instead of the rising tone, however, the high tone was generally employed, as, e. g.

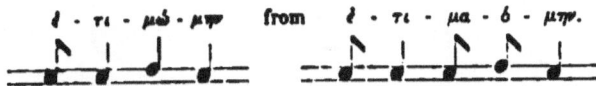

That the quantity of the final syllable had an influence on the accent of the preceding syllable is a common error. Still everybody writes γλῶτται and ἄνθρωποι, etc., although the last syllable is long in quantity. That, however, the genitive is accented ἀνθρώπου, and not ἄνθρωπου, arises from the fact that this form comes from ἀνθρώποο, it being an old law of the Greek language that the high tone could not stand farther back than upon the third syllable from the last. When now the last two syllables were contracted, it still held its accustomed place. Similarly in most other cases.

5. It is, therefore, a great mistake to regard the circumflex as a mark of protraction. Not infrequently monosyllabic English words, even those with a sharp vowel, have the falling tone, as *bread*, to be written in order to represent the pronunciation βρε͂δ, never βρῆδ. Such words, however, are often pronounced with a single tone, βρέδ or βρὲδ. Compare *go!* = γῶ, *go along!* = γὼ ἀλόγγ (ἐλόγγ), *go! go!* = γώ, γώ. The vowel in this word is in no case made sharp, γό, γὸ. The accent, as used to mark its different tones, does not affect its protraction, but the word always remains protracted, whatever accent it may happen to have.

The French language shows the greatest misuse of the accents; é, è, and ê, that is, are entirely different sounds. It should here be noticed that é is indeed protracted, but is not long, being pronounced very rapidly, as e. g. *été* = $\overset{\smile\smile}{ete}$.

6. The theory of elevation of tone is called *prosody*. Giving a syllable another tone than the middle tone is called *accenting* (*betonen*) it, *accentuation*. The former expression is generally confounded with "quantity" and "vowel-articulation," the latter with "intonation."

Second Book.

METRIC.

§ 6. Origin of the Forms of Poetry and Music.

1. In the ὁπλοποιία in *Il.* XVIII. 567 *sq.*, there is a beautiful picture of an old national dance (ὁ λίνος):

> παρθενικαὶ δὲ καὶ ἠίθεοι ἀταλὰ φρονέοντες
> πλεκτοῖς ἐν ταλάροισι φέρον μελιηδέα καρπόν.
> πᾶσιν δ' ἐν μέσσοισι πάις φόρμιγγι λιγείῃ
> ἱμερόεν κιθάριζε, λίνον δ' ὑπὸ καλὸν ἄειδεν
> λεπταλέῃ φωνῇ· τοὶ δὲ ῥήσσοντες ἁμαρτῇ
> μολπῇ τ' ἰυγμῷ τε ποσὶ σκαίροντες ἕποντο.

A youth standing in the middle sings a song and accompanies it with his lyre; round about him dance young men and maidens and join in his song. They dance chiefly to the music of the song, while the single lyre is of little significance and serves only to accompany it. And such is the origin of all music and singing in regulated measure (metre): both have their source in the dance and march.

Of the simplest sort, and yet of the exactest regularity, are the movements of soldiers in marching. When marching in order they first tread all at the same time with the left foot, and then again all at the same time with the right. The time, or in other words the step to the music, is kept with the left foot. This makes the tread of the left foot the more prominent (although theoretically it is no heavier than that of the right foot), and thus the time is divided into exactly equal portions, to the first half of which the natural tendency is to give the greater weight, *left, right* | *left, right* | etc.

The movements of a dancer are somewhat more complicated; but these too have a regular succession. To illustrate, in the "polka-mazurka," a very simple dance, there are three different movements equal in time. With "one" the dancer treads heavily with the right foot, with "two" more lightly with the left, and with "three" the right foot is brought into position behind the left. Then the feet change their rôle, and so on. By these movements the time is divided into equal portions of three parts each.

These small portions of time with their regular division are called *measures*, πόδες, *pedes*. The preparatory tread in marching corresponds to the anacrusis. The measures cited above in march and dance are respectively *measures of two parts each* (*equal measures*) and *measures of three parts each* (*unequal measures*). The Greek terminology is γένος ἴσον, γένος διπλάσιον. Measures of four parts each are about the same as those of two parts; these also are equal measures. But *measures of five parts each* form a new class: these are now very rare, but were more frequent among the Greeks, and are called γένος ἡμιόλιον.

2. If the song is to correspond to these dance and march movements, it also must be divided into measures. The beginning of every measure must be intoned (§ 4, 5) more forcibly in order to have the right relation to the more vigorous movement of the body; the remaining syllables correspond to the weaker movements.

This, then, is the first requirement in rhythmical composition, that it be divided into equal measures the first part of each of which shall have the ictus. Now, there is need in song of an exacter law for the relation of syllables to one another with reference to their length than prevails in prose, where their relative length does not conform to any strict mathematical ratio. This law (already stated in § 3, 6) is, that every long syllable is equal to two short ones, $- = \cup \cup$.

Further, since the beginning of every measure must be intoned more strongly, the measure, according to § 4, 4, 2, must be introduced by a long syllable. The short syllables are then assigned to the lighter part of the measure; yet a long syllable is allowed here, since not every long is necessarily given with an ictus. Consequently both ♩ ♪ ♪ ($-\cup\cup$) and ♩ ♩ ($- -$) are proper $2/4$ measures.

Song is further distinguished by an exact regulation of the relations of its tones. Since, now, even prose had a varying usage in reference to these tones (many syllables e. g. with the acute under certain circumstances — in connected discourse — took the grave in its place), so, as the art of music developed itself more and more independently, the relations of its tones were less and less restricted by preceding usage.

§ 6. ORIGIN OF THE FORMS OF POETRY AND MUSIC.

3. This, then, is rhythmical speech, one divided into portions of equal length with regularly distributed ictuses. In song, to attain still greater regularity, there is added the exact determination of the tones.

Song, therefore, is

1) *Metrically* divided into equal portions (of which the smallest, the measures, are first to be considered).

2) These portions become *rhythmical* in consequence of regularly distributed ictuses.

3) Song becomes *musical* through the exactly regulated intervals between its tones.

4. But little by little musical instruments were perfected, so that they ceased to serve simply for accompaniment, and produced the melodies independently. Thus arose *music without words*. It had the same rhythm, the same tones, as song; but metrically must early have gone beyond it. While, therefore, the measure of four parts e. g., which has the duration of about four eighth-notes (♪♪♪♪), cannot well have more than four syllables, since their pronunciation always requires a certain time, — while indeed a quarter-note must generally be used for the first two eighth-notes, (♩ ♪ ♪, — ∪ ∪, not often ∪ ∪ ∪ ∪), since otherwise a stronger ictus must be given to a short syllable than by nature it should have; there is, on the other hand, no difficulty in expressing this measure on stringed instruments with eight sixteenth-notes (♬♬♬♬), etc.

Therefore, *vocal music has, in the nature of language, considerable metrical limitations.* Syllables sung with extraordinary rapidity would not allow the sense of the language to be understood. And these limitations were in vocal music always observed by the Greeks in the classical period of their language. Trills, runs, and so on, used in modern music, would have been a horror to the Greeks, at least in their vocal music. To this noble simplicity, which nevertheless produced the highest effect and an extraordinarily artistic division into measures, sentences, verses, and periods, do we owe it that it is yet possible for us in the texts that have been preserved to learn the metrical values of the syllables and to determine the entire rhythmical construction.

For from the principle that the long syllable has exactly the value of two short ones, there was not in their poetry, even when more fully developed, any considerable departure, and it is everywhere possible to determine the degree of this departure.

On the development of the forms of poetry and music, cf. further § 25.

§ 7. Preliminary Statements concerning the Measures.

1. Only measures consisting of long and short syllables used with their ordinary value will here be discussed. Their metrical forms are the common ones in which the greater number of poems is composed.

2. The first note of the measure, as already stated, is intoned more strongly than the rest, and has, therefore, the chief ictus. Take e. g. the four-eighth measure:

$$\overset{\text{Ἄν - δρα}}{\underset{- \; \cup \; \cup}{\text{♩ ♪ ♪}}} \Big| \overset{\text{ἔν - νε - πε}}{\underset{- \; \cup \; \cup}{\text{♩ ♪ ♪}}}$$

In music this ictus, as readily understood, is not commonly marked.

This more strongly intoned part of the measure was called θέσις, since in beating time the foot was here set down, while the lighter part of the measure, during the utterance of which the foot was raised, was called ἄρσις:

$$\underset{\text{θέσις} \quad \text{ἄρσις}}{\overset{\text{ἄν - δρα μοι}}{\text{♩ ♪ ♪}}} \Big| \underset{\text{θέσις} \quad \text{ἄρσις}}{\overset{\text{ἔν - νε - πε}}{\text{♩ ♪ ♪}}}$$

Now, however, it is customary to call θέσις, arsis, and ἄρσις, thesis, and thereby to pervert the signification of the Greek terms. This use of these terms agrees with the modern practice of pronouncing the more heavily intoned part of the measure with the high-tone (the voice being "raised"), the lighter part with the middle-tone (which in contrast with the high-tone seems a "lowered" tone). Cf. § 5, 3. We should, however, and this will be in accordance with our own practice in beating time, employ the terms as they were used by the Greeks themselves, i. e. call the *downward* beat *thesis*, and the *upward* beat *arsis*.

3. In course of the development of Greek poetry the principle that long syllables were to stand in the *thesis*, short ones in the *arsis*, was not strictly maintained. So that the $^3/_8$ measure could be expressed not only by ♩ ♪ (e. g. τοῦτο), but also by ♪ ♪ ♪ (e. g. διότι). That is, two short syllables are used in place of the long one, a process which is called *resolution* (διάλυσις). Further, it was possible to use a long syllable in place of two short ones (in the arsis), e. g. ♩ ♩ (as κεῖνοι), for ♩ ♫. This is called *contraction*.

§ 7. PRELIMINARY STATEMENTS CONCERNING THE MEASURES. 23

This license is expressed as follows:

Resolution, i. e. ♪♪ for ♩, by 𝅘𝅥𝅮𝅘𝅥𝅮 or ⌣⌣

Contraction, i. e. ♩ for ♪♪, by 𝅘𝅥𝅮𝅘𝅥𝅮 or ⏑⏑

If it is immaterial whether one long or two short syllables be employed, this can be expressed by 𝅘𝅥𝅮𝅘𝅥𝅮. For this there is no metrical sign.

Since, now, in the hexameter the light dactyl ♩ ♪ ♪ is the common, the heavy dactyl the unusual form, except in the last measure where the heavy dactyl alone can occur, the first mentioned form must not be considered as a resolution of the latter, but, directly contrary to this, the latter must be regarded as a contraction of the former. Thus:

or ♩ 𝅘𝅥𝅮𝅘𝅥𝅮 | ♩ 𝅘𝅥𝅮𝅘𝅥𝅮 | ♩ 𝅘𝅥𝅮𝅘𝅥𝅮 | ♩ 𝅘𝅥𝅮𝅘𝅥𝅮 | ♩ 𝅘𝅥𝅮𝅘𝅥𝅮 | ♩ ♩

not — ⏑⏑ | — ⏑⏑ | — ⏑⏑ | — ⏑⏑ | — ⏑⏑ | — —

♩ 𝅘𝅥𝅮𝅘𝅥𝅮 | ♩ 𝅘𝅥𝅮𝅘𝅥𝅮 | or — ⌣⌣ | — ⌣⌣ |

4. If we consider the value of the measure as a rhythmical element designed originally for dance and march, we see at once that in measures of equal length different ictus-relations could nevertheless prevail. It is possible to intone ♩ 𝅘𝅥𝅮𝅘𝅥𝅮 either ⊥ ⌣ ⌣ or ⊤ ⌣ ⌣; i. e. the chief ictus can outweigh the secondary, or be comparatively less prominent, according as the movements in the dance and march, though equal in time, are more or less vigorous. It is natural that also in music this difference should appear as characteristic, and give it a peculiar stamp. Waltzes have only one strong ictus: ⊥ _ _ (this is the fundamental form of their measures), but in the polka-mazurka there is another tolerably strong secondary ictus: ⊥ _ ⊤.

What ictus-relations prevailed in the Greek texts can be judged from their metrical peculiarities. If it is possible for resolutions of the thesis and contractions of the arsis to occur at will, it is certain that the arsis could not have had a relatively unimportant ictus. If the $4/8$ measure, for example, is not only ⊥ ⌣ ⌣, but also ⊥ _, it is not yet obvious, to be sure, that the arsis had a strong secondary ictus; but this must have been the case, if also the form ⌣ ⌣ _ was allowed, so that the general

24 § 7. PRELIMINARY STATEMENTS CONCERNING THE MEASURES.

scheme of the measure was ⌣ ⌢. For since the long syllables have by the rule the heavier ictuses, it would have been impossible in a measure like ♫ ♫ | ♫ ♫ | etc. for the ictus of the first part of the measure, which frequently fell upon short syllables while at the same time the arsis had a long syllable, to preponderate to any great extent.

It is, therefore, possible to determine the ictus-relations in the measures of the different rhythms by the frequency of resolution and contraction.

5. Not all melodies and consequently not all verses begin with a full measure, i. e. with a syllable having an ictus. Frequently the unintoned part of the measure precedes. This is called by Hermann the *anacrusis* (ἀνάκρουσις). Take e. g. the following first part of an iambic trimeter:

$$\mathring{\omega} \quad \text{κοινόν} \quad \text{αὐ-τά-δελ-φον} \quad \ldots$$
$$\quad \overset{>}{\quad} \quad \overset{>}{\quad} \quad \overset{>}{\quad}$$
♩ : ♩ ♪ | ♩ ♪ | ♩ ♪ | ...

Just as this verse in $^3/_8$ measure begins with an anacrusis, so can every other. The effect is to make the rhythm livelier, since the first syllable or syllables (for two syllables also can constitute the anacrusis according to the kind of measure) give, so to speak, a sort of invitation or encouragement to begin the rhythmical movement proper.

It is the law that *the anacrusis must not be greater than the arsis;* according to the rule it also must not be less. In the $^4/_8$ measure the arsis = $^2/_8$, consequently the anacrusis also = $^2/_8$, not $^1/_8$ or $^3/_8$. Thus

⌢ : _ ⌢ | _ ⌢ etc., not
⌣ : _ ⌢ | _ ⌢ etc., or
_ ⌣ : _ ⌢ | _ ⌢ .....

An irrational syllable, however, which will hereafter be indicated by this mark, >, can in most cases constitute the anacrusis, as in ὦ κοινὸν αὐτάδελφον, apparently _ for ⌣. See on this § 13.

6. The grammarians carefully distinguished verses with and without anacrusis. Nevertheless in their theoretical systems they sometimes became confused on this very point, and made the anacrusis the first part of the measure, as e. g.

Καὶ δὴ 'πίκουρος ὥστε Κὰρ κεκλήσομαι. Arch.
> ≐ | ⌣ ≐ | ⌣ ≐ | ⌣ ≐ | ⌣ ≐ | ⌣ ≐

§ 8. FUNDAMENTAL FORMS OF THE MEASURES. 25

In consequence of this they distinguished two kinds of the $3/8$ measure, trochees ($\perp \cup$) and iambi ($\cup \perp$). But if only the anacrusis be detached, the ictus will fall on the first syllable, as well in the one kind of measure as in the other. The "iambic" verse quoted above should therefore be written:

$$> \vdots \perp \cup \mid \perp \cup \mid \perp \cup \mid \perp \cup \mid \perp \cup \mid \perp \wedge \parallel$$

($\wedge$ signifies an eighth pause).

7. In the case of paeons and choriambi (cf. § 8) it is best to distinguish two theses of different grades, which can be called primary and secondary thesis. That the grammarians did not make this distinction arose from the fact that they concerned themselves principally with relations of numbers, and never put the practical value of their theories to the test. Paeons, moreover (but not choriambi), have anacrusis, though seldom. Cf. § 23, 3.

On this point see further Schmidt, *Compositionslehre*, § 4.

§ 8. Fundamental Forms of the Measures.

1. *Extension*, *division*, and *intonation* determine the character of the measures. According to their extension we distinguish $3/8$, $4/8$, $5/8$, $6/8$ measures. But the division of e. g. a measure of six eighths can be twofold; it can be divided into a thesis of $3/8$ and an arsis of $3/8$, $\perp \cup \perp \cup \mid$, and then it is called a $6/8$ measure; or into a thesis of $4/8$ and an arsis of $2/8$ ($4/8 + 2/8$), $\perp \perp \cup \cup \mid$, and then it is customary to call it a $3/4$ measure. The former is an equal measure, since thesis and arsis are equal; the latter is an unequal measure.

Finally, measures of the same extension and division may be different in intonation, as e. g. $\perp \perp \mid$ and $\perp \perp \mid$.

Whether in any particular measure the ground-form occurs or the equivalent forms arising from resolution or contraction, is of secondary importance, provided that the division of the measure and its intonation be not thereby affected. Cf. § 7, 3.

2. The following are the fundamental forms of the measures that commonly occur. The more common "resolutions" and "contractions" are noted in metrical and musical characters; as examples simple words are given, but where anacrusis ordinarily occurs, parts of verses.

§ 8. FUNDAMENTAL FORMS OF THE MEASURES.

A. Equal Measures (γένος ἴσον).

I. $\overset{\llcorner}{\smile}\smile$ or ♩ ♫, *dactyl* (εἴπετο).

It is a $^4/_8$ measure with weak secondary ictus.

The form with contracted arsis ($\overset{\llcorner}{\;}\overset{\lrcorner}{\;}$) is generally (but incorrectly) named *spondee*. We distinguish light dactyls, $\overset{\llcorner}{\smile}\smile$, and heavy dactyls, $\overset{\llcorner}{\;}\overset{\lrcorner}{\;}$.

II. $\overset{\llcorner}{\smile}\smile$, $\overset{\llcorner}{\;}\overset{\lrcorner}{\;}$, $\smile\smile\overset{\lrcorner}{\;}$, or ♪♪ ♫, *anapaest*, always with anacrusis. Cf. § 10, II.

ἐλελεῦ, ἐλελεῦ ⏑⏑ ┆ _ ⏑⏑ | _ . . . .

III. $\overset{\llcorner}{\;}\overset{\lrcorner}{\;}$ or ♩ ♩, *spondee* (κεῖνοι).

A $^2/_4$ measure with strong secondary ictus.

It is distinguished from the anapaest especially by its slower time, also by infrequency of resolutions, and generally by absence of anacrusis. Cf. § 10, III.

IV. $\overset{\llcorner}{\smile}\overset{\lrcorner}{\smile}$ or ♩♪ ♩♪, *dichoree* (ἐκτρέπεσθε).

A $^6/_8$ measure with the division $^3/_8 + ^3/_8$.

B. Unequal Measures (γένος διπλάσιον).

V. $\overset{\llcorner}{\smile}$ or ♩ ♪, *choree.*

A $^3/_8$ measure with weak secondary ictus.

Without anacrusis it is called *trochee* (εἶπε); with anacrusis, *iambus*:

κράτος βία τε ⏑ ┆ _ ⏑ | _ ⏑ | ...

resolved (⏑⏑⏑), *tribrach* (λέγετε).

VI. $\overset{\llcorner}{\;}\overset{\lrcorner}{\smile}\smile$ or ♩ ♩ ♫, *ionic* (ἐκλείπετε).

A $^3/_4$ measure with the division $^2/_4 + ^1/_4$ and the weakest ictus in the arsis.

Without anacrusis it is called *ionicus a majore;* with anacrusis, *ionicus a minore:*

σέβομαι μὲν προσιδέσθαι ⏑⏑ ┆ _ _ ⏑⏑ | _ _ ...

VII. $\overset{\llcorner}{\smile}\smile\overset{\lrcorner}{\;}$ or ♩ ♫ ♩, *choriambus* (ἐκτρέπομαι).

A $^3/_4$ measure with the division $^2/_4 + ^1/_4$ and strong secondary ictus in the arsis.

VIII. $\overset{\llcorner}{\;}\_\_$ or ♩ ♩ ♩, *molossus* (βούλεσθαι).

A very slow $^3/_4$ measure without resolution and with a comparatively light ictus.

§ 9. SHORTENED FINAL MEASURES. 27

C. Quinquepartite Measures (γένος ἡμιόλιον).

IX. $-\cup-$ or ♩ ♪ ♩, *paeon* (βούλομαι).
A $5/8$ measure with the division $3/8 + 2/8$.
The names of the forms are:
$-\cup-$, *amphimacer* or *cretic* (βούλομαι).
$-\cup\cup\cup$, *paeon primus* (ἐκτρέπετε).
$\cup\cup\cup-$, *paeon quartus* (καταλέγω).
$\cup\cup\cup\cup\cup$, *resolved paeon* (παρεγένετο).

X. $--\cup$ or ♩ ♩ ♪, *bacchius*.
A $5/8$ measure, usually with anacrusis:
τίς ἀχώ, τίς ὀδμά ∪ : _ _ ∪ | _ _ ...

§ 9. Shortened Final Measures.

1. Before the characteristics of the different measures are given, it should be remarked that the final measure of a series, and especially of a verse, whether sung or recited, may be incomplete, and end with a pause instead of the arsis. This pause is denoted in music and in metric by different characters according to its length:

the eighth-pause 𝄾, ∧;
the quarter-pause 𝄽, 𝈖;
the $3/8$-pause 𝄽·, 𝈖·;
the half-pause 𝄼, 𝈗.

2. To close a series with a shortened measure is called κατάληξις, and the verse itself so closing is called *catalectic* (στίχος καταληκτικός, μέτρον καταληκτικόν). If, on the other hand, the verse closes with a full measure it is called *acatalectic* (ἀκατάληκτος).

E. g. the following verse is acatalectic:

"Ἄνδρα μοι ἔννεπε, Μοῦσα, πολύτροπον, ὃς μάλα πολλὰ
_ ∪ ∪ |_∪ ∪ | _ ∪ ∪||_ ∪ ∪ | _ ∪ ∪ | _ _ ||

Catalectic, on the other hand, is:

νῦν δ' ἐπικεκλομένα   Aesch. *Suppl.* I. str. a' (v. 41).
_ ∪ ∪ |_∪∪|_ 𝈖 ||

In the following strophe the first and third verses are acatalectic, the second and fourth catalectic:

§ 10. EXAMPLES OF THE DIFFERENT KINDS OF MEASURE.

Tell me not in mournful numbers,
"Life is but an empty dream!"
For the soul is dead that slumbers,
And things are not what they seem.
      Longfellow.

_ ◡ | _ ◡ | _ ◡ | _ ◡ ‖
_ ◡ | _ ◡ | _ ◡ | _ ⋀ ‖, etc.

§ 10. Examples of Verses in the different Kinds of Measure.

I. *Dactyls* are a solemn and slow measure, and are, therefore, used (especially in choric poetry) to denote an exalted, God-trusting state of mind, or to express warnings with solemn earnestness. Sometimes anacrusis occurs:

Κύριός εἰμι θροεῖν ὅδιον κράτος αἴσιον ἀνδρῶν ἐκτελέων·
ἔτι γὰρ θεόθεν καταπνείει πειθὼ μολπᾶν, ἀλκὰν σύμφυτος αἰών.
     Λεscη. *Agam.* I. *str. a'* (104 – 107).

_ ◡ ◡ | _ ◡ ◡ | _ ◡ ◡ | _ ◡ ◡ ‖ _ ◡ ◡ | _ _ | _ ◡ ◡ | _ ⋀ ‖
◡ ◡ : _ ◡ ◡ | _ ◡ ◡ | _ _ | _ _ ‖ _ _ | _ _ | _ ◡ ◡ | _ _ ‖

Further, they are the measure in which the solemnly recited epic hexameter (so called) is composed:

Ἄνδρα μοι ἔννεπε, Μοῦσα, πολύτροπον, ὃς μάλα πολλὰ
πλάγχθη ἐπεὶ Τροίης ἱερὸν πτολίεθρον ἔπερσε. *Od.* I. 1, 2.

_ ◡ ◡ | _ ◡ ◡ | _ ◡, ◡ ‖ _ ◡ ◡ | _ ◡ ◡ | _ _ ‖
_ ◡ ◡ | _ _ | _, ◡ ◡ ‖ _ ◡ ◡ | _ ◡ ◡ | _ _ ‖

They have quicker time in lamentations, and yet the religious element exists here also, since lamentation for the dead was a religious act:

Ἀλλ' ἐμέ γ' ἁ στονόεσσ' ἄραρεν φρένας,
ἅ Ἴτυν, αἰὲν Ἴτυν ὀλοφύρεται,
ὄρνις ἀτυζομένα, Διὸς ἄγγελος.
    Soph. *El.* I. *ant. a'* (147 – 149).

_ ◡ ◡ | _ ◡ ◡ | _ ◡ ◡ | _ ◡ ◡ ‖
_ ◡ ◡ | _ ◡ ◡ | _ ◡ ◡ | _ ◡ ◡ ‖
_ ◡ ◡ | _ ◡ ◡ | _ ◡ ◡ | _ ◡ ◡ ‖

II. *Anapaests* are the proper march measure, and consequently occur in the march-songs (in particular those of the Spartans) of which fragments have been preserved. The chorus in tragedy also generally entered the orchestra (in the *parodos*) and left it (in the *exodos*) while reciting anapaests, the recitation in both cases being in a chanting tone. Of course, as is also the case in our own marches, the ictuses were

§ 10. EXAMPLES OF THE DIFFERENT KINDS OF MEASURE.

marked by the tread. Take as an example the entrance of the chorus of the Danaïdes in the *Supplices* of Aeschylus:

    Ζεὺς μὲν ἀφίκτωρ ἐπίδοι προφρόνως
    στόλον ἡμέτερον νάιον ἀρθέντ᾽
    ἀπὸ προστομίων λεπτοψαμάθων
    Νείλου· δίαν δ᾽ ἐκλείπουσαι
    χθόνα σύγχορτον Συρίᾳ φεύγομεν, κ. τ. λ.

    _ ⋮ ᴗ ᴗ _ | _ ᴗ ᴗ | _ ᴗ ᴗ | _
    ᴗ ᴗ ⋮ _ ᴗ ᴗ | _ _ | ᴗ ᴗ | _
    ᴗ ᴗ ⋮ _ ᴗ ᴗ | _ _ | _ ᴗ ᴗ | _
    _ ⋮ _ _ | _ _ | _
    ᴗ ᴗ ⋮ _ _ | _ ᴗ ᴗ | _ _ | ᴗ ᴗ

It should be noticed how great the difference is between these measures and dactyls which have anacrusis, as in the example cited above from the *Agamemnon* of Aeschylus, where it would be impossible for measures like ᴗ̇ ᴗ ᴗ̱ to occur.

III. *Spondees*, in which resolutions even of the arsis are seldom allowed, are the measure used in religious hymns, extremely measured and slow, to which they are even better adapted than dactyls. Their name arose from the drink-offerings (σπονδαί). Take as an example the following from a *Hymn to Helios* by Dionysius:

    Εὐφαμείτω πᾶς αἰθήρ,
    γῆ καὶ πόντος καὶ πνοιαί,
    οὔρεα, τέμπεα σιγάτω,
    ἦχοι φθόγγοι τ᾽ ὀρνίθων·
5   μέλλει γὰρ πρός γ᾽ ἡμᾶς βαίνειν
    Φοῖβος ἀκερσεκόμας εὐχαίτας.

    _ _ | _ _ | _ _ | _ ⋏ ‖
    _ _ | _ _ | _ _ | _ ⋏ ‖
    _ ᴗ ᴗ | _ ᴗ ᴗ | _ _ | _ ⋏ ‖
    _ _ | _ _ | _ _ | _ ⋏ ‖
5   _ _ | _ _ | _ _ | _ _ ‖
    _ ᴗ ᴗ | _ ᴗ ᴗ | _ _ | _ _ ‖

These true spondees must be carefully distinguished from heavy dactyls which are like them in their outward form (_ _ for _ ᴗ ᴗ), but are used solely to relieve the tiresome uniformity of dactylic verses.

We best get a clear conception of the real nature of the spondee from church hymns. These are frequently composed in spondaic measure, though with less restrictions than in ancient poetry. Anacrusis is frequent.

30 § 10. EXAMPLES OF THE DIFFERENT KINDS OF MEASURE.

Thou who didst leave Thy Father's breast,
Eternal Word sublime!
And cam'st to aid a world distressed
In Thine appointed time.

The melody is:

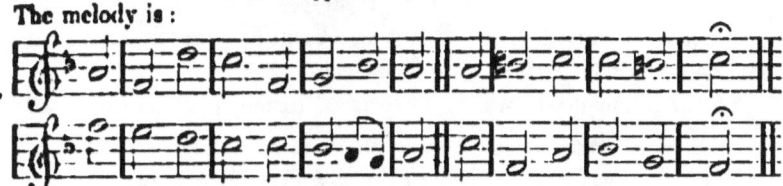

If this solemn melody with its slow time be compared with the vigorous music of a march, the difference between spondees and anapaests will be perfectly clear; and it will further be evident that spondees are not to be spoken of as occurring in anapaestic verse, in hexameter, in trimeter, etc.

IV. *Chorees* are a somewhat vivacious measure serving for the expression of individual feeling, especially when they occur with anacrusis (as *iambi*). Without it (as *trochees*) they are much less lively.

> Ἔσθ᾽ ὅπου τὸ δεινὸν εὖ,
> καὶ φρενῶν ἐπίσκοπον
> δεῖ μένειν καθήμενον.
> AESCH. *Eum.* IV. *ant.* β' (517 – 519).

_ ∪ | _ ∪ | _ ∪ | _ ∧ ǁ
_ ∪ | _ ∪ | _ ∪ | _ ∧ ǁ
_ ∪ | _ ∪ | _ ∪ | _ ∧ ǁ

> Δι᾽ αἷματ᾽ ἐκποθένθ᾽ ὑπὸ χθονὸς τροφοῦ
> τίτας φόνος πέπηγεν οὐ διαρρύδαν.
> Id. *Cho.* I. *str.* γ' (66, 67).

∪ ⋮ _ ∪ | _ ∪ | _ ∪ | _ ∪ | _ ∪ | _ ∧ ǁ
∪ ⋮ _ ∪ | _ ∪ | _ ∪ | _ ∪ | _ ∪ | _ ∧ ǁ

The measure becomes somewhat more vivacious if, as is frequently the case, resolution occurs. Compare the song between Antigone and Ismene in Aesch. *Sept.* IX. *pr.* (962 – 964), where in the metrical scheme, each verse being divided between the two singers, the comma will be used to denote the point of division.

A. δορὶ δ' ἔκανες.   I. δορὶ δ' ἔθανες.
A. μελεόπονος.   I. μελεοπαθής.
A. ἴτω δάκρυα.   I. ἴτω γόος.

∪ ⋮ ∪ ∪ ∪ | _, ∪ | ∪ ∪ ∪ | _ ∧ ǁ
∪ ⋮ ∪ ∪ ∪ | _, ∪ | ∪ ∪ ∪ | _ ∧ ǁ
∪ ⋮ _ ∪ | ∪ ∪, ∪ | _ ∪ | _ ∧ ǁ

§ 10. EXAMPLES OF THE DIFFERENT KINDS OF MEASURE. 31

V. The *ionic* measure is used in giving expression to a greatly excited frame of mind. In this measure the loud shout of victory, or the feeling of joy at deliverance from great danger, breaks forth. The enthusiasm, moreover, of the priestesses of Bacchus and of noisy drinkers is expressed by it. But it also beautifully expresses that deep inner anxiety which cries aloud for rescue.

Cf. the following, in which is expressed certainty of victory:

Πεπέρακεν μὲν ὁ περσέπτολις ἤδη
βασίλειος στρατὸς εἰς ἀντίπορον γείτονα χώραν,
λινοδέσμῳ σχεδίᾳ πορθμὸν ἀμείψας.

AESCH. *Pers.* I. *str.* α' (65 – 67).

∪∪ ⋮ _ _ ∪∪ | _ _ ∪∪ | _ _ 𝜦 ‖
∪∪ ⋮ _ _ ∪∪ | _ _ ∪∪ ‖ _ _ ∪∪ | _ _ 𝜦 ‖
∪∪ ⋮ _ _ ∪∪ | _ _ ∪∪ | _ _ 𝜦 ‖

Cf. also the following, in which the shout of joy of the rescued Danaïdes (X.) breaks forth, who sing alternately with their attendants (Θ.):

    X. Κύπριδος δ' οὐκ ἀμελεῖ θεσμὸς ὅδ' εὔφρων.
    δύναται γὰρ Διὸς ἄγχιστα σὺν Ἥρᾳ·
    τίεται δ' αἰολόμητις
    θεὸς ἔργοις ἐπὶ σεμνοῖς.
5   Θ. Μετάκοινοι δὲ φίλᾳ ματρὶ πάρεισιν
    πόθος, ᾇ τ' οὐδὲν ἄπαρνον
    τελέθει θέλκτορι Πειθοῖ.
    δέδοται δ' Ἁρμονίας μοῖρ' Ἀφροδίτᾳ
    ψεδυροὶ τρίβοι τ' Ἐρώτων.

AESCH. *Suppl.* IX. *str.* β' (1035 – 1042).

∪∪ ⋮ _ _ ∪∪ | _ _ ∪∪ | _ _ 𝜦 ‖
∪∪ ⋮ _ _ ∪∪ | _ _ ∪∪ | _ _ 𝜦 ‖
∪∪ ⋮ _ _ ∪∪ | _ _ 𝜦 ‖
∪∪ ⋮ _ _ ∪∪ | ⊥ _ 𝜦 ‖
5 ∪∪ ⋮ _ _ ∪∪ | _ _ ∪∪ | _ _ 𝜦 ‖
∪∪ ⋮ _ _ ∪∪ | _ _ 𝜦 ‖
∪∪ ⋮ _ _ ∪∪ | _ _ 𝜦 ‖
∪∪ ⋮ _ _ ∪∪ | _ _ ∪∪ | _ _ 𝜦 ‖
∪∪ ⋮ _ ∪ _ ∪ | _ _ 𝜦 ‖

A dichoree is substituted in the last verse, a practice of which more hereafter.

VI. *Choriambi* are used especially for the expression of the highest degree of despair and indignation, and are apt to form very long verses. They do not often occur.

§ 10. EXAMPLES OF THE DIFFERENT KINDS OF MEASURE.

Take for illustration the following:

Παῖδα μὲν αὑτᾶς πόσιν αὑτᾷ θεμένα
τοιῷδ᾽ ἔτεχ᾽, οἱ δ᾽ ὧδ᾽ ἐτελεύτασαν ὑπ᾽ ἀλλαλοφόνοις χερσίν ...
AESCH. Sept. VIII. ant. γ΄ (929 – 933).

$$\_\cup\cup\_ \mid \_\cup\cup\_ \mid \_\cup\cup\_ \parallel$$
$$\_\cup\cup\_ \mid \_\cup\cup\_ \mid \_\cup\cup\_ \parallel \_\cup\cup\_ \mid \_\cup...$$

Anacrusis is not allowed. Ionic verses often follow choriambic. These also denote violent states of mind, but those less violent than are expressed by choriambic verses.

Δεινὰ μὲν οὖν, δεινὰ ταράζει σοφὸς οἰωνοθέτας
οὔτε δοκοῦντ᾽ οὔτ᾽ ἀποφάσκονθ᾽ · ὅ τι λέξω δ᾽ ἀπορῶ.
πέτομαι δ᾽ ἐλπίσιν οὔτ᾽ ἐνθάδ᾽ ὁρῶν οὔτ᾽ ὀπίσω.
SOPH. Oed. R. II. str. β΄ (483 – 486).

$$\_\cup\cup\_ \mid \_\cup\cup\_ \parallel \_\cup\cup\_ \mid \_\cup\cup\_ \parallel$$
$$\_\cup\cup\_ \mid \_\cup\cup\_ \parallel \_\cup\cup\_ \mid \_\cup\cup\_ \parallel$$
$$\cup\cup \vdots \_\_\cup\cup \mid \_\_\cup\cup \parallel \_\_\cup\cup \mid \_\overset{\cdot}{\cup} \parallel$$

VII. *Dichorees* consist of chorees in pairs. In a long verse a succession of such small measures as ♩ ♪ or $\_\cup$ with ictuses of equal weight would be tiresome. But this would be relieved by uniting them in pairs in a $^6/_8$ measure: $\overset{\cdot}{\_}\cup\overset{\cdot}{\_}\cup$ |, which is to be carefully distinguished from the succession: $\overset{\cdot}{\_}\cup \mid \overset{\cdot}{\_}\cup$, where both ictuses of the long syllables have the same emphasis and, therefore, the two $^3/_8$ measures do not appear as a unit. It seems natural to divide a series of four or six iambi into dichorees, so that the above examples in IV. would be given:

Ἔσθ᾽ ὅπου τὸ δεινὸν εὖ
$$\_\cup\_\cup \mid \_\cup\_\wedge \parallel$$
Δι᾽ αἵματ᾽ ἐκποθένθ᾽ ὑπὸ χθονὸς τροφοῦ
$$\cup \vdots \_\cup\_\cup \mid \_\cup\_\cup \mid \_\cup\_\wedge \parallel$$

This division of iambic and trochaic verses into dichorees is the reason for not calling e. g. an iambic verse of six measures an hexameter, but trimeter, since it is divided thus:

$\cup \vdots \_\cup\_\cup \mid \_\cup\_\cup \mid \_\cup\_\wedge \parallel$,
not
$\cup \vdots \_\cup \mid \_\cup \mid \_\cup \mid \_\cup \mid \_\cup \mid \_\wedge \parallel$.

In like manner we speak of a trochaic tetrameter, when composed of eight single trochees, i. e. four ditrochees. But if it be observed that in long choreic verses, as for example the hexapody, the first, third, and fifth measures naturally have a heavier ictus than the second, fourth, and

§ 10. EXAMPLES OF THE DIFFERENT KINDS OF MEASURE. 33

sixth, it will be seen that the difference between $\_\cup|\_\cup|\_\cup|\_\wedge\|$ and $\_\cup\_\cup|\_\cup\_\wedge\|$ lies, in fact, only in the way in which they are written; for

$\overset{\cdot}{\_}\cup|\overset{\cdot}{\_}\cup|\overset{\cdot}{\_}\cup|\overset{\cdot}{\_}\wedge\|$ is exactly equal to $\overset{\cdot}{\_}\cup\overset{\cdot}{\_}\cup|\overset{\cdot}{\_}\cup\overset{\cdot}{\_}\wedge\|$

Since, now, the first method of writing is necessary in many choreic strophes, as for example in the case of pentapodies like $\cup\vdots\_\cup|\_\cup|\_\cup|\_\cup|\_\wedge\|$, which certainly have not the value of three full dichorees, since so incomplete a measure as the last would then destroy the rhythm and consequently the melody also, — it is best to adopt generally the first method of writing, namely as chorees, which can be done in every case without difficulty. We shall, therefore, give the preference to the division into $3/8$ measures, and only in a single instance (§ 23, 2) divide into $6/8$ measures. In the case of a division into $3/8$ measures the verses are named differently: dimeter = tetrapody, trimeter = hexapody, tetrameter = octapody.

In like manner it is customary, with less reason, to regard two anapaestic measures as a single one, so that e. g. the tetrapody

$\overline{\cup\cup}\vdots\underline{\cup\cup}\ \overline{\cup\cup}\ |\ \underline{\cup\cup}\ \overline{\cup\cup}\ |\ \underline{\cup\cup}\ \overline{\cup\cup}\ |\ \underline{\cup\cup}$

is also called dimeter.

VIII. The *Molossus*, like the spondee, was used in solemn religious melodies. Only a single refrain in this measure has been preserved, in Eur. *Ion*, I. 125 – 127 and 141 – 143:

Ὦ Παιάν, ὦ Παιάν,
εὐαίων, εὐαίων
εἴης, ὦ Λατοῦς παῖ.

$\_\_\_|\_\_\_\|$
$\_\_\_|\_\_\_\|$
$\_\_\_|\_\_\overset{\cdot}{\_}\|$

IX. *Paeonics* denote extreme excitement of mind, either finding vent in overwhelming enthusiasm, or, on the contrary, manifesting itself in great uncertainty, wavering, and helplessness. They are sometimes used, therefore, in the urgent prayers and entreaties of those who have been forsaken. Since this measure is seldom used, particular attention should be directed to its quantities. Measures like $\_\cup\_,\_\cup\cup\cup,\cup\cup\cup\_,\cup\cup\cup\cup\cup$ should be counted off accurately:

βούλομαι, βουλόμεθα, etc.
1.2. 3. 4.5.   1.2. 3. 4. 5.
$\overset{\cdot}{\_}\cup\overset{\cdot}{\_}\quad\overset{\cdot}{\_}\cup\overset{\cdot}{\cup}\cup$

§ 11. PROLONGATION OF LONG SYLLABLES.

Φρόντισον, καὶ γενοῦ πανδίκως
εὐσεβὴς πρόξενος·
τὰν φυγάδα μὴ προδῷς,
τὰν ἕκαθεν ἐκβολαῖς
δυσθέοις ὁρμέναν.
    AESCH. *Suppl.* III. *str. a'* (418 – 422).

‿ _ _ | _ ⏑ _ | _ ⏑ _ ‖
_ ⏑ _ | _ ⏑ _ ‖
_ ⏑ ⏑ ⏑ | _ ⏑ _ ‖
_ ⏑ ⏑ ‿ | _ ⏑ _ ‖
_ ⏑ _ | _ ⏑ _ ‖

Aristophanes has frequently employed this measure with exceedingly comical effect, as e. g. in *Ach.* IV. *str.* (299 – 301):

Οὐκ ἀνασχήσομαι· μηδὲ λέγε μοι σὺ λόγον·
ὡς μεμίσηκά σε Κλέωνος ἔτι μᾶλλον, ὃν
κατατεμῶ τοῖσιν ἱππεῦσι καττύματα.

_ ⏑ _ | _ ⏑ _ ‖ _ ⏑ ⏑ ⏑ | _ ⏑ ⏑ ⏑ ‖
_ ⏑ _ | _ ⏑ ⏑ ⏑ ‖ _ ⏑ ⏑ ⏑ | _ ⏑ _ ‖
⏑ ⏑ ⏑ _ | _ ⏑ _ ‖ _ ⏑ _ | _ ⏑ _ ‖

X. *Bacchii*, which are seldom independently used in great number, denote a much stronger uncertainty and wavering than the paeonics, and also astonishment and surprise.

Τίς ἀχώ, τίς ὀδμὰ προσέπτα μ' ἀφεγγής; AESCH. *Prom.* 115.

⏑ ⁝ _ _ ⏑ | _ _, ⏑ ‖ _ _ ⏑ | _ _ ∧ ‖

B. Στενάζω; τί ῥέξω; γελῶμαι πολίταις.
ἔπαθον, ὦ, δύσοιστα.
Γ. ἰώ, ὦ, μεγάλα τοι κόραι δυστυχεῖς
Νυκτὸς ἀτιμοπενθεῖς. Id. *Eum.* V. *str. a'* (789 – 792).

⏑ ⁝ _ _ ⏑ | _ _, ⏑ ‖ _ _ ⏑ | _ _ ∧ ‖
⏑ ⁝ ⏑ ⏑ _ ⏑ | _ _ ∧ ‖
⏑ ⁝ _ _ ⏑ | ⏑ ⏑ _, ⏑ ‖ _ _ ⏑ | _ 𝈖 ‖
> ⁝ ⏑ ⏑ _ ⏑ | _ _ ∧ ‖

§ 11. Prolongation of Long Syllables (τονή).

1. The following are two lines of a common ballad:

    And over the meadows the mowers came,
    And merry their voices rang; etc.

If the syllables with the chief ictuses are marked, we have:

§ 11. PROLONGATION OF LONG SYLLABLES.

$$\begin{array}{l} -\, \vdots\, \underline{\cdot}\, -\, -\, |\, \underline{\cdot}\, -\, -\, |\, \underline{\cdot}\, -\, |\, \underline{\cdot} \\ -\, \vdots\, \underline{\cdot}\, -\, -\, |\, \underline{\cdot}\, -\, |\, \underline{\cdot} \end{array}$$

No attempt is made in the above notation to express the metre of the lines. The long (—) marks simply the syllables.

Without regard either to the anacrusis or to the final measure of the verse, which latter, according to § 9, can be shortened, there are seen to be within the verse rhythmical divisions of sometimes two, sometimes three syllables. But it would be impossible to sing the above words in measures like the following, which constantly vary, being sometimes equal and sometimes unequal:

 etc.

We do not, moreover, even recite the words so, since we involuntarily pronounce these rhythmical divisions as measures of equal length:

And | over the | meadows the | mowers | came;

i. e. four divisions equal in time. How, now, is this equality in time produced? The music, expressed in $^3/_8$ time, is:

In the measures of two syllables the syllable with the ictus is given double time, and thereby equality of the measures is obtained.

2. The last measure, moreover, has set against it only the word *rang*. In measures of this sort, consisting of only a single syllable, it is possible either to prolong the syllable until it becomes equal to the other measures, or else to make a pause after it, as here.

Cases similar to this will often occur, if the song is recited so as to observe the rhythm of the melody, a thing that the Greeks always did. For otherwise the splendid creations of their poets would have become, when recited, mere prose.

3. In the Greek language there can be given to the *long syllable which begins the measure*, and so constitutes the thesis, in poetry as well as in music, a value greater than that of two shorts: this is called *prolongation*, τονή. Moreover, the long syllable may fill out an entire measure, so that it comprehends in itself both thesis and arsis: this is called *syncope*.

In this way, therefore, there arise notes of greater value than the quarter-notes. But since Greek music always remained essentially a vocal music (at least only this can be had in mind when the rhythm

§ 11. PROLONGATION OF LONG SYLLABLES.

of Greek texts is under consideration), it is clear that the prolongation of the notes must have been limited by fixed bounds. The Greeks in *singing* never ignored the *words;* at least in the period of their classical literature they did not go so far as to engraft upon meaningless texts, the understanding of which was of no consequence, an over-artificial music. They did not, therefore, give the long syllable e. g. the value of eight ordinary short syllables, by which according to our notation there would have arisen a whole note (𝅝). They went no further really than the $^4/_8$ note, and when a $^5/_8$ note seems to occur it is only apparent. No longer notes than this ever occur.

The rhythmical time-values, therefore, of Greek poetry, and consequently also of Greek vocal music, expressed in musical and metrical characters, are the following:

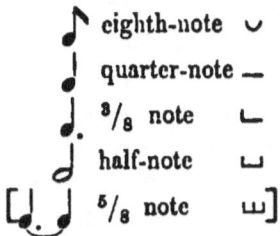

4. In this way was removed the very great sameness which all melodies must have had, if composed only of an interchange of quarter and eighth-notes. But how is it possible to determine in the texts the value of the long syllables, when these values can be so different?

We are treating of rhythmic, and rhythmic is a sort of applied mathematics. It must therefore be possible to find simple and exact laws, which in the different cases will lead with certainty to a knowledge of the value of the long syllables. The different ways of arriving at this knowledge are briefly as follow:

1) If it is possible from the sum total of the metrical facts to determine in what measure a song is written, it will be right to admit at all points longer notes, if thus the equality of the measures is preserved.

2) In this way rhythmical series of various forms will arise, which have all their fixed character. Just as the kind of measure in general must be suited to the meaning of the text, so also must the metrical form of the series be adapted to its meaning. Whether these are in conflict or agreement will make it possible to determine whether we have combined rightly or not.

§ 11. PROLONGATION OF LONG SYLLABLES. 37

3) Other quite positive grounds for determining the value of the long syllables are given in Book V. (on "Eurhythmy"), in § 34 – 37.

4) These positive external grounds, i. e. those based on form, must be substantiated by reasons from within; the *thought* of the forms in music and recited rhythm must be clear. Since the music of the Greeks was less complex and easier to be understood than modern music, there must have arisen among them a *limited* number of forms which were used in their whole poetical literature. In the general conformity of their *entire* literature to these laws lies the main proof that they are valid.

5. The use of the longer notes will now be explained. It is necessary to presuppose that the reader already understands the nature of the rhythmical " sentence," for which see below, § 18.

6. *Syncope* occurs the oftenest. It is found in the following kinds of measure:

I. Very frequently in *chorees* (syncopated chorees) in choric lyrical poetry. Syncope in the next to the last measure of the verse (and sentence) gives it a melancholy character, if these syncopated sentences constitute the main body of a strophe or of a greater part of it. Such sentences or verses may be named " falling " sentences or verses.

      Πνοαὶ δ' ἀπὸ Στρυμόνος μολοῦσαι
      κακόσχολοι, νήστιδες, δύσορμοι,
      βροτῶν ἄλαι, νεῶν τε καὶ πεισμάτων ἀφειδεῖς,
      παλιμμήκη χρόνον τιθεῖσαι
5   τρίβῳ, κατέξαινον ἄνθος Ἀργείων.
                          AESCH. *Agam.* I. *str.* δ' (192 – 197).

    ⏑ ⋮ — ⏑ | ⌊ | — ⏑ | — ⏑ | ⌊ | — ∧ ‖
    ⏑ ⋮ — ⏑ | ⌊ | — ⏑ | — ⏑ | ⌊ | — ∧ ‖
    ⏑ ⋮ — ⏑ | — ⏑ | — ⏑ | ⌊ ‖ — ⏑ | — ⏑ | ⌊ | — ∧ ‖
    ⏑ ⋮ ⌊ | ⌊ | — ⏑ | — ⏑ | ⌊ | — ∧ ‖
5   ⏑ ⋮ — ⏑ | ⌊ | — ⏑ | — ⏑ | ⌊ | — ⏑ ‖

A verse in which syncope occurs in the next to the last measure, and in which the last measure is at the same time *full*, is adapted to the expression of the unexpected and overpowering, as in the last verse of the above illustration. Verses of six measures of this sort with anacrusis are called *choliambic* (" halting iambi ") and were used in entire poems with comic effect, especially by the old iambographers Hipponax and Ananius, later by Babrius in his fables.

§ 11. PROLONGATION OF LONG SYLLABLES.

Δύ' ἡμέραι γυναικός εἰσιν ἥδισται,
ὅταν γάμῃ τις κἀκφέρῃ τεθνηκυῖαν. HIPP.

⏑⁝ _⏑ | _⏑ | _⏑ | _⏑ | ∟ | _⏑ ‖
⏑⁝ _⏑ | _⏑ | _⏑ | _⏑ | ∟ | _⏑ ‖

An example of the "halting" trochaic tetrameter:

ἔαρι μὲν χρόμιος ἄριστος, ἀνθίας δὲ χειμῶνι. AN.

⏑⏑⏑ | _⏑ | ⏑⏑⏑ | _⏑ ‖ _⏑ | _⏑ | ∟ | _⏑ ‖

In case the verse is divided into dichorees in place of chorees, either part of the measure may be syncopated, i. e. in place of

_⏑_⏑ | can occur either ∟ _ _ ⏑ or _ ⏑ ∟.

Remark. With reference, therefore, to their final measure there are the following kinds of verses (and likewise sentences):

1. *Acatalectic*, as e. g.:
$$\_\cup | \_\cup | \_\cup | \_\cup \|$$
ξυμβολεῖ φέρων φέροντι.

2. *Catalectic*:
$$\_\cup | \_\cup | \_\cup | \_ \wedge \|$$
καὶ κενὸς κενὸν καλεῖ.

3. *Falling*:
$$\_\cup | \_\cup | \llcorner | \_ \wedge \|$$
οὐκ ἄνολβος ἔσται.

4. *Halting*:
⏑⁝ _⏑ | _⏑ | _⏑ | _⏑ | ∟ | _⏑ ‖
δύ' ἡμέραι γυναικός εἰσιν ἥδισται. AN.

II. The so-called *paroemiac* (οἶμος, *a way:* therefore, "march-verse"), an anapaestic verse of which entire march-songs were composed, has been regarded a "falling rhythm." The ground-form has been thought to be:

⏑⏑⁝ _⏑⏑ | _⏑⏑ | ⊔ | _

But this is clearly erroneous, for forms like the following occur:

⏑⏑⁝ _⏑⏑ | ⏑⏑⏑⏑ | ⏑⏑ _ |
πόδα παρθένιον ὅσιον ὁσίας. EUR. *Iph. Taur.* 130,

in which the last two short syllables allow no such τονή. If the paroemiac is pronounced without syncopation:

⏑⏑⁝ _⏑⏑ | _⏑⏑ | _ _ ‖

it sounds much more warlike and vigorous, and is especially adapted to give force and life to the march-songs in which it is used, as in the following fragment of Tyrtaeus:

§ 11. PROLONGATION OF LONG SYLLABLES. 39

"Αγετ', ὦ Σπάρτας εὐάνδρου
κοῦροι πατέρων πολιατᾶν,
λαιᾷ μὲν ἴτυν προβάλεσθε,
δόρυ δ' εὐτόλμως πάλλοντες
5 μὴ φείδεσθαι τᾶς ζωᾶς·
οὐ γὰρ πάτριον τᾷ Σπάρτᾳ.

```
∪∪ : _ _ | _ _ | _ _ | ⊼
 _ : _∪∪ | _∪∪ | _ _ | ⊼
 _ : _∪∪ | _∪∪ | _ _ | ⊼
∪∪ : _ _ | _ _ | _ _ | ⊼
5  _ : _ _ | _ _ | _ _ | ⊼
 _ : _∪∪ | _ _ | _ _ | ⊼
```

How dragging and unwarlike would these verses be if they were regarded a falling rhythm. The pauses, moreover, at the close of each verse, during which the soldier marches without singing, give the necessary rest to the voice. This is still more necessary in the parodos and exodos of Attic tragedy, where long sections close with this verse.

Τελαμώνιε παῖ, τῆς ἀμφιρύτου
Σαλαμῖνος ἔχων βάθρον ἀγχιάλου,
σὲ μὲν εὖ πράσσοντ' ἐπιχαίρω·
σὲ δ' ὅταν πληγὴ Διὸς ἢ ζαμενὴς
5 λόγος ἐκ Δαναῶν κακόθρους ἐπιβῇ,
μέγαν ὄκνον ἔχω καὶ πεφόβημαι
πτηνῆς ὡς ὄμμα πελείας. SOPH. *Aj.* 134 *sq.*

```
∪∪ : _∪∪ | _ _ | _∪∪ | _
∪∪ : _∪∪ | _∪∪ | _∪∪ | _
∪∪ : _ _ | _∪∪ | _ _ | ⊼
∪∪ : _ _ | _∪∪ | _∪∪ | _
5 ∪∪ : _∪∪ | _∪∪ | _∪∪ | _
∪∪ : _∪∪ | _ _ | _∪∪ | _
 _ : _ _ | _∪∪ | _ _ | ⊼
```

Cf. further § 31.

III. In dactyls syncope is allowed in various places, yet is not frequent in the next to the last measure. It is most worthy of note at the end of a "sentence" within a verse. The elegiac verse, for example, which united with the "heroic hexameter" forms a kind of short strophe, the "distichon," of which elegies are composed, consists of two sentences of three measures each, each of which ends with syncope, as in the following fragment of Solon:

Πολλοὶ μὲν πλουτεῦσι κακοί, ἀγαθοὶ δὲ πένονται·
ἀλλ' ἡμεῖς αὐτοῖς οὐ διαμειψόμεθα

§ 11. PROLONGATION OF LONG SYLLABLES.

τῆς ἀρετῆς τὸν πλοῦτον, ἐπεὶ τὸ μὲν ἔμπεδον αἰεί,
χρήματα δ' ἀνθρώπων ἄλλοτε ἄλλος ἔχει.

_ _ | _ _ | _ ◡, ◡ ‖ _ ◡ ◡ | _ ◡ ◡ | _ _ ‖
_ _ | _ _ | ⌴, ‖ _ ◡ ◡ | _ ◡ ◡ | ⌴ ‖
_ ◡ ◡ | _ _ | _ ◡, ◡ ‖ _ ◡ ◡ | _ ◡ ◡ | _ _ ‖
_ ◡ ◡ | _ _ | ⌴, ‖ _ ◡ ◡ | _ ◡ ◡ | ⌴ ‖

At the close of a verse — $\overline{\wedge}$, of course, can be written in place of ⌴.

IV. No other cases of syncope than these occur, for those found in logaoedic verse are not at all different from those in choreic.

According to § 9 only the last measure of every verse can be incomplete. This is, of course, true of paeonic and bacchiic verses as well as of the rest. If, now, a paeonic verse ends in a measure with only one syllable, this can be given the value of five eighths (♩ ♪ or ⌴), though it is quite as correct to regard what is lacking supplied by a pause:

_ ◡ _ | _ ◡ _ | ∟ $\overline{\wedge}$ ‖, likewise
◡ : _ _ ◡ | _ _ ◡ | _ $\overline{\curlywedge}$ ‖ or
◡ : _ _ ◡ | ⌴ ∧ ‖

7. *Prolongation* of the long syllables of the thesis (always to the value of four eighths) occurs

1) in *ionics*, where apparent measures like _ ◡ ◡ have the value ⌴ ◡ ◡.

Ἔμαθον δ' εὐρυπόροιο θαλάσσας
πολιαινομένας πνεύματι λάβρῳ
ἐσοράν πόντιον ἄλσος.

AESCH. *Pers.* I. ant. γ′ (108 – 111).

◡ ◡ : _ _ ◡ ◡ | ⌴ ◡ ◡ | _ _ $\overline{\wedge}$ ‖
◡ ◡ : ⌴ ◡ ◡ | _ _ ◡ ◡ | _ _ $\overline{\wedge}$ ‖
◡ ◡ : _ _ ◡ ◡ | _ _ $\overline{\wedge}$ ‖

2) in *dochmii*, a discussion of which will be given in § 23, 4.

8. Under no circumstances is it allowable to assume a *pause* in the middle of a verse by which to complete a measure. For since, with few exceptions, there is no fixed place in the middle of the verse at which a word shall end, a pause must frequently thereby have occurred in the middle of a word. If this had been allowed at all, it must have been allowed also after short syllables, so that we should be able to regard e. g. λέγομαι as a paeon (◡ ◡ ∧ _). But luckily the Greeks never did this. Had they done so, there would be no Greek metric and rhythmic, since almost every verse of a lyrical song would allow the most varied arrangements.

§ 12. Doric Melodies.

1. Dactylic melodies consisting of an unbroken interchange of ♩ ♫ and ♩ ♩, rarely with single measures of ♩, would necessarily have been monotonous, and would have possessed little life and variety. It is true that their measured, powerful movement could have produced a great effect; yet this effect must have been so much the greater when more lively series intervened. Now, equal measures of ♩ ♪ are extremely common in all music. The Greeks too used them frequently, yet very seldom in immediate succession: ♩. ♪ | ♩. ♪ | ♩. ♪ | ♩. ♪ ‖ , but generally in such a way that the heavier measure followed the livelier: ♩. ♪ | ♩ ♩ | ♩. ♪ | ♩ ♩ ‖. This succession is exceedingly common in our own melodies, but the converse arrangement: ♩ ♩ | ♩. ♪ | , etc., is rare, and the Greeks never used it at all. The livelier measure could not end the series.

We will call this form of measure the *Doric*. The so-called Doric strophes consist of rhythmical sentences of ♩. ♪ | ♩ ♩ | and pure dactylic sentences, e. g. ♩ ♫ | ♩ ♫ | ♩ ♩ ‖ . They occur chiefly
1) in a great number of the triumphal odes of Pindar;
2) in the choruses of several of the tragedies.

The writers on metric, who distinguished only long and short syllables, naturally wrote series like ♩. ♪ | ♩ ♩ | ♩. ♪ | ♩ ♩ ‖ or ‿ ∪ | _ _ | ‿ ∪ | _ _ ‖ in this way : _ ∪ _ _ _ ∪ _ _, and so imagined that there was some such measure as _ ∪ _ _, which they called ἐπίτριτος δεύτερος.

The fact that in measures like ‿ ∪ | thesis and arsis are not in the right ratio (the ratio in the γένος ἴσον being 2 : 2) can be expressed, though imperfectly, by _ >, i. e. _ > | _ _ | _ > | _ _ ‖. This means only that the short syllable has *apparently* the value of a long.

> Ἔστιν ἀνθρώποις ἀνέμων ὅτε πλείστα
> χρῆσις, ἔστιν δ᾽ οὐρανίων ὑδάτων
> Ὀμβρίων, παίδων νεφέλας.
> εἰ δὲ σὺν πόνῳ τις εὖ πράσσοι, μελιγάρυες ὕμνοι
> 5 ὑστέρων ἀρχαὶ λόγων
> τέλλεται καὶ πιστὸν ὅρκιον μεγάλαις ἀρεταῖς.
>   PIND. *Ol*. X. *str.*

§ 12. DORIC MELODIES.

⌣ ‿ | _ _ | _ ‿ ‿ | _ ‿ ‿ | _ _ ‖
⌣ ‿ | _ _ | _ ‿ ‿ | _ ‿ ‿ | _ ⏞ ‖
⌣ ‿ | _ _ | _ ‿ ‿ | _ ⏞ ‖
⌣ ‿ | ⌣ ‿ | ⌣ ‿ | _ _ ‖ _ ‿ ‿ | _ ‿ ‿ | _ _ ‖
5   ⌣ ‿ | _ _ | ⌣ ‿ | _ ⏞ ‖
⌣ ‿ | _ _ | ⌣ ‿ | ⌣ ‿ ‖ _ ‿ ‿ | _ ‿ ‿ | _ ⏞ ‖

2. It has already been seen in (§ 4, 4, 2), that the tendency in Greek was to give the long syllables a heavier intonation (ictus). If, now, among dactyls (not anapaests, where the arsis also has a prominent ictus) we conceive measures of the form ♪♪ ♩, which were necessary to make the melodies more various, these could not have been well expressed by the syllables ‿ ‿ _, as e. g. by λέγομαι, since in such a case a Greek would always have been inclined to give the last syllable a strong ictus and thereby confuse the measure. And, in fact, these measures were hardly ever so expressed in their language. What they did do was to use three short syllables, e. g. λέγετε. In this case it was very easy to dwell with the voice on the last syllable for a comparatively long time, without giving it a heavier ictus through protracted articulation. Thus, then, apparent tribrachs stand in the place of dactyls, an infrequent case, however. This is best indicated by ‿ ‿ >, since here the short syllable is really employed otherwise than in its general use. The notes, however, remain ♪♪ ♩ |.

Ταχὺ δὲ Καδμείων ἀγοὶ χαλκέοις ἀθρόοι σὺν ὅπλοις ἔδραμον·
ἐν χερὶ δ᾽ Ἀμφιτρύων κολεοῦ γυμνὸν τινάσσων φάσγανον
ἵκετ᾽, ὀξείαις ἀνίαισι τυπείς. τὸ γὰρ οἰκεῖον πιέζει πάνθ᾽ ὁμῶς·
εὐθὺς δ᾽ ἀπήμων κραδία κᾶδος ἀμφ᾽ ἀλλότριον.

PIND. *Nem.* I. *ep.* γ΄.

‿ ‿ > | _ _ | _ ‿ | _ _ ‖ _ ‿ ‿ | _ ‿ ‿ | _ ‿ ‿ | _ ⏞ ‖
_ ‿ ‿ | _ ‿ ‿ | _ ‿ ‿ | _ _ ‖ _ ‿ | _ _ | _ ‿ | _ ∧ ‖
⌣ ‿ | _ _ ‖ _ ‿ ‿ | _ ‿ ‿ | _ ‿ ‿ | _ _ ‖ _ ‿ | _ _ | ⌣ ‿ | _ ⏞ ‖
_ : ⌣ ‿ | ⌣ | _ ‿ ‿ | ⌣ ‖ _ ‿ | _ _ | _ ‿ | _ ⏞ ‖

The notes are:

§ 13. LOGAOEDICS. 43

3. This same use of a short syllable as a long arsis sometimes occurs among dactyls in the apparent measure $\_ \cup$, of the value of $\_ >$, not $\_\_ \cup$. This use is clear when the strophe apparently has $\_ \cup$, while the antistrophe in the same place has $\_ \_$; this case is to be marked by $\_ >$. So in Doric strophes there occurs not infrequently the series $\_ \cup \mid \_ > \mid \_ \cup \mid \_ \_ \parallel$, etc.

§ 13. Logaoedics.

1. In the preceding paragraph, "Doric melodies," dactylic series of somewhat complex construction, have been treated. There is still a measure to be considered among chorees, which has the value of an ordinary choree as respects length, but not the same ictus relations. It was found that in the $^3/_8$ measure the ictus relations were $\overset{\perp}{\_} \cup$, $\overset{\cdot}{\cup} \cup \cup$. But there is also a $^3/_8$ measure with the ictuses:

$$\overset{\perp}{\_} \overset{\cdot}{\cup}, \overset{\cdot}{\cup} \cup \overset{\cdot}{\cup},$$

or, which is the same:

$$\overset{\perp}{\_} \cup, \overset{\cdot}{\cup} \cup \cup.$$

This is the *logaoedic* measure. The name arises from the apparently irregular interchange in this sort of verse of different forms of measure (or, according to the old theory, of really different measures), which made the verse seem like prose (λόγος).

2. According to § 12, 2, and § 4, 4, 2), the Greeks were inclined to put a heavier intonation on the long syllables. If, therefore, it is desired to express a heavier secondary ictus, $\overset{\perp}{\_} \overset{\cdot}{\cup}$ in distinction from $\overset{\perp}{\_} \cup$, this is best effected by having a long syllable on which this ictus shall fall; this long syllable has then the time-value of only a short: but a stronger intonation. This syllable also is denoted by $>$, to show that an apparent long syllable is given the time of a short one, as e. g.:

$$\_ \cup \mid \_ > \mid \_ \cup \mid \_ \wedge \parallel$$

The measure $\_ >$ is an "*irrational choree* (trochee)."

It is used interchangeably with $\_ \cup$. The two together, the choree coming first, are then similar in form to the so-called ἐπίτριτος δεύτερος, $\_ \cup \_ >$, or possibly $\_ > \_ >$. The succession $\_ > \_ \cup$ is not allowed. Whether now the apparent $\_ \cup \mid \_ \_ \mid \_ \cup \mid \_ \wedge \parallel$ is to be regarded as a Doric series $\_ \cup \mid \_ \_ \mid \_ \cup \mid \_ \overline{\wedge} \parallel$ or a logaoedic $\_ \cup \mid \_ > \mid \_ \cup \mid \_ \wedge \parallel$ is to be judged from the *sum total of the facts*, from which it is always to be determined whether a series is in $^4/_8$ or $^3/_8$ measure.

§ 13. LOGAOEDICS.

It may be asked, why all logaoedic measures cannot be irrational, instead of, for the most part, only those in the even places, viz. the second, fourth, and sixth. Because Greek vocal music always paid strict regard to the text; the poet was not only composer but also reciter, and in recitation a succession of none but long syllables would necessarily have seemed like spondees and been heavy and measured, while, in consequence of the heavier ictuses of the arses, the rhythm in logaoedic verse ought to become not less but more vivacious than in choreic. The first, third, and fifth measures contributed to this, since by means of their short syllables they made the movement lighter. The shorts, however, kept the same heavier intonation.

Analogously to the succession in Doric melodies ⌣ ∪ | — — |, the succession here is always — ∪ | — > |, the heavier measure in both cases, even in merely recited poetry, following the livelier, lighter measure.

3. Besides this there occurs quite frequently in logaoedic melodies another form of measure, the so-called "cyclic dactyl," i. e. the note succession ♩♪♪, expressed by the syllables — ∪ ∪. Entire series can be composed of these measures, which then look like dactylic series; but the sum of the facts in a strophe always enables us to determine what we have. The long syllable is pronounced and sung more rapidly, and together with the next short, — which loses half its value and becomes a $1/16$ note, ♬, — has the time only of a quarter-note. Therefore this combination of these two syllables was called τροχαῖος δίσημος, "two-timed trochee." It can be written metrically ⌢∪, so that the cyclic dactyl is to be expressed : ⌢∪ ∪.

Irrational as well as rational chorees can be interchanged with these cyclic dactyls in any order, so that they can occur, when in connection with these, also as first and third measure :

— ⏑ | ⌢∪∪ | — ∪ | — ∧ ||
— ⏑ | — ⏑ | ⌢∪∪ | — ∪ ||

4. Since, now, contracted measures occur frequently also among logaoedics, and that too in all the places, logaoedic measures have the following forms :

§ 13. LOGAOEDICS. 45

The secondary ictus is wanting, of course, in syncopated measures, by which the rhythm becomes so much the more varied.

As examples of the great variety of logaoedic melodies, cf. Soph. *Ant.* I., II., III., IV.

5. Since at first glance what has been stated concerning the logaoedic measure and its different forms seems to be somewhat arbitrary, it is proper that certain main proofs be given as briefly as possible. The best test of the theory, however, will be the practical application of it, after it is thoroughly understood, to different logaoedic compositions. But cf. also § 22, 11.

I. If it be insisted upon that every long syllable must have had exactly the value of two shorts, it follows that it would have been impossible, even allowing anacrusis, either to recite rhythmically or to sing any strophe whatsoever. This can easily be shown from the two verses that follow:

Τίς, ὄντιν' ἁ θεσπιέπεια Δελφὶς εἶπε πέτρα
ἄρρητ' ἀρρήτων τελέσαντα φοινίοισι χερσίν;
Soph. *Oed. R.* II. str. α' (463 – 465).

If these verses be divided into so-called feet, there results, even if anacrusis be allowed, as is proper, the following:

∪ : _ ∪ _ | _ ∪ ∪ | _ ∪ | _ ∪ | _ ∪ | _ _ ‖
_ _ | _ _ | _ ∪ ∪ | _ ∪ | _ ∪ | _ ∪ | _ ∪ ‖

In musical characters this would be:

♪ ⁞ ♩ ♪ | ♩ ♪ ♪ | ♩ ♪ | ♩ ♪ | ♩ ♪ | ♩ ♩ |

♩ ♩ | ♩ ♩ | ♩ ♪ ♪ | ♩ ♪ | ♩ ♪ | ♩ ♪ | ♩ ♪ |

There is no musician in the world who would regard it possible to execute such a combination of bars. It is equally impossible to recite such verses if the value of the notes be observed. And yet it would have been easy to cite verses much more difficult than these. If, on the other hand, the following values be given the syllables, not only will the musician regard both verses as rhythmical and impressive, but it will also be possible to recite them in such a way as to produce a beautiful effect:

∪ : _ ∪ | ∟ | _ᴗᴗ | _ ∪, ‖ _ ∪ | _ ∪ | ∟ | _ ∧ ‖
_ > | _ > | _ᴗᴗ | _ ∪, ‖ _ ∪ | _ ∪ | ∟ | _ ∧ ‖

§ 13. LOGAOEDICS.

♪:♩♪|♩. |♩. ♪♪|♩♪||♩♪|♩♪|♩♪|♩.|♩ ⁊||
♩♪|♩♪|♩. ♪♪|♩♪||♩♪|♩♪|♩.|♩ ⁊||

This is a negative proof of the correctness of the theory. It should, moreover, be remarked that the people of all lands recite logaoedics in this way. Even scholars do so, however false the values may be which they give the notes upon paper. They never recite as they have theorized, but in actual practice recite correctly, though they do so unconsciously. It is altogether another question whether, according to the theories that have prevailed, the strophes have been properly divided into verses, etc., or not. As to this there have been as many views as writers, and the utmost confusion has prevailed.

II. A positive proof of the correctness of the forms of the measures that have been given is the fact that in the antistrophe an apparent _ _ (i. e. _ >) can and often does stand as the equivalent of _ ᴗ in the strophe, and *vice versa*. This proves conclusively that _ _ and _ ᴗ have the same time-value, _ > = _ ᴗ.

Compare e. g. Soph. *Ant.* V. *str.* and *ant.* α′, v. 3 (810 and 828):

str. α′. κοὔποτ' αὖθις· ἀλλά μ' ὁ παγκοίτας Ἀίδας ζῶσαν ἄγει
ant. α′. πετραία βλάστα δάμασεν, καί νιν ὄμβροι τακομέναν
i. e.   _ ᴗ | _ ᴗ | ‿ᴗ | ∟ || _ > | _ > | ‿ᴗ | _ ∧ ||
        _ ᴗ | _ > | ‿ᴗ | ∟ || _ ᴗ | _ > | ‿ᴗ | _ ∧ ||

And likewise in numberless other cases. Chorees, also, designed for recitation, as e. g. the common trimeter, are an additional proof of this. If we say here that "spondees occur in place of iambi," the words are meaningless; unless one is ready to affirm seriously that 4 is equal to 3.

III. The cyclic dactyl is likewise used as the equivalent of _ ᴗ and _ >. This indeed does not occur often in lyric strophes, because ‿ᴗ is comparatively so vivacious a measure that if any other be used for it the melody seems to be essentially modified. It does occur, however, in the trimeter, especially in that of the comedians, the dialogue of whose dramas was distinguished from that of the tragedians by greater liveliness. This is seen in the first verses of the *Clouds* of Aristophanes. (With reference to the character ω in v. 2, see § 15.)

Ὦ Ζεῦ βασιλεῦ, τὸ χρῆμα τῶν νυκτῶν ὅσον
ἀπέραντον· οὐδέποθ' ἡμέρα γενήσεται;
καὶ μὴν πάλαι γ' ἀλεκτρυόνος ἤκουσ' ἐγώ·

§ 13. LOGAOEDICS.

$$> \mid -\cup\cup \mid \_ > \mid \_\cup \mid \_ > \mid \_\cup \mid \_\wedge \parallel$$
$$\omega \mid \_\cup \mid -\cup\cup \mid \_\cup \mid \_\cup \mid \_\cup \mid \_\wedge \parallel$$
$$> \mid \_\cup \mid \_\cup \mid \_\cup \mid \cup\cup > \mid \_\cup \mid \_\wedge \parallel$$

It is beyond question that the different forms of measure that occur here, $\_\cup$, $\_>$, $\cup\cup>$, and $-\cup\cup$ (the tribrach, $\cup\cup\cup$, does not happen to occur here) have the same time-value, since the kind of verse remains the same, however much the forms of the measures change.

IV. That there is a strong secondary ictus on the arsis of the logaoedic measure is proved, first by the correspondence of $\_\cup$ and $\_>$ in strophe and antistrophe; and then by the fact that the cyclic dactyl, $-\cup\cup$, is admitted as a form of the measure. For if we dwell for a considerable length of time on a note like ♪ and then pass rapidly over the second short one, ♪, the third note of twice the value of this, ♪, is naturally made prominent, that is, is given a strong secondary ictus. This bar, ♪ ♪ ♪, is very common in the music of all nations, and must have been used by the Greeks. Even in recitation, verses in which $-\cup\cup$ interchanges with $\_\cup$ and with $\_>$ are to-day so pronounced.

So there arises the logaoedic measure, a measure of very lively character, which distinguishes it from the less vivacious chorees and still less vivacious dactyls. If the subject-matter of poetry in logaoedic measure be considered, it will be seen that it has the same spirited character that distinguishes the measure, which is an additional proof of the correctness of the theory.

V. This theory, when applied to the productions of the Greek poets, shows a regularity in their rhythmical construction and a beauty of composition which must remove the last trace of doubt. From verse to verse we see how exactly thought and form correspond, and are filled with wonder at those mighty masters who were at once poets and musicians. What, moreover, the true division of the strophes into verses is, will be so obvious if the various criteria and rules are carefully observed, that in no case can there be doubt. To make such an application as the one suggested above, in detail, is beyond the province of a mere Introduction. The reader is referred for this to the larger volumes of Dr. Schmidt mentioned in the Preface.

§ 14. Further Use of the "Two-timed Trochee."

Cf. the preceding paragraph, 3.

1. In unmistakably paeonic strophes, measures like $\_\cup\_\cup$, with the value of $\_\cup\smile$, i. e. ♩ ♪ ♫ |, are seldom met. We may conclude that they do occur only when there are the most certain indications that the verse is not choreic; for, generally, verses like

have the notation
$$\_\cup\_\_\cup\_\_\cup\_\cup\_\cup\_$$
$$\_\cup\mid\llcorner\mid\_\cup\mid\llcorner\parallel\_\cup\mid\_\cup\mid\_\cup\mid\_\wedge\parallel,$$

not
$$\_\cup\_\mid\_\cup\_\parallel\_\cup\smile\mid\_\cup\_\mid$$

Undoubtedly such a paeonic measure occurs in Ar. *Eq.* IV. *ant.* (684 – 687):

> Εὗρε δ' ὁ πανοῦργος ἕτερον πολὺ πανουργίαις
> μείζοσι κεκασμένον, καὶ δόλοισι ποικίλοις
> ῥήμασίν θ' αἱμύλοις.

$$\_\cup\cup\cup\mid\_\cup\cup\cup\parallel\_\cup\cup\cup\mid\_\cup\_\parallel$$
$$\_\cup\cup\cup\mid\_\cup\_\parallel\_\cup\smile\mid\_\cup\_\parallel$$
$$\_\cup\_\mid\_\cup\_\parallel$$

2. Quite as seldom do ionic measures of the form $\smile\_\cup\cup$, i. e. ♫ ♩ ♫, occur.

> Ὑμέναιον ὃς τότ' ἐπέρρεπε
> γαμβροῖσιν ἀείδειν.

AESCH. *Ag.* III. *ant.* a' (707, 708).

$$\cup\cup\vdots\smile\_\cup\cup\mid\_\cup\_\wedge\parallel$$
$$\_\_\cup\cup\mid\_\_\overline{\wedge}\parallel, \text{ i. e.}$$

♫ ⁚ ♫ ♩ ♫ | ♩ ♪ ♩ 𝄾 ‖
♩ ♩ ♫ | ♩ 𝄾 ‖

(Concerning the final measure of the first verse, cf. § 23, 2.)

3. The combination ♫ is as frequent in the music of *all* nations as in the poetry and music of the Greeks. "Superfluous" syllables are treated in a similar way in our recitation of English poetry. For example:

> Then, methought, I heard a hollow sound,
> Gathering up from all the lower ground;
> Narrowing in to where they sat assembled,
> Low, voluptuous music, winding, trembled.
>
> *Tennyson.*

§ 15. SIXTEENTH NOTES. 49

```
_ ⌣ | _ ⌣ | _ ⌣ | _ ⌣ | _ ∧ ‖
⌣⌣ ⌣ | _ ⌣ | _ ⌣ | _ ⌣ | _ ∧ ‖
⌣⌣ ⌣ | _ ⌣ | _ ⌣ | _ ⌣ | _ ⌣ ‖
_ ⌣ | ⌣⌣ ⌣ | _ ⌣ | _ ⌣ | _ ⌣ ‖
```

Syllables without ictus may be treated not only as shorts, but also as "half-shorts" (𝅘𝅥𝅮 for 𝅘𝅥𝅯).

§ 15. Sixteenth Notes.

1. One use of the sixteenth-note has already been explained, namely in the *trochaeus disemus* in the formation, first of a cyclic dactyl (§ 13, 3), then of an "irrational" paeon (§ 14, 1), and then of an "irrational" ionic (§ 14, 2).

Besides this, two united sixteenths occur now and then in choreic measures, i. e. 𝅘𝅥𝅯𝅘𝅥𝅯 for 𝅘𝅥𝅯, forming with preceding long syllables whole series of 𝅘𝅥 𝅘𝅥𝅯𝅘𝅥𝅯, which outwardly appear like real dactyls or cyclic dactyls, but probably do not belong even to the latter. We will write two half-shorts ω, so that _ ω = 𝅘𝅥 𝅘𝅥𝅯𝅘𝅥𝅯.

A fine example occurs in AESCH. *Ag.* IV. ant. α' (987 – 993):

Πεύθομαι δ' ἀπ' ὀμμάτων νόστον, αὐτόμαρτυς ὤν·
τὸν δ' ἄνευ λύρας ὅμως ὑμνῳδεῖ
θρῆνον Ἐρινύος αὐτοδίδακτος ἔσωθεν
θυμός, οὐ τὸ πᾶν ἔχων ἐλπίδος φίλον θράσος.

```
_ ⌣ | _ ⌣ | _ ⌣ | ⌞  ‖ _ ⌣ | _ ⌣ | _ ⌣ | _ ∧ ‖
_ ⌣ | _ ⌣ | _ ⌣ | _ ⌣ | ⌞   | _ ∧ ‖
_ ω | _ ω | _ ω | _ ω | ⌞   | _ ∧ ‖
_ ⌣ | _ ⌣ | _ ⌣ | ⌞  ‖ _ ⌣ | _ ⌣ | _ ⌣ | _ ∧ ‖
```

2. The combination ⌣ ⌣ ω, i. e. 𝅘𝅥𝅯𝅘𝅥𝅯 𝅘𝅥𝅯𝅘𝅥𝅯, was too quick a measure for the Greeks; to understand the *words* (for we are now always speaking of vocal music only) would scarcely have been possible, if they had been pronounced so quickly. Therefore the cyclic "proccleusmatic," as this form has been named, does not occur. An exception hardly worthy of notice will be considered in § 17, 4.

3. It is not inconsistent to regard the combination of syllables _ ⌣ ⌣ in the iambic trimeter on the one hand as ⌣⌣ ⌣, in lyric strophes in choreic measure on the other as _ ω. For in the last the character of the measure is very carefully preserved. The combination _ ⌣ ⌣, when it is to be regarded ⌣⌣ ⌣ in a choreic strophe or part of a

strophe, hardly ever occurs in considerable number, and generally only where there is a transition into logaoedic verse. Verses like $-\cup\cup\,|$ $-\cup\cup\,|-\cup\cup\,|-\cup\cup\,|\sqcup\,|-\wedge\,\|$ would fairly destroy the unity of the measure, while a verse like $-\omega\,|-\omega\,|-\omega\,|-\omega\,|\sqcup\,|-\wedge\,\|$ is beautifully adapted to it; for a combination like ♩ ♫ cannot, in the nature of things, have a strong secondary ictus on the last short syllable which is pronounced so rapidly as scarcely to be heard. On examination it will be seen that in all verses of this sort the contents correspond exactly to the rhythm $-\omega$. In the above verse, e. g.,

$$\theta\rho\tilde{\eta}\nu o\nu\ \text{'E}\rho\iota\nu\acute{\nu}o\varsigma\ a\mathring{\upsilon}\tau o\delta\acute{\iota}\delta a\kappa\tau o\varsigma\ \mathring{\epsilon}\sigma\omega\theta\epsilon\nu,$$

the heavy complaint of the chorus that breaks forth impetuously is adequately expressed first by the strong ictus placed each time on $-$, and then by the quick movement of ω. (The final measures $\sqcup\,|-\wedge\,\|$ are in strong contrast to those that precede.)

In the iambic trimeter, on the other hand, the apparent dactyl that sometimes occurs is not to be regarded $-\omega$, but $-\cup\cup$, since the trimeter is in its character more or less logaoedic. It will be noted, further, that in the solemn trimeter of tragedy the apparent dactyl occurs almost only in proper names and then from necessity. This rule was strictly observed until the time of Euripides, but he is somewhat freer. The propriety, on the other hand, of the admission of the lively cyclic dactyl into comedy is obvious.

§ 16. Recitative Chorees.

1. The combination of syllables $-\cup\,|--\,|$, however it may be regarded musically, whether as $\sqcup\cup\,|--\,|$ or as $-\cup\,|->\,|$, nevertheless always puts last that measure which, with reference to its syllables, is heavier and less rapid than the other. It is very frequent in recitative chorees, both iambi and trochees, but, on the other hand, occurs very seldom among chorees that were sung. In the iambic trimeter, then, the second and fourth measures, in the trochaic tetrameter also the sixth, may be "irrational," i. e. an apparent spondee.

$$\overset{\text{\~}}{\omega}\ \kappa o\iota\nu\grave{o}\nu\ a\mathring{\upsilon}\tau\acute{a}\delta\epsilon\lambda\phi o\nu\ \text{'I}\sigma\mu\acute{\eta}\nu\eta\varsigma\ \kappa\acute{a}\rho a$$
$$>\,\vdots\,-\cup\,|-\cup\,|-\cup\,|->\,|-\cup\,|-\wedge\,\|$$

$$\mathring{a}\rho'\ o\mathring{\iota}\sigma\theta'\ \mathring{o}\ \tau\iota\ Z\epsilon\grave{\upsilon}\varsigma\ \tau\tilde{\omega}\nu\ \mathring{a}\pi'\ O\mathring{\iota}\delta\acute{\iota}\pi o\upsilon\ \kappa a\kappa\tilde{\omega}\nu$$
$$>\,\vdots\,-\cup\,|->\,|-\cup\,|-\cup\,|-\cup\,|-\wedge\,\|$$

§ 16. RECITATIVE CHOREES.   51

ὦ πάτρας Θήβης ἔνοικοι, λεύσσετ', Οἰδίπους ὅδε,
ὃς τὰ κλείν' αἰνίγματ' ᾔδη καὶ κράτιστος ἦν ἀνήρ,
εἰς ὅσον κλύδωνα δεινῆς συμφορᾶς ἐλήλυθεν.
         Soph. *Oed. R.* 1524 *sq.*

_ ∪ | _ > | _ ∪ | _ > ‖ _ ∪ | _ ∪ | _ ∪ | _ ∧ ‖
_ ∪ | _ > | _ ∪ | _ > ‖ _ ∪ | _ ∪ | _ ∪ | _ ∧ ‖
_ ∪ | _ ∪ | _ ∪ | _ > ‖ _ ∪ | _ ∪ | _ ∪ | _ ∧ ‖

2. It is further to be remarked concerning the tragic trimeter, that it admits, though seldom, the cyclic dactyl in each of the five complete measures, though generally only in case of proper names. Its occurrence also in the first and fifth measure is rare, since thereby the character of the verse would have been too considerably changed.

Τέκνον τυφλοῦ γέροντος Ἀντιγόνη, τίνας
χώρους ἀφίγμεθ', ἢ τίνων ἀνδρῶν πόλιν;
         Soph. *Oed. Col.* 1, 2.

∪ ⁝ _ ∪ | _ ∪ | _ ∪ | ⌣∪ | _ ∪ | _ ∧ ‖
> ⁝ _ ∪ | _ ∪ | _ ∪ | _ > | _ ∪ | _ ∧ ‖

The dissyllabic anacrusis is also allowed, as e. g. Aesch. *Pers.* 327:

Κιλίκων ἔπαρχος, εἷς ἀνὴρ πλεῖστον πόνον
ἐχθροῖς παρασχών, εὐκλεῶς ἀπώλετο.

ω ⁝ _ ∪ | _ ∪ | _ ∪ | _ > | _ ∪ | _ ∧ ‖.

But cyclic proceleusmatics are not to be admitted, and such a trimeter as

∪ _ ∪ _ ∪ ∪ ∪ ∪ _ ∪ _ ∪ _

should not be divided

∪ ⁝ _ ∪ | _ ∪ | ∪ ∪ ω | _ ∪ | _ ∪ | _,

but ∪ ⁝ _ ∪ | ⌣∪ | ∪ ∪ ∪ | _ ∪ | _ ∪ | _ ∧ ‖.

The cyclic dactyl and the tribrach occur much more frequently in the trimeter of comedy, which thereby becomes much more lively (cf. § 15, 3). The irrational choree, moreover, may be resolved and appear as ∪∪ > (♫ ♪, the last eighth being expressed by a long syllable).

Ἰοὺ ἰού·
ὦ Ζεῦ βασιλεῦ, τὸ χρῆμα τῶν νυκτῶν ὅσον
ἀπέραντον. οὐδέποθ' ἡμέρα γενήσεται;
καὶ μὴν πάλαι γ' ἀλεκτρυόνος ἤκουσ' ἐγώ. Ar. *Nub.* 1-4.

> ⁝ ⌣∪ | _ ∪ | _ ∪ | _ > | _ ∪ | _ ∧ ‖
ω ⁝ _ ∪ | ⌣∪ | _ ∪ | _ ∪ | _ ∪ | _ ∧ ‖
> ⁝ _ ∪ | _ ∪ | _ ∪ | ∪ ∪ > | _ ∪ | _ ∧ ‖

§ 17. Metrical Correspondence.

1. The Greeks generally divided their songs, as do modern nations, into portions called strophes (cf. § 33, 1), exactly corresponding to each other rhythmically and metrically and having the same melody. These usually correspond so exactly that at the same places in the strophes *the same forms of the measure occur;* e. g. the one strophe, with very few exceptions, cannot have a cyclic dactyl where the other has a choree, etc.

2. There are, however, two exceptions to this rule:

I. Two shorts may in most cases correspond to the simple long. Accordingly, a verse like
$$- \cup | - \cup | - \cup | - \wedge \|$$
may in any one of the strophes also read
$$- \cup | \cup \cup \cup | - \cup | - \wedge \|,$$
where $\cup \cup \cup = -\cup$.

Such a correspondence is indicated by writing the one over the other, as here: $- \cup | \underset{\cup\cup}{-} \cup | - \cup | - \wedge \|$, which shows that the long had two tones which in the following strophe fell to the two shorts that took its place.

In like manner the following cases may occur: $- \cup \underset{\cup\cup}{-}$, $\underset{\cup\cup}{-} \cup -$, $- \underset{\cup\cup}{-} \cup$, seldom $- \underset{\cup\cup}{-} \cup \cup$, etc.

II. An irrational syllable in the arsis may correspond to a rational. Four cases of this occur:

A. The long may correspond to the short in the arsis of the $^3/_8$ measures (chorees and logaoedics), being used to moderate the too lively movement of a choreic series, or to show more distinctly the heavier, secondary ictus of the logaoedic:
$$- \cup | - \overset{\frown}{\cup} | - \cup | - \wedge \|,$$
$$- \overset{\frown}{\cup} | - \cup \cup | - \cup | - \wedge \|.$$

B. In equal measures (commonly in Doric melodies, less often in the case of true dactyls), the short, which is allowed on account of the weak ictus of the arsis, may answer to the real long:
$$\cup \cup | - \overset{\frown}{\geq} | \cup \cup | - \overline{\wedge} \|.$$

C. Short and irrational syllables may correspond in every anacrusis; also in the arses of the dochmii (concerning which see § 23, 4):
$$\overset{\frown}{\geq} : \overset{\frown}{\cup} \cup | - \cup | - \wedge \|,$$
$$\overset{\frown}{\geq} : - \cup | - \cup | - \cup | - \wedge \|.$$

§ 17. METRICAL CORRESPONDENCE. 53

D. In the cyclic dactyl in a few cases a short stands in place of the initial long: ⏑⏑⏑ for —⏑⏑. It is then more convenient to write ⩺⏑⏑, since the unusual value of the syllables is especially noticeable in the first. The notes remain the same, even the apparent tribrach then having the value of 𝅘𝅥𝅮𝅭 𝅘𝅥𝅮.

If it be observed that the value of 𝅘𝅥𝅮 stands between 𝅘𝅥 and 𝅘𝅥𝅮, it is clear that the short syllable could just as well be used in its place (𝅘𝅥𝅮 for 𝅘𝅥𝅮) as the long (𝅘𝅥 for 𝅘𝅥𝅮). But quite naturally this was avoided as much as possible, because on the one hand it did not so easily allow the heavy ictus and on the other hand stood too near the following short, which was to have only a third of its value ($𝅘𝅥𝅮 = 1/3\ 𝅘𝅥𝅮$).

3. But under no circumstances may the prolonged long syllable (⌊⏤ or ⌊⏝) be replaced by two shorts. If, therefore, e. g. a choreic series _⏑__⏑_⏑_⏑_ is to be divided _⏑ | ⌊⏤ | _⏑ | _⏑ | _⏑ | _∧‖, it would not be at all possible for two short syllables in the antistrophe to correspond to the second long. For the metrical correspondence ⏑⏑/⌊⏤ is an impossibility.

The prolonged long syllables of three and four times cannot, moreover, be replaced by any other combinations of syllables, e. g. ‾⏑, ⏑⏑⏑/⌊⏤, although ⌊⏤, _⏑, and ⏑⏑⏑ have the same time-value. Through "prolongation" a syllable or tone receives an uncommon weight, which would be lost in the resolution (_⏑ or ⏑⏑⏑ = ⌊⏤), and the result of this would be that the melodies would not exactly correspond.

4. Pindar has two instances of somewhat freer correspondence.

I. He has several times used in logaoedic strophes an apparent iambus for a tribrach, i. e. ⏑⏜_ corresponding to ⏑⏑⏑, i. e. ⏑⏝. There thus arises the measure 𝅘𝅥𝅮⏜ 𝅘𝅥 |, that does not occur elsewhere. Cf. *Ol.* I. *str. β'*, v. 9:

ἐς ἔρανον φίλαν τε Σίπυλον
⏑⏑⏑ | _⏑ | ⌊⏤ | ⏑⏑⏑ | _∧‖

and *ant. β'*, v. 9:
μαχαίρᾳ τάμον κατὰ μέλη

that is
⏑_ | _⏑ | ⌊⏤ | ⏑⏑⏑ | _∧‖,

⏑⏝ | ⸝⏑ | ⌊⏤ | ⏑⏑⏑ | ⸝∧‖.

II. In two places he has ⏑⏑ω (a cyclic proceleusmatic) answering to the apparent dactyl _ω. One of the cases is *Pyth.* XI. *str. α'*, v. 5:

μᾱτρὶ πὰρ Μελίαν χρυσέων ἐς ἄδυτον τριπόδων
_⏑ | _ω | _> | ⌊⏤ ‖ ⏑⏑⏑ | ⏝⏑ | _∧‖

§ 17. METRICAL CORRESPONDENCE.

and *ant. a', v.* 5 :

ὄφρα θέμιν ἱερὰν Πυθῶνά τε καὶ ὀρθοδίκαν.

that is

$\_\cup\,|\,\cup\cup\bullet\,|\_>|\,\llcorner\,\|\,\cup\cup\cup\,|\,\smile\cup\,|\_\wedge\,\|$

$\_\cup\,|\,\underline{\smile}\bullet\,|\_>|\,\llcorner\,\|\,\cup\cup\cup\,|\,\smile\cup\,|\_\wedge\,\|$

The poet first had in mind, as he composed, a verse with ⌣⌣⌣ or with ⎯ ⚬; but he did not hesitate to use other combinations of syllables when these occurred to him in one of the antistrophes, i. e. ⌣⎯ and ⌣⌣⚬. The case is different from what it would have been if these measures had been used independently throughout in all the strophes, where they probably would have had the notes ♩ ♩ and ♪ ♪ ♫, while here ⌣⎯ must have had the notes ♩ ♬, and in ⌣⌣⚬ both the first tones could have had the same pitch, e. g. ·

, which makes the two eighth-notes about the same as the single quarter-note.

5. To conclude this general subject, it may be remarked that other combinations of notes in measures than those that have been given cannot be inferred from the texts that have come down to us; and that they would conflict with the principles of the writers on rhythmic and metric, who even reduce the number of forms still more, though wrongly. The Greek composer was at the same time poet, and did no violence to his speech even in music. Modern composers, on the contrary, dispose of the texts of songs in the most arbitrary manner, so that very frequently there arise entirely different musical measures from what the text authorizes. For example, Burns's ballad begins,

    O wert thou in the cauld blast,
    On yonder lea, on yonder lea;
    My plaidie to the angry airt,
    I 'd shelter thee, I 'd shelter thee; etc.,

i. e.   ⌣ ⋮ ⎯ ⌣ | ⎯ ⌣ | ⎯ ⌣ | ⎯‿ | ⎯
    ⌣ ⋮ ⎯ ⌣ | ⎯ ⌣ | ⎯ ⌣ | ⎯

Mendelssohn's music begins:

♩ ♪ ♪ ♪ ♪ | ♫ ♩. ♪ | ♪ ♪ ♪. ♪ | ♪. ♪ ♩.

that is   ⎯ ⌣ ⌣ ⌣ ⌣ | ⌣ ⎯ ⌣ | ⌣ ⎯ ⌣ | ⌣ ⎯.

Third Book.

RHYTHMIC.

§ 18. The Rhythmical Sentence (κῶλον).

1. Measures have a rhythmical as well as a metrical value. The doctrine of their ictuses belongs properly to rhythmic, which teaches us how these small divisions of the verse, having exactly the same value in time, correspond to one another in ictus. But to fix the constitution of these measures, to determine what given notes shall stand in them, is the province of metric, which teaches us the use of the syllables of speech for this purpose. From this point on, only the rhythmical values of the measures will be regarded.

2. Measures are such small divisions of time that their continued repetition, without separation into well-divided groups, could not have sufficed either for dance or march. The dance especially would have been nothing else than a series of always equal movements, in which no art could have been displayed. It came about, therefore,' that as in spoken language the words were united into grammatical sentences, so in the rhythmical language of song the measures were united into rhythmical sentences. And further on we shall see the union of these sentences into periods. The following correspondences, therefore, can be traced out:

1. Note.
2. Measure.
3. Rhythmical sentence.
4. Rhythmical period.

1. Syllable.
2. Word.
3. Grammatical sentence.
4. Grammatical period.

§ 18. THE RHYTHMICAL SENTENCE.

3. A grammatical sentence sounds to the ear as such

1) from the principal ictus which is given to one of the words, the ictuses of the other words being only secondary.

In the sentence

    Caesar, beware of Brutus,

we have the ictuses:

    $\dot{-}\,{-},\ {-}\,\dot{-},\ {-},\ \dot{-}\,{-}.$

The word "Brutus" has the principal ictus of the sentence, so that the syllable -*ware*, though it has the chief word-ictus in "beware," nevertheless appears in the sentence as a syllable with secondary ictus only.

If two or more grammatical sentences are united into a period, each of them has its own chief ictus, e. g.

    Caesar, beware of Brutus; Decius Brutus loves thee not,

that is

    $\dot{-}\,{-},\ {-}\,\dot{-},\ {-},\ \dot{-}\,{-};\ \smile\,{-},\ \dot{-}\,{-},\ \dot{-},\ {-},\ \dot{-}.$

It is customary to distinguish the ictus-syllables of single sentences by higher or lower tones. Beyond this the relations of the ictuses in grammatical periods are much confused in consequence of the ellipses, incorporations, etc., that may occur.

2) The sentence cannot overstep a fixed length. This is so in the nature of the case, since in a simple sentence there can be but one subject, etc. For the sentence " Gold and riches do not make one happy " is really an elliptical contraction of two sentences : " Gold does not make one happy " and " Riches do not make one happy." But on still other grounds a fixed length cannot be overstepped. In too long sentences the syllable with the chief ictus would no longer appear as such with sufficient distinctness: the voice would have to admit in other places one or more syllables with equal emphasis. Suppose that we construct the sentence : "*An occurrence in all respects exceedingly distressing has cast the entire population of this world-renowned city into the most extraordinary excitement and unwonted alarm.*" — Where here is the single chief ictus? Would not every one divide this sentence into three groups and give each of these three groups its own chief ictus?

  An occurrence in all respects exceedingly distressing |
 has cast the entire population of this world-renowned city |
 into the most extraordinary excitement and unwonted alarm. |

Such a sentence, then, is a rhythmical anomaly, which a good writer will allow himself seldom and only for a fixed purpose, — for prose, too, is controlled by the principles of rhythm.

3) Every grammatical sentence is distinctly separated from the remaining sentences by a pause. There are different degrees of separation, which are distinguished by the comma, colon, period, etc. Generally the period shows that a sentence is not further closely connected with what follows, but this is not necessarily the case.

4. *A rhythmical sentence is a series of almost always equal measures, which appear as a unit through the chief ictus that falls on one of them.*

A fixed length cannot be overstepped.

Rhythmical sentences were originally separated from one another by pauses. The pauses within the periods had afterwards their regular places; after many sentences also they might be wanting.

This closely resembles the construction of the period in prose. For even the want of rhythmical pauses has there its exact analogy in the case of periods complexly constructed. Because of the displacement of their parts many sentences in such periods cannot be accurately separated by pauses.

§ 19. Close of Sentences.

1. All melodies consist of such rhythmical sentences as these with fixed succession of tones.

The rhythmical sentence corresponds in general to the *line* in an English stanza. The line is either completely isolated by a pause at its close, or it is closely united to the following line, the pause being scarcely noticeable. The music e. g. of the lines

    We have lived and loved together
    Through many a changing year

is as follows:

  We have lived and loved together Through many a changing year.

In this case the first line is separated from the second by a pause, though it is true that the first note of the second line falls in the last measure of the first.

§ 19. CLOSE OF SENTENCES.

The relation is different in the following:

> When other lips and other hearts
> Their tales of love shall tell.

When other lips and oth - er hearts Their tales of love shall tell.

Here the anacrusis of the second line constitutes the arsis of the final measure of the first. This is very common; but it also often happens that the first line ends with full measure, and the second begins immediately likewise with full measure.

2. All these relations are common in Greek poetry. But in addition it is allowed to begin a new rhythmical sentence in the middle of a word without any pause whatever. The following, then, are the four cases fully stated:

I. There is a pause of unfixed length after the sentence; *then it constitutes a verse, whose close is always to be recognized* by the following facts:

1) The sentence ends with the end of a word, the final vowel of which is seldom elided.

2) Hiatus is allowed with the beginning of the next sentence.

3) The last syllable is *of variable value* (συλλαβὴ ἀδιάφορος, *syllaba anceps*), i. e. the long syllable may have the value of a short one, the short of a long.

> Ἀμηχανῶ, φροντίδος στερηθεὶς
> εὐπάλαμον μέριμναν
> ὅπα τράπωμαι, πίτνοντος οἴκου.
> AESCH. *Ag.* VII. *str.* γ´ (1530–1532).

$$\cup \stackrel{\cdot}{:} \_ \cup | \_ | \_ \cup | \_ \cup | \_ | \_ \wedge \|$$
$$\_ \cup \cup | \_ \cup | \_ | \_ \wedge \|$$
$$\cup \stackrel{\cdot}{:} \_ \cup | \_ | \_ \cup | \_ \cup | \_ | \_ \wedge \|$$

At the close of the second verse -ᾶν has the value of a long syllable, though the next word (ὅπα) begins with a vowel.

II. The sentence must indeed end with a complete word, but

1) the final syllable cannot be *anceps*, so that e. g. a short syllable could not be used as a long one.

2) Hiatus is, with very few exceptions, forbidden.

§ 19. CLOSE OF SENTENCES.

Such a sentence, consequently, cannot end the verse. This sort of close is called *diaeresis* (διαίρεσις).
The following is an example;

δυσάνεμον στόνῳ βρέμουσιν ἀντιπλῆγες ἀκταί.
SOPH. *Ant.* III. *str.* a' (591, 592).
⏑ ⋮ _ ⏑ | _ ⏑ | _ ⏑ | _ ⏑, ‖ _ ⏑ | _ ⏑ | ட | _ ⋀ ‖.

III. The sentence ends with the thesis, to which the following sentence furnishes the arsis.
This sort of close is called *caesura* (τομή).
This caesura is well known e. g. in the hexameter, which consists of two sentences of three measures each. The last measure of the first sentence is not metrically complete without the arsis, which is regarded as a sort of anacrusis to the second sentence; a new word begins after the third thesis, yet not necessarily immediately, since it may begin after the first short syllable of the arsis. Therefore, if the caesura is indicated by a comma, either

and
_ ∞ | _ ∞ | _, ⏑ ⏑ ‖ _ ∞ | _ ∞ | _ _ ‖

or also
_ ∞ | _ ∞ | _, _ ‖ _ ∞ | _ ∞ | _ _ ‖

_ ∞ | _ ∞ | _ ⏑, ⏑ ‖ _ ∞ | _ ∞ | _ _ ‖

The first sort of this caesura is called "masculine caesura," as e. g.

Μῆνιν ἄειδε, θεά, Πηληϊάδεω 'Αχιλῆος.
_ ⏑ ⏑ | _ ⏑ ⏑ | _, _ ‖ _ ⏑ ⏑ | _ ⏑ ⏑ | _ _ ‖

The second is called "feminine caesura," as e. g.

"Ανδρα μοι ἔννεπε, Μοῦσα, πολύτροπον, ὃς μάλα πολλά.
_ ⏑ ⏑ | _ ⏑ ⏑ | _ ⏑, ⏑ ‖ _ ⏑ ⏑ | _ ⏑ ⏑ | _ _ ‖

In this way two sentences are very beautifully united with each other, the second linking into the first. In the music, also, sentences are united in the same way, as is to be seen in songs like the one cited above: " We have lived and loved together, through many a changing year." This would have been regarded by the Greeks as one verse, divided by a caesura into two members (musical and rhythmical sentences), like the heroic hexameter. Though in the melody a new series of tones begins with the word "through," still metrically it belongs to the first sentence, whose final measure is not complete without it.

The caesura is of more weight in melic than in merely rhythmical verse, but is still of especial importance in recitation, on account of which it will be discussed more at length under the "recitative types."

IV. The new sentence may begin anywhere within a word.

Here, therefore, regard is no longer paid to grammatical speech: the music is predominant and, within the bounds of the limitations given in Book II., arranges its notes at will without reference to the spoken word. This practice could have arisen only in a language whose words were spoken very rapidly even when separated by marks of punctuation.

This sort of close of the sentence needs no especial name, since the melody is not affected by the absence of the word-pause. It is obvious e. g. in the second English illustration in this paragraph, "When other lips," etc., that the melody would not be affected, if in place of the words that fall to the last two notes of the second full bar and the first note of the third, a *single* word should occur, if that were possible. In Greek poetry that was sung the caesura certainly did not signify a pause. In a verse, therefore, like

_ ∪ | ‿∪ ∪ | ‿∪ ∪ | _ , ∪ ‖ _ ∪ | _ ∪ | ∟ | _ ∧ ‖,

if a new part of the melody begins just after the comma, we shall use the expression "caesura," no matter whether a word end at this point or not. In the same way we regard it a case of "diaeresis," in the trochaic tetrameter e. g.,

_ ∪ | _ ∪ | _ ∪ | _ ∪, ‖ _ ∪ | _ ∪ | _ ∪ | _ ∧ ‖,

even if the first sentence ends in the middle of a word.

If, on the other hand, the first sentence end with a syncopated measure (§ 11, 3), so that two theses come together without intervening arsis, as in the following example from Aeschylus, we have what may be called "break." Such verses are "asynartete." The Greek expression is στίχοι ἀσυνάρτητοι.

> Ἰλίῳ δὲ κῆδος ὀρ|θώνυμον τελεσσίφρων
> Μῆνις ἤλασεν τρυπέ|ζας ἀτίμωσιν ὑστέρῳ χρόνῳ
> καὶ ξυνεστίου Διός,
> πρασσομένα τὸ νυμφότι|μον μέλος ἐκφάτως τίοντας.
>   AESCH. *Ag.* III. *ant. a'* (700 – 706).

_ ∪ | _ ∪ | _ ∪ | ∟ ‖ _ ∪ | _ ∪ | _ ∪ | _ ∧ ‖
_ ∪ | _ ∪ | _ ∪ | ∟ ‖ _ ∪ | ∟ | _ ∪ | _ ∪ | _ ∪ | _ ∧ ‖
_ ∪ | _ ∪ | _ ∪ | _ ∧ ‖
‿∪ | _ ∪ | _ ∪ | ∟ ‖ ‿∪ | _ ∪ | _ ∪ | _ ∪ ‖

In asynartete verses also, as well as in those with caesura or diaeresis, the first sentence may end either with a word, as in the verse,

Οὐδ' ὅστις πάροιθεν ἦν μέγας, παμμάχῳ θράσει βρύων,
AESCH. *Ag.* I. ant. β' (168, 169);

or in the middle of a word, as in the corresponding verse,

Ζεύς, ὅστις ποτ' ἐστίν, εἰ τόδ' αὐτῷ φίλον κεκλημένῳ,
AESCH. *Ag.* I. str. β' (160, 161).

These examples, being the corresponding verses of strophe and antistrophe, also show that the character of the melody is in no respect changed, whether the first sentence ends with a word or in the middle of it. Marking the place where the first sentence ends with a word by a colon, the following notation shows the two verses exactly equal:

⌴ | ⌴ | ‿ ∪ | ‿ ∪ | ‿ ∪ | ⌴ : ‖ ‿ ∪ | ‿ ∪ | ‿ ∪ | ‿ ∧ ‖

and ⌴ | ⌴ | ‿ ∪ | ‿ ∪ | ‿ ∪ | ⌴ ‖ ‿ ∪ | ‿ ∪ | ‿ ∪ | ‿ ∧ ‖.

§ 20. Intonation of Sentences.

1. The science of Greek rhythm was early reduced to systems philosophically developed. Here, as in almost all the sciences, instead of simply a statement of the facts and a development of categories from the facts, the categories were developed *a priori*, and the facts had to be interpreted in accordance with these logically refined schemes.

The sentences, like the measures, were divided into equal, unequal, and quinquepartite.

The equal sentences were the dipody, consisting of $1 + 1$, and the tetrapody, of $2 + 2$ measures; the unequal, the tripody, of $2 + 1$, and the hexapody, of $4 + 2$; the quinquepartite, the pentapody, of $3 + 2$.

According to this division θέσις and ἄρσις were again distinguished. Each had its fixed number of measures, as follows:

Dipody: θέσις had 1 measure,   ἄρσις had 1 measure.
Tetrapody: "   " 2 measures,   "   " 2 measures.
Tripody: "   " 2 measures,   "   " 1 measure.
Hexapody: "   " 4 measures,   "   " 2 measures.
Pentapody: "   " 3 measures,   "   " 2 measures.

Now, according to this division, there ought to be an exact regulation of the ictuses of the sentence, so that in the case of equal division, e. g., there should be only two strong ictuses, the stronger on the thesis, the weaker on the arsis.

§ 20. INTONATION OF SENTENCES.

$$\text{́} \cup | \text{́} \cup \|$$
$$\text{́} \cup \_ \cup | \text{́} \cup \_ \cup \|$$
$$\underbrace{\text{́} \cup \cup | \_ \cup \cup}_{\theta\acute{\epsilon}\sigma\iota s} | \underbrace{\text{́} \cup \cup | \_ \cup \cup}_{\check{a}\rho\sigma\iota s} \|$$

In the case of unequal division three sentence-ictuses were distinguished, two stronger ones for the thesis, and a weaker one for the arsis, e. g.

$$\underbrace{\text{́} \cup \cup}_{\theta\acute{\epsilon}\sigma\iota s} | \underbrace{\text{́} \cup \cup | \text{́} \cup \cup}_{\check{a}\rho\sigma\iota s} \|$$

The relation was still more varied in quinquepartite sentences. Beyond this it was not fixed whether a sentence should begin with the thesis (i. e. the stronger ictus) or the arsis (i. e. the weaker). The arrangement, therefore, of the sentence, with reference to its tones might be:

$$\underbrace{\text{́} \cup \cup}_{\check{a}\rho\sigma\iota s} | \underbrace{\text{́} \cup \cup | \text{́} \cup \cup}_{\theta\acute{\epsilon}\sigma\iota s} \|$$

And this last sort, indeed, was regarded the more common.

2. But in actual practice the poems were recited with those ictuses which the feeling in the different passages prompted. The poet marked them neither for the text nor the musical notes, in which hardly more than the ictuses of the measures were given, and these not always. And doubtless different reciters intoned the sentences differently, each being from his own point of view correct. No one, however, paid attention to philosophic theories, of which, therefore, there is here need of but brief mention. If the ictuses of the measures are observed, and the syllables are given their true metrical value, the correct intonation of the sentence will follow as a necessary consequence.

It should be remarked, however, that it is not best, especially in poems of simple construction, to put the heaviest ictus on the first measure. E. g. the following,

ποικιλόθρον', ἀθάνατ' 'Αφροδίτα

should be $\quad \text{́} \cup | \text{́} \cup | \text{́} \cup \cup | \text{́} \cup | \text{́} \cup \|$

or something like it. But in choric strophes it is well always to give the strongest ictus to the first measure, especially if the sentence does not begin a verse. E. g.

Κύριός εἰμι θροεῖν ὅδιον κράτος αἴσιον ἀνδρῶν ἐκτελέων.

AESCH. *Ag.* I. *str.* α' (104, 105).

$$\text{́} \cup \cup | \_ \cup \cup | \_ \cup \cup | \_ \cup \cup \| \text{́} \cup \cup | \_ \_ | \_ \cup \cup | \_ \overline{\wedge} \|$$

Other suggestions in regard to the position of the sentence-ictus might perhaps be made, but no fixed rules can be given.

§ 21. Length of Sentences.

1. The verse, whose definition will be more fully given further on, must first of all be carefully distinguished from the rhythmical sentence. In English as well as in Greek poetry there are lines (verses) composed of two sentences, as e. g. in the strophes of Longfellow's poem, "The Belfry of Bruges":

> In the market-place of Bruges stands the belfry old and brown;
> Thrice consumed and thrice rebuilded, still it watches o'er the town.

$$\_\cup\mid\_\cup\mid\_\cup\mid\_\cup, \parallel \_\cup\mid\_\cup\mid\_\cup\mid\_\wedge\parallel$$
$$\_\cup\mid\_\cup\mid\_\cup\mid\_\cup, \parallel \_\cup\mid\_\cup\mid\_\cup\mid\_\wedge\parallel$$

Each of these lines consists of two sentences of four measures each. But sometimes the sentences are written separately as independent lines, even if they have no metrical pauses between them, as e. g. those cited in § 19, 1:

> "When other lips and other hearts
> Their tales of love shall tell,"

which are separated by no musical pause, as has there been shown.

Before proceeding to the illustrations that follow, it should be remarked that in modern musical composition the number of measures of the recited poem is often arbitrarily diminished or increased, though never beyond the hexapody. It cannot be admitted that this arbitrary practice existed among the Greeks; if it had, we should not be able to show the beautiful conformity of their poetic creations to the laws of musical composition.

A. *The dipody.*

> Over hill, over dale,
> Through bush, through brier,
> Over park, over pale,
> Through flood, through fire.
>
> *Midsummer Night's Dream,* II. 1.

$$\infty\mid\_\infty\mid\_$$

It would be possible to write $\infty : \_\infty \mid \_ \overline{\wedge} \parallel$, though it is very questionable whether the notation

$$\cup\cup : \_\cup\cup\mid\_, \_\mid\_\_\mid\_, \cup\cup\mid\_\cup\cup\mid\_, \text{etc.,}$$

where there is no noticeable pause between the sentences, is not preferable. In Greek, with few exceptions, no arbitrary pause was allowed until the verse had come to an end.

§ 21. LENGTH OF SENTENCES.

B. **The tripody**, often following a tetrapody, but also alone.

> The rivers rush into the sea,
>   By castle and town they go;
> The winds behind them merrily
>   Their noisy trumpets blow. — LONGFELLOW.

$$\smile \vdots \_ \smile | \_ \smile | \_ \smile | \_$$
$$\smile \vdots \smile\smile | \_ \smile | \_$$

> Hail to thee, blithe spirit!
> Bird thou never wert,
> That from heaven or near it
> Pourest thy full heart
> In profuse strains of unpremeditated art. — SHELLEY.

$$\_\smile | \_ \smile | \_ \smile \|$$
$$\_\smile | \_ \smile | \_ \wedge \|$$
$$\_\smile | \smile\smile | \_ \smile \|$$
$$\_\smile | \_ \smile | \_ \wedge \|$$
$$\smile \vdots \_ \smile | \_ \smile | \_ \smile | \_ \smile | \_ \smile | \_ \wedge \|$$

C. **The tetrapody**, the most common sentence.

> Now the hungry lion roars,
> And the wolf behowls the moon;
> Whilst the heavy ploughman snores,
> All with weary task fordone.
>   *Midsummer Night's Dream*, V. 2.

$$\_\smile | \_ \smile | \_ \smile | \_$$
$$\_\smile | \_ \smile | \_ \smile | \_$$

D. **The pentapody**, most known as "blank verse," in which the English dramas commonly are written.

> Now, fair Hippolyta, our nuptial hour
> Draws on apace: four happy days bring in
> Another moon; but O, methinks, how slow
> This old moon wanes! she lingers my desires,
> Like to a step-dame, or a dowager,
> Long withering out a young man's revenue.
>   *Midsummer Night's Dream*, I. 1.

$$\smile \vdots \_ \smile | \_ \smile | \_ \smile | \_ \smile | \_$$

E. **The hexapody**, commonly called the "Alexandrine Verse," most used by the French in their tragedies.

> Oui, je viens dans son temple adorer l'Éternel
> Je viens, selon l'usage antique et solennel,
> Célébrer avec vous la fameuse journée,
> Où, sur le mont Sinn, la loi nous fut donnée. — RACINE.

§ 21. LENGTH OF SENTENCES.

In English poetry this verse is seldom used, because heavy and dragging. It closes the Spenserian stanza, the other eight verses of which are pentapodies, and is found occasionally among the pentapodies of the blank verse of Shakespeare. Pope's lines, the second of which is itself an Alexandrine, will be recalled to mind:

> A needless Alexandrine ends the song,
> Which like a wounded snake drags its slow length along.

The first stanza of the "Faerie Queene" ends:

> Full iolly knight he seemed, and faire did sitt,
> As one for knightly giusts and fierce encounters fitt.

$$\smile | \_\smile | \_\smile | \_\smile | \_\smile | \_$$
$$\smile | \_\smile | \_\smile | \_\smile | \_\smile | \_\smile | \_$$

2. Greek poetry has the same sentences. But a pentapody or a hexapody, if consisting of long measures like the $^6/_8$ ($\_ \_ \smile\smile$ or $\_ \smile\smile \_$ or $\_ \smile \_ \smile$), would be too long a sentence, — one in which it would be difficult to let only a single chief ictus be heard. The ancient writers on rhythmic saw this and formulated rules for the allowed length of the sentences as determined by the length of the measure. Their division of the sentences (§ 20), moreover, aided in determining their length; where there were the least ictuses, that is in the case of equal division, the sentences were allowed to be of limited extent only; the greatest length was allowed in quinquepartite division, when the different grades of intonation gave the sentence the appearance of a well-divided unit.

The rules of the ancient writers on this subject can be accepted intact, since they harmonize with the facts, are inherently probable, and have their analogies in the poetry of other nations.

If the eighth-note or common short syllable be named a "mora" (χρόνος), the rules are as follows:

1) *Sentences equally divided* (i. e. *equal* sentences, see § 20, 1) *can be extended only to* 16 *morae;*

2) *Unequal sentences to* 18;

3) *Quinquepartite sentences to* 25.

According to this:

I. Chorees and logaoedics can be extended to series of six measures ($6 \times {}^3/_8 = 18$ morae).

II. Dactyls and anapaests to pentapodies ($5 \times {}^4/_8 = 20$ morae); so also Doric groups and spondees.

§ 21. LENGTH OF SENTENCES.

III. Paeonics and bacchii to tripodies ($3 \times {}^5/_8 = 15$ morae); the tetrapody is not allowed ($4 \times {}^5/_8 = 20$ morae, which exceeds the extent granted to equally divided sentences); but the pentapody again is allowed ($5 \times {}^5/_8 = 25$ morae).

IV. Ionics, choriambi, and dichorees to tripodies ($3 \times {}^6/_8 = 18$ morae).

3. The anacrusis is not reckoned in these estimates. Syncopated measures are, of course, reckoned as full measures, as e. g. ‿ ‖ ⌐ ‖ ‿ ‖ ‿ ⌐ ‖, i. e. four measures of three morae each $= 12$ morae.

4. The number of rhythmical and musical sentences is, therefore, very limited, and yet, in consequence of the many metrical forms which the measures that compose them may assume, they are of the greatest variety.

Many of these forms are very frequent and characteristic; these have received particular names. Some of these names are ambiguous, and are, therefore, not to be used. Those that are not ambiguous will be given in the next paragraph.

It should be remembered that long and short syllables cannot be assumed at pleasure. If e. g. the choreic series

$$\smile - - - \smile - \smile - \smile$$

is given, we are not under any circumstances to think of

$$\smile \vdots \_ > \mid \_ \smile \mid \_ \smile \mid \_ \smile \|,$$

since the irrational measure cannot stand in the odd place (§ 13, 2; § 16, 1). There is nothing to do, therefore, but to write

$$\smile \vdots \sqcup \mid \sqcup \mid \_ \smile \mid \_ \smile \mid \_ \smile \|,$$

or better

$$\smile \vdots \sqcup \mid \sqcup \mid \_ \smile \mid \_ \smile \mid \sqcup \mid \_ \wedge \|.$$

The laws determining the length of the sentence that have been given above are proved to be valid: 1) by the fact that the entire literature presents no facts that contradict them; 2) by their inherent probability, the sentences which they authorize being exactly adapted to the proper expression of the necessary musical thought; 3) by the important results in Eurhythmy (see Book V.) which arise from them. It is not to be feared, therefore, that the determination of the length of the sentences of which a description follows in § 22, rests upon arbitrary grounds.

§ 22. Sentences Occurring Most Frequently.

1. *Dactylic sentences*.

Pure dactylic strophes consist oftenest of tripodies and tetrapodies; the pentapody occurs less often; still less often the dipody (only as "interlude," see § 32, 4).

The pentapody as an independent verse, with contraction of the arsis allowed only in the first measure, is called Σαπφικὸν τεσσαρεσκαιδεκασύλλαβον. — Theocr. *Id.* 29 is composed of such sentences.

κἄμμε χρὴ μεθύοντας ἀλαθέας ἔμμεναι.
— — | — ∪ ∪ | — ∪ ∪ | — ∪ ∪ | — ∪ ∪ ||

2. *Doric sentences*.

The chief sentences of which Doric melodies are composed are the following:

I. The *dactylic tripody*:
— ∪ ∪ | — ∪ ∪ | — — ||

εἷς δ' ἐσόρουσε βοάσαις. PIND. *Ol.* VIII. *ep. β'*.

Or catalectic — ∪ ∪ | — ∪ ∪ | — ⋀ ||, to be written within the verse thus, — ∪ ∪ | — ∪ ∪ | ⊔ ||.

κίονα δαιμονίαν. Ib. *str. β'*.

It may here be remarked in general that catalexis is essentially the same whether it occurs at the close of a verse or within it (the last being technically a case of *syncope*, § 11, 3); so that it will be sufficient to note the first only in the different kinds of sentences to be enumerated.

II. The *epitritic* (*Doric*) *dipody and tetrapody*:
⌊ ∪ | — — || or ⌊ ∪ | — ⋀ ||,
⌊ ∪ | — — | ⌊ ∪ | — — || or ⌊ ∪ | — — | ⌊ ∪ | — ⋀ ||, both sentences also with anacrusis.

III. The *first encomiologicum*:
— ∪ ∪ | — ∪ ∪ | — — | ⌊ ∪ | — — ||,

and the *second encomiologicum*:
⌊ ∪ | — — | — ∪ ∪ | — ∪ ∪ | — — ||.

Both sentences also catalectic.

Ἔστιν ἀνθρώποις ἀνέμων ὅτε πλεῖστα
χρῆσις, ἔστιν δ' οὐρανίων ὑδάτων.
PIND. *Ol.* X. *str. α'*.

IV. The *iambelegus* (ἰαμβέλεγος):

$$\_\,\vdots\,\llcorner\,\cup\,|\,\_\,\_\,|\,\_\,\cup\,\cup\,|\,\_\,\cup\,\cup\,|\,\_\,\overline{\wedge}\,\|$$

κλεινᾶν Συρακοσσᾶν θάλος 'Ορτυγία. PIND. *Nem.* I. *str. a'*.

V. The not infrequent use of the *dactylic dipody* is also to be noticed; in addition to these many other sentences occur.

3. *Anapaestic sentences.*

Since these constitute a peculiar "type," they will be separately treated in § 31.

4. *Spondaic sentences.*

Pure spondees seem to have occurred most in tetrapodies and tripodies. For an example, see § 10, III.

Spondees with anacrusis, a variety of anapaests that frequently occurs in tragic monodies (especially in Euripides), cannot be treated in a mere Introduction, whose limits indeed forbid the discussion of the construction of monodies at all.

5. *Choreic sentences.*

Choreic strophes were especially perfected by Aeschylus. They consist almost entirely of tetrapodies and hexapodies. The most noteworthy forms are:

A. *Tetrapodies.* Why these are called tetrapodies and not dimeters is explained in § 10, VII.

$$\_\,\cup\,|\,\_\,\cup\,|\,\_\,\cup\,|\,\_\,\check{\cup}\,\|,\text{ acatalectic trochaic dimeter.}$$

Κολχίδος τε γᾶς ἔνοικοι. AESCH. *Prom.* II. *str. β'* (415).

$$\_\,\cup\,|\,\_\,\cup\,|\,\_\,\cup\,|\,\_\,\wedge\,\|\text{ (much more common), catalectic trochaic dimeter.}$$

μάντιν οὕτινα ψέγων. Id. *Ag.* I. *ant. γ'* (185).

$$\cup\,\vdots\,\_\,\cup\,|\,\_\,\cup\,|\,\_\,\cup\,|\,\_\,\wedge\,\|,\text{ iambic dimeter.}$$

ἐπεὶ κατῆλθες ἐς πύλιν. Id. *Sept.* IX. *ep.* (992).

$$\cup\,\vdots\,\_\,\cup\,|\,\_\,\cup\,|\,\llcorner\,|\,\_\,\wedge\,\|\text{ and }\_\,\cup\,|\,\_\,\cup\,|\,\llcorner\,|\,\_\,\wedge\,\|,\text{ falling dimeters.}$$

The first of these two forms, the one with anacrusis, was much used, under the name of ἡμίαμβος, in short poems by the Anacreontic writers.

Then various other forms occur with resolution and syncope, as e. g.

$$\cup\,\vdots\,\_\,\cup\,|\,\llcorner\,|\,\_\,\cup\,|\,\_\,\wedge\,\|$$

μένει δ' ἀκοῦσαί τί μου
μέριμνα νυκτηρεφές.

Id. *Ag.* II. *ant. γ'* (459, 460).

§ 22. SENTENCES OCCURRING MOST FREQUENTLY. 69

∪ ː ⌴ | ⌴ | ⌣ ∪ | ⌣ ∧ ‖
ἰδέσθω δ' εἰς ὕβριν. Id. Suppl. I. ant. ε' (112).

∪ ː ⌴ | ⌣ ∪ | ⌴ | ⌣ ∧ ‖
πρόκεισαι κατακτάς. Id. Sept. IX. pr. (965).

> ː ⌴ | ⌴ | ⌴ | ⌴ ‖
πρόστερνοι στολμοί. Id. Cho. I. str. α' (29).

∪ ∪ ∪ | ⌣ ∪ | ⌣ ∪ | ⌣ ∧ ‖
φύλακος εὐμενεστάτου. Id. Ag. VII. str. α' (1452).

∪ ∪ ∪ | ⌴ | ∪ ∪ ∪ | ⌣ ∧ ‖
ἐπὶ δὲ τῷ τεθυμένῳ
τόδε μέλος, παρακοπά. Id. Eum. III. str. α' (341, 342).

B. *Hexapodies*. (See § 10, VII.) The common forms, which any one will easily name for himself, are, in Aeschylus:

∪ ː ⌣ ∪ | ⌣ ∪ | ⌣ ∪ | ⌣ ∪ | ⌣ ∪ | ⌣ ∧ ‖
πόθεν δέ μοι γένοιτ' ἂν αἰθέρος θρόνος; Suppl. VII. str. β' (792).

⌣ ∪ | ⌣ ∪ | ⌣ ∪ | ⌣ ∪ | ⌴ | ⌣ ∧ ‖
τὸν δ' ἄνευ λύρας ὅμως ὑμνῳδεῖ. Ag. IV. ant. α' (990).

∪ ː ⌣ ∪ | ⌴ | ⌣ ∪ | ⌴ | ⌣ ∧ ‖
ἄναξ δ' ὁ πρέσβυς τόδ' εἶπε φωνῶν. Ib. I. ant. δ' (205).

∪ ː ⌴ | ⌴ | ⌣ ∪ | ⌣ ∪ | ⌴ | ⌣ ∧ ‖
Διὸς πλαγὰν ἔχουσιν εἰπεῖν. Ib. II. str. α' (367).

∪ ː ⌣ ∪ | ⌴ | ⌣ ∪ | ⌴ | ⌣ ∪ | ⌣ ∧ ‖
λιποῦσα δ' ἀστοῖσιν ἀσπίστορας. Ib. str. β' (403).

∪ ː ⌣ ∪ | ⌴ | ⌣ ∪ | ⌣ ∪ | ⌣ ∪ | ⌣ ∧ ‖
ἰὼ ἰώ, δῶμα δῶμα καὶ πρόμοι. Ib. (410).

6. *Ionic sentences*
and
7. *Choriambic sentences*.

Dipodies are more frequent than tripodies.

8. *Dichoreic sentences* are included under choreic; cf. § 10, VII.

9. *Paeonic sentences* are rare in Aeschylus, and are for the most part dipodies. In Aristophanes, besides the dipody and the somewhat less common tripody, the pentapody also occurs. For examples, see § 10, VIII.

10. The *bacchii*, which are rare, occur almost only as dipodies.

11. The forms of *logaoedic sentences* show the greatest variety. It must here suffice to give a selection merely.

A. *Dipodies.* Such a one is —∪∪ | — ∪ ‖, the *versus Adonius*, which closes the Sapphic strophe.

B. *Tripodies.*

—∪∪ | — ∪ | — ∪ ‖, catalectic —∪∪ | — ∪ | — ∧ ‖, *first Pherecratean*, Φερεκράτειον.

βυρσότονον κύκλωμα. EUR. *Bacch.* I. ant. β' (123).
αἴλινον αἴλινον. SOPH. *Aj.* IV. str. β' (627).

— ⏓ | —∪∪ | — ∪ ‖, catalectic — ⏓ | —∪∪ | — ∧ ‖, *second Pherecratean*, 'Αριστοφάνειον.

παιδὸς δύσφορον ἄταν. SOPH. *Aj.* IV. ant. β' (643).
ἐχθίστων ἀνέμων. Id. *Ant.* I. str. β' (137).

Besides these there occur forms with two cyclic dactyls, with anacrusis, and with syncope, as e. g.

—∪∪ | —∪∪ | — ∧ ‖
ποῦ σφαγίων ἔφοροι; EUR. *Rhes.* I. str. (30).

∪ ⋮ —∪∪ | —∪∪ | — ∧ ‖
τίς εἷσ' ἐπὶ Πανθοίδαν; Ib. (28).

∪ ⋮ L_ | —∪∪ | — ∧ ‖
πόνῳ τρυχόμενος. SOPH. *Aj.* IV. str. α' (605).

Finally, many sentences occur without cyclic dactyls, but then frequently with tribrachs; this form e. g. is found in *Aj.* III. str. γ' (403):

∪ ⋮ ∪∪∪ | — > | — ∧ ‖

C. *Tetrapodies.* These are the commonest. The ground forms are:

—∪∪ | — ∪ | — ∪ | — ∪ ‖ and —∪∪ | — ∪ | — ∪ | — ∧ ‖, *first Glyconic.*

νῦν γὰρ ἐμοὶ μέλει χορεῦσαι. SOPH. *Aj.* V. str. (701).
σίμαλον εἶδον ἐν χορῷ. ANACR.

— ⏓ | —∪∪ | — ∪ | — ∪ ‖ and — ⏓ | —∪∪ | — ∪ | — ∧ ‖, *second Glyconic* (the catalectic form called also 'Ανακρεόντειον ὀκτωσύλλαβον).

σφαίρῃ δηὖτέ με πορφυρέῃ. ANACR. *fr.* 14.

The acatalectic form seldom occurs.

Falling tetrapodies are frequent, as

— ⏓ | —∪∪ | L_ | — ∧ ‖
χἀ γλαυκῶπις 'Αθάνα. SOPH. *Oed. C.* III. str. β' (706).

This must not be regarded a Pherecratean (— ⏓ | —∪∪ | — ∪).

§ 22. SENTENCES OCCURRING MOST FREQUENTLY. 71

Further, several cyclic dactyls frequently occur in succession; indeed, even all four measures may consist of them.

⌣ ⁝ ⌞ | —⌣⌣ | —⌣⌣ | ⌟ ‖

ξυναλγεῖν μετὰ τοῦδε τυπείς. SOPH. *Aj.* II. *ant.* (255).

On the other hand, what appear to be choreic sentences are found in logaoedic strophes, as e. g.

⌣ ⁝ ⌞⌣ | ⌞⌣ | ⌞⌣ | ⌞ ‖ ⌞⌣ | ⌞⌣ | ⌞⌣ | ⌞ ∧ ‖

ὅμοιον ὥστε ποντίαν οἶδμα δυσπνόοις ὅταν . . .
                                    SOPH. *Ant.* III. *str. a'* (586, 587).

Euripides is beyond all others rich in forms, which he used for the purpose of bringing variety into successions of series which would otherwise have been too uniform. As an example take the following:

Ἡδὺς ἐν οὔρεσιν, εὖτ' ἂν
ἐκ θιάσων δρομαίων
πέσῃ πεδόσε, νεβρίδος ἔχων
ἱερὸν ἐνδυτόν, ἀγρεύων
αἷμα τραγοκτόνον, ὠμοφάγον χάριν,
ἱέμενος εἰς ὄρεα Φρύγια, Λύδια.
                                   Bacch. I. *ep.* (135 – 140).

—⌣⌣ | —⌣⌣ | ⌞ | ⌞ ∧ ‖
—⌣⌣ | ⌞⌣ | ⌞ | ⌞ ∧ ‖
⌣ ⁝ ⌞ ⌣ | ⌣⌣⌣ | ⌣⌣⌣ | ⌞ ∧ ‖
⌣⌣⌣ | —⌣⌣ | ⌞⌣ | ⌞ ∧ ‖
—⌣⌣ | —⌣⌣ | —⌣⌣ | —⌣⌣ ‖
⌣ ⁝ ⌣⌣⌣ | ⌞ | ⌣⌣⌣ | ⌣⌣⌣ | ⌞⌣ | ⌞ ∧ ‖

We should observe also the tetrapody

◡ ⁝ —⌣⌣ | ⌞⌣ | ⌞⌣ | ⌞⌣ ‖, μέτρον Πραξίλλειον,

which was much used (in unvarying form) in the construction of strophes (in Aeolic poetry).

πλήρης μὲν ἐφαίνετ' ἁ σελάννα,
αἱ δ' ὡς περὶ βῶμον ἐστάθησαν. SAPPHO.

And the two tetrapodies which occur in the "Alcaïc strophe" (§ 29, 4, II.):

◡ ⁝ ⌞⌣ | ⌞ ◡ | ⌞⌣ | ⌞⌣ ‖, *Alcaicus enneasyllabus,*
and   —⌣⌣ | —⌣⌣ | ⌞⌣ | ⌞⌣ ‖, *Alcaicus decasyllabus.*

ὦ Βύκχι, φάρμακον δ' ἄριστον
οἶνον ἐνεικαμένοις μεθύσθην. ALC.

D. *Pentapodies.*

Pentapodies were used in Aeolic lyric poetry, in the treatment of its favorite subjects, in the following forms:

§ 22. SENTENCES OCCURRING MOST FREQUENTLY.

1) $\_ \check{\smile} \mid \smile \smile \mid \_ \smile \mid \_ \smile \mid \_ \smile \parallel$, *Phalaecēum hendecasyllabum.*
Παλλὰς Τριτογένει', ἄνασσ' Ἀθηνᾶ. *Scolium.*

2) $\_ \smile \mid \_ \check{\smile} \mid \smile \smile \mid \_ \smile \mid \_ \smile \parallel$, *Sapphicum hendecasyllabum.*
ποικιλόθρον', ἀθάνατ' Ἀφροδίτα. SAPPHO.

The Sapphic strophe is constructed mainly of this verse (§ 29, 5, II.). The last verse of this strophe shows that we are not to regard 2) a hexapody with syncope of the next to the last measure ($\_ \smile \mid \_ \check{\smile} \mid \smile \smile \mid \_ \smile \mid \_ \wedge \parallel$), to which we naturally incline:

$$\_ \smile \mid \_ \check{\smile} \mid \smile \smile \mid \_ \smile \mid \_ \smile \parallel \smile \smile \mid \_ \smile \parallel$$

πυκνὰ δινεῦντες πτέρ' ἀπ' ὠράνω αἰθέρος διὰ μέσσω. SAPPHO.

The short in the fifth measure, since it does not close the verse, cannot be regarded as long, and consequently cannot constitute a measure by itself.

3) $\smile \vdots \_ \smile \mid \_ \check{\smile} \mid \smile \smile \mid \_ \smile \mid \_ \smile \parallel$, *Alcaicum dodecasyllabum.*
Ἰόπλοκ' ἄγνα μελλιχόμειδε Σάπφοι. ALC.

4) $\smile \vdots \_ \smile \mid \_ \check{\smile} \mid \smile \smile \mid \_ \smile \mid \_ \wedge \parallel$, *Alcaicum hendecasyllabum.*
οὐ χρὴ κακοῖσι θῦμον ἐπιτρέπην. ALC.

Of this the "Alcaïc strophe" was formed (§ 29, 4, II.).

In choric poetry the logaoedic pentapody is comparatively infrequent, and yet it occurs in many forms:

$$\smile \smile \mid \smile \smile \mid \smile \smile \mid \smile \smile \mid \_ \wedge \parallel$$
$$\smile \smile \mid \_ \mid \smile \smile \mid \_ \mid \_ \wedge \parallel$$

τῶν μεγάλων Δαναῶν ὑπὸ κληζομέναν,
τὰν ὁ μέγας μῦθος ἀέξει.

SOPH. *Aj.* II. *str.* (225, 226).

$$\smile \smile \mid \smile \smile \mid \_ \mid \smile \smile \smile \mid \_ \wedge \parallel$$

ὤμοι ἐγώ, τί πάθω, τέκνον ἐμόν;—
ἀλλ' ἐρῶ· οὐ γὰρ ἔχω κατακρυφάν.

Id. *Oed. Col.* I. (216 and 218).

F. *Logaoedic hexapodies* likewise occur in various forms and somewhat more frequently than pentapodies. Two illustrations from the *Ajax* and the *Antigone* will suffice:

$$\smile \smile \mid \smile \smile \mid \_ \smile \mid \_ \smile \mid \_ \mid \_ \wedge \parallel$$
$$\_ > \mid \smile \smile \mid \_ \smile \mid \_ \smile \mid \_ \smile \mid \_ \wedge \parallel$$

ἀλλ' ἄνα ἐξ ἑδράνων, ὅπου μακραίων
στηρίζει ποτὲ τᾷδ' ἀγωνίῳ σχολᾷ.

Aj. I. *ep.* (194, 195).

§ 23. INTERCHANGE OF MEASURES. 73

```
>⋮⌣∪│⌣∪│_∪│_∪│ ⌊ │_∧‖
_∪│_>│⌣∪│⌣∪│ ⌊ │_∧‖
_∪│_>│⌣∪│⌣∪│_∪│_∪‖
```

εὐδαίμονες, οἷσι κακῶν ἄγευστος αἰών.
οἷς γὰρ ἂν σεισθῇ θεόθεν δόμος, ἄτας
οὐδὲν ἐλλείπει γενεᾶς ἐπὶ πλῆθος ἕρπον.

Ant. III. *str.* α' (582 – 585).

§ 23. Interchange of Measures.

1. Since quantity is not to any considerable extent an element in modern languages, these languages are not adequate to the expression of the rhythm of series consisting of measures of varying metrical forms. Often, therefore, in order to treat understandingly of rhythmical facts, we shall be compelled to resort to dance-melodies.

The "Rheinländer" is distinguished from other dances by being composed of $4/8$ measures of changing form. Some of the measures have only one chief ictus; others a strong secondary ictus, so that they are divided, so to speak, into two $2/8$ measures.

There follows the first part of the best known dance of this sort:

In metrical characters:

```
ω⋮ ὐ ∪ ὐ ∪ │ ὐ ∪ ω ω │ ὐ ∪ ω ω │ ὐ ω ∪, ω ‖
   ὐ ∪ ὐ ∪ │ ὐ ∪ ω ω │ ὐ ∪ ω ω │ ὐ ω ∪ ∧ ‖
```

The different changes of direction in this dance are allowed, as is known, only at the ictuses. This is the peculiar and original significance of the ictuses. But they also determine the character of the music, and moreover exercise the greatest influence upon the metrical forms of the measures, and can therefore in turn themselves be determined from these.

§ 23. INTERCHANGE OF MEASURES.

2. In Greek poetry sentences of interchanging $^6/_8$ and $^3/_4$ measures, i. e. ionics and dichorees, are very common. The latter, where they predominate to the exclusion of ionics, are easily distinguished from simple chorees by the ionic anacrusis of two short syllables, as e. g. the series

is not to be classified as ⏑⏑ _ ⏑ _ ⏑ _ ⏒

but
⏒ : _ ⏑ | _ ⏑ | _ ⏑ ‖,
⏑⏑ : _ ⏑ _ ⏑ | _ _ ⏥ ‖.

This substitution of the dichoree for the ionic is called ἀνάκλασις (*breaking up*). Cf. § 30. Many of the Anacreontic poems are written in this rhythm.

In these melodies the intermixed dichorees can have the forms

_ > _ ⏑ | and ⌊ _ _ ⏑ | or _ ⏑ ⌊.

τόδε μειλίσσοντες οὖδας. AESCH. *Suppl.* IX. *ant.* a´ (1030).

⏑⏑ : _ > _ ⏑ | _ _ ⏥ ‖

The choriambus also (a $^6/_8$ measure with still other ictus-relations) is sometimes admitted, though very seldom; and quite as seldom the two-timed anacrusis is shortened or omitted, as in Aesch. *Sept.* VI. *str.* a´ (720):

πέφρικα τὰν ὠλεσίοικον,

⏑ : _ ⏑ ⌊ | _ ⏑ ⏑ _ | ⌊ ⏥ ‖

where the rare forms occur in unusual number. Aeschylus is disposed to begin his ionic strophes with such seemingly irregular series, for which see Schmidt, *Metrik*, § 14, 10.

If, now, it be added that the ionic measure besides this admits resolution of its longs and contraction of its shorts, it will be seen that ionic melodies may be of exceedingly various metrical forms. In the following series the measures are arranged according to the frequency of their occurrence:

$^3/_4$ *measures.* $^6/_8$ *measures.*

§ 23. INTERCHANGE OF MEASURES. 75

It should, however, be remarked that forms of such varied character as those in the example given above occur only in Aeschylus, and there for peculiar reasons. For these, see Schmidt, *Metrik, l. c.*

The following sentences, common in the lyric poets, should be noted:

1. ∪ ∪ ː _ _ ∪ ∪ | ⊔ ⊼ ‖, Τιμοκρεόντειον.

    Σικελὸς κομψὸς ἀνὴρ
    ποτὶ τὰν ματέρ' ἔφα. ΤΙΜ.

2. ∪ ∪ ː _ ∪ _ ∪ | _ _ ⊼ ‖, *ionicus anaclomenus.*

    Ἀπὸ μουσικῶν μελάθρων
    λογικοὶ νέοι μολεῖτε. ΑΝΑCR.

A good example of the interchange of the measures occurs in *Pers.* I. *ep.* (93 – 100).

Δολόμητιν δ' ἀπάταν θεοῦ τίς ἀνὴρ θνατὸς ἀλύξει;
τίς ὁ κραιπνῷ ποδί, πηδήματος εὐπετής, ἀνᾴσσων;
φιλόφρων γὰρ παρασαίνει βροτὸν εἰς ἄρκυας ἄτας,
ὅθεν οὐκ ἔστιν ὕπερθεν ἀλύξαντα φυγεῖν.

∪ ∪ ː _ _ ∪ ∪ | _ _, ∪ ∪ ‖ _ _ ∪ ∪ | _ _ ⊼ ‖
∪ ∪ ː _ _ ∪ ∪ | _ _, ∪ ∪ ‖ _ ∪ _ ∪ | _ _ ⊼ ‖
∪ ∪ ː _ _ ∪ ∪ | _ _, ∪ ∪ ‖ _ _ ∪ ∪ | _ _ ⊼ ‖
∪ ∪ ː _ _ ∪ ∪ | ⊔ ∪, ∪ ‖ _ _ ∪ ∪ | ⊔ ⊼ ‖

An example that illustrates the resolutions, contractions, and prolongations that may occur is found in Eur. *Bacch.* III. *ep.* (570 – 575).

διαβὰς Ἀξιὸν εἰλισσομένας Μαινάδας ἄξει
Λυδίαν τε, τὸν εὐδαιμονίας ὀλβοδόταν
πατέρα τε, τὸν ἔκλυον εὔιππον χώραν
ὕδασιν καλλίστοισι λιπαίνειν.

∪ ∪ ː _ _ ∪ ∪ | _ _ ∪ ∪ ‖ _ _ ∪ ∪ | _ _ ⊼ ‖
∪ ∪ ː _ ⊔ ∪ ∪ | _ _ ∪ ∪ ‖ _ _ ∪ ∪ | ⊔ ⊼ ‖
∪ ∪ ː ∪ ∪ ∪ ∪ ∪ ∪ | _ _ _ | _ _ ⊼ ‖
∪ ∪ ː _ _ _ | ⊔ ∪ ∪ | _ _ ⊼ ‖

The rhythm of an enthusiastic song like this will not appear unless the time of the syllables is given with accuracy.

3. The interchange of paeonic and bacchiic measures is analogous to that just described. A beautiful example occurs in Pindar *Ol.* II. *str. a':*

Ἀναξιφόρμιγγες ὕμνοι,
τίνα θεόν, τίν' ἥρωα, τίνα δ' ἄνδρα κελαδήσομεν;
ἤτοι Πίσα μὲν Διός· Ὀλυμπιάδα δ' ἔστασεν Ἡρακλέης
ἀκρόθινα πολέμου.

§ 23. INTERCHANGE OF MEASURES.

$\cup \vdots - \cup - | - \cup - | - \bar{\lambda} \|$
$\cup \vdots \cup \cup - \cup | - \_ \cup | \cup \cup - \cup \| \cup \cup - \cup | - \bar{\lambda} \|$
$- \vdots - \cup - | - \cup \cup \cup | - \cup \cup \cup \| - \_ \cup | \_ \_ \cup | - \bar{\lambda} \|$
$\quad - \cup - | \cup \cup \cup - \|$

4. But the interchange of measures of unequal length is of quite another kind. In Greek poetry only one sentence with such interchange occurs, the so-called *dochmius* (δόχμιος), the ground-form of which is: $\quad \cup \vdots \_ \_ \cup | - \wedge \|$,

i. e. a bacchius (with anacrusis) with following (shortened) choree. If several dochmii follow one another in a verse, they are generally separated by caesura,

$$\cup \vdots \_ \_ \cup | \_, \cup \| \_ \_ \cup | - \wedge \|.$$

Resolution is frequent; the commonest form is

$$\cup \vdots \cup \cup \_ \cup | - \wedge \|,$$

less frequent are
$\cup \vdots \_ \cup \cup \cup | - \wedge \|,$
$\cup \vdots \cup \cup \cup \cup \cup | - \wedge \|,$
$\cup \vdots \cup \cup \cup \cup \cup | \cup \cup \wedge \|,$ etc.

The anacrusis can, as usual, be irrational, even when serving as a short to the preceding choree. So also the short of the bacchius, since it serves in a certain sense as anacrusis to the choree. Therefore dochmii like the following are found:

$> \vdots \_ \_ \cup | - \wedge \|$
$\cup \vdots \_ \_ \cup | \_, > \| \_ \_ \cup | - \wedge \|$
$\cup \vdots \_ \_ > | - \wedge \|$
$> \vdots \_ \_ > | \_, > \| \_ \_ \cup | - \wedge \|.$

Accordingly Seidler, who even more than the ancient writers on metric gives every long, even when irrational, the value of a metrical long, exhibits thirty-two different forms, all of which, however, are by no means in use.

A more accurate statement of the facts is made in the *Griechische Metrik*, § 22, from which the following table is taken. All forms of which no illustration is given in this table are not in use, for reasons given in the *Metrik*. Three of the illustrations are in parentheses. These parentheses show that in the corresponding strophe another form of the measure occurs than the one given in the table, the latter slipping into use through the carelessness of the poet. Accordingly, of the thirty-two forms which have been supposed to exist, only nineteen in fact occur (and some of these very seldom), excluding the three in parentheses which occur each but once.

§ 23. INTERCHANGE OF MEASURES. 77

I.   a. ∪ ⋮ _ _ ∪ | _.   δυσαλγεῖ τύχᾳ.   *Ag.* V. *str.* ζ' (1165).
     b. > ⋮ _ _ ∪ | _.   ἐν γᾷ τᾷδε, φεῦ.   *Eum.* V. *str.* α' (781).
     c. ∪ ⋮ _ _ > | _.   φεροίμαν βοσκάν.   *Eum.* II. (264).
     d. > ⋮ _ _ > | _.   οἰοῖ δᾶ, φεῦ φεῦ.   *Eum.* V. *str.* β' (841).

II. a. ∪ ⋮ ∪ ∪ _ ∪ | _.   πτεροφόρον δέμας.   *Ag.*V. *ant.* ς' (1147).
     b. > ⋮ ∪ ∪ _ ∪ | _.   μισόθεον μὲν οὖν.   *Ag.* V. *str.* γ' (1090).
     c. ∪ ⋮ ∪ ∪ _ > | _.   βαρύδικος Ποινά.   *Cho.* VI. *str.* α' (936).
     d. > ⋮ ∪ ∪ _ > | _.   φεῦ, κατὰ γᾶς οἰκεῖν. *Eum.*V.*str.* β'(838).
                                                                 [(1198).

III. a. ∪ ⋮ ∪ ∪ ∪ ∪ ∪ | _.   μεγάλα μεγάλα καὶ.   *Bacch.* IX. *ant.*
     b. > ⋮ ∪ ∪ ∪ ∪ ∪ | _.   οὔποτε διὰ φρενός.   *Herc. Fur.* IV.
     c. ∪ ⋮ ∪ ∪ ∪ ∪ > | _.   [(745).
     d. > ⋮ ∪ ∪ ∪ ∪ > | _.
                                                      [VII. *str.* α' (1314).

IV. a. ∪ ⋮ ∪ ∪ ∪ ∪ ∪ | ∪ ∪.   νέφος ἐμὸν ἀπότροπον.   *Oed. R.*
     b. > ⋮ ∪ ∪ ∪ ∪ ∪ | ∪ ∪.   τὰν λιποπάτορα λιπό|γαμόν θ' ἃ
                                πλείστους | ἔκανεν Ἑλλάνων. *Or.*V.(1305).
     c. ∪ ⋮ ∪ ∪ ∪ ∪ > | ∪ ∪.   δι' ἐμὲ κατεδήσατο.   *Hel.* IV. (687).
     d. > ⋮ ∪ ∪ ∪ ∪ > | ∪ ∪.

V.   a. ∪ ⋮ _ ∪ ∪ ∪ | _.   ἰὼ πρόμαχ' ἐμῶν.   *Sept.* IV. *str.* β' (482).
     b. > ⋮ _ ∪ ∪ ∪ | _.   σκύμνου δυσελένας.   *Or.* VI. (1388).
     c. ∪ ⋮ _ ∪ ∪ > | _.
     d. > ⋮ _ ∪ ∪ > | _.

VI. a. ∪ ⋮ ∪ ∪ _ ∪ | ∪ ∪.   διὰ πύλας ἔμολεν.   *Hipp.* V. (586).
     b. > ⋮ ∪ ∪ _ ∪ | ∪ ∪.   εἰς γόον, εἰς δάκρυα.   *Bacch.* VIII.
                                                                  (1162).
     c. ∪ ⋮ ∪ ∪ _ > | ∪ ∪.   (ὅτε τε σύριγγες ἔ|κλαγξαν ὀλοίτρο-
     d. > ⋮ ∪ ∪ _ > | ∪ ∪.   [χοι.   *Sept.* II. *str.* α', 205.)

VII. a. ∪ ⋮ _ _ ∪ | ∪ ∪.   τὰ δ' ἔξω νόμιμα.   *Bacch.*VI. *ant.*(1010).
     b. > ⋮ _ _ ∪ | ∪ ∪.   τοὐμὸν τίς τίς ἔλα|χε τέκος, ἔννεπε.   *Tro.*
                                                                 II. (247).
     c. ∪ ⋮ _ _ > | ∪ ∪.   (τί φῄς ὦ παῖ, τίνα.   *Ant.*VIII. *ant.* α',
     d. > ⋮ _ _ > | ∪ ∪.   [1289.)

VIII. a. ∪ ⋮ _ ∪ ∪ ∪ | ∪ ∪.   (θεὸς τότ' ἄρα τότε.   *Ant.* VIII. *str.*
      b. > ⋮ _ ∪ ∪ ∪ | ∪ ∪.   [β', 1273.)
      c. ∪ ⋮ _ ∪ ∪ > | ∪ ∪.
      d. > ⋮ _ ∪ ∪ > | ∪ ∪.

78   § 23. INTERCHANGE OF MEASURES.

The sentence rarely closes with full measure. But it should be observed that in the bacchiic measure the first syllable may absorb the second:

∪ ⋮ ⊔ ∪ | _ ∧ ‖.

This can occur, however, only when a very strong emphasis rests on this syllable, as in cries of pain and joy and in those words whose passion is expressed mainly by their repetition. Cf. Soph. *Elec.* V. *str.* (1232 – 1234):

∪ ⋮ ⊔ ∪ | _ ∧ ‖
∪ ⋮ _ _ ∪ | _, ∪ ‖ _ _ ∪ | _ ∧ ‖

Ἰώ, γοναί,
γοναὶ σωμάτων ἐμοὶ φιλτάτων,

and in the antistrophe (1253 – 1255):

Ὁ πᾶς ἐμοί,
ὁ πᾶς ἂν πρέποι παρὼν ἐννέπειν . . .

We can obtain from examples like these, though they are brief in extent, some idea of the exact agreement of thought and form in Greek poetry. Many hundreds of the most various sorts might be added. Cf. *Compositionslehre*, § 4, 5, and *Monodien*, § 8, 6.

5. Dochmiac sentences occur in the following still different forms also, though rarely:

I. The first measure may be a paeon (*paeonic dochmius*), in which case the anacrusis may be wanting.

ἐπεύχομαι δὴ τῷδε μὲν εὐτυχεῖν.   Sept. IV. *str.* β′ (481).

∪ ⋮ _ ∪ _ | _, > ‖ ∪ ∪ _ ∪ | _ ∧ ‖

II. The *amphidochmius* consists of two quinquepartite measures, which enclose a tripartite measure.

ἔτυψεν δίκαν διφρηλάτου.   AESCH. *Eum.* I. *str.* β′ (156).

∪ ⋮ _ _ ∪ | _ ∪ | _ ∪ _ ‖

See for this Schmidt, *Eurhythmie*, p. 248, where this very remarkable form is explained.

III. In the *inverted dochmius* the three-timed measure precedes the five-timed.

ὑπὸ φρένας, ὑπὸ λοβόν.   AESCH. *Eum.* I. *str.* β′ (159).

∪ ⋮ ∪ ∪ ∪ | ∪ ∪ ∪ _ ‖

Further than this Greek poetry and Greek vocal music did not allow interchange of measures. In this the Greek practice is in strong contrast with the modern.

§ 24. The Rhythmical Period.

1. In the preceding paragraphs it has been shown how common speech is made rhythmical, 1) by dividing it into small parts, called measures, that are exactly equal to one another; and 2) by uniting these measures into sentences with only one chief ictus. The word and the simple sentence correspond grammatically to these two divisions. Now in rhythmical as in common speech the sentences are united into periods. And the rhythmical period is no more recognizable by means of one chief ictus than the grammatical (§ 18, 3).

But the grammatical period is a unit not only because of the logical connection of its members, but also because of the manner of their arrangement. There are in particular two forms of arrangement: the *anaphoric*, e. g. *ama bonos, obsta maleficis.*

$$\underbrace{A\,B}\ \underbrace{A\,B}$$

and the *chiastic*, e. g. *ama bonos, maleficis obsta.*

Again, the different sentences in the grammatical period have a fixed ratio of length, since at least very long and very short sentences are united in a period only under given conditions. Moreover, the close of such a period is marked by a longer pause, which is indicated by the mark of punctuation.

2. The rhythmical period must, of course, show a much greater conformity to law. This is seen, 1) in the exact way in which it groups its forms, not indeed according to the parts of the sentences (as above in the Latin examples, where the position of the predicate and object varies), but according to the sentences themselves; 2) in the strict limitation of the length of the sentences; 3) in the fact that even if the period is not always closed by a long pause, this pause is still enough to give the music a satisfactory close. This can be seen even in the simple rhythm of the recited poem.

The theory of rhythmical periods (*periodology*), however, if it is to be comprehensive, cannot be given without a previous discussion of the different types of poetry. We, therefore, proceed to a new subject, "typology," in which will be discussed the types themselves, and the forms of the periods which prevail in them.

Fourth Book.
TYPOLOGY.

§ 25. Introductory.

1. Poetry and music had their origin in dance and march (§ 6, 1). But when the forms had once been found, when the song, designed originally for accompaniment, became in itself a source of pleasure to the hearer, — then it grew and developed independently. Songs arose which were no longer accompaniments to dance or march. Since the art of writing was not yet known, or remained for a long time the possession of a very few, melodies were propagated orally as songs of the people, and were composed, since they were the possession of whole tribes, in fixed forms generally known and easy to understand. It was natural that these forms should lose much, when they no longer served as a basis for complex dances. Many musical series affect the feelings pleasingly, which would not be a fit accompaniment to the dance.

Then arose a new tendency. The Greek nation, like other nations, had its era of heroes, during which after various struggles it came into possession by conquest of permanent places of residence, and established its independence against other nations. The rich recollections of this time were preserved in great poems, in which it was no longer possible that a well-rounded melody should be repeated *ad infinitum* without satiety and weariness. With the loss of the melody, the poem was also no longer divided into strophes. This was inevitable. For otherwise the narrative would have been divided into parts in too complex a manner to be adapted to whole masses of people, a manner, too, which would have affected the narration. So the poems were solemnly chanted according to the feeling of each reciter. In this way there arose recitative poetry, especially the epic and the didactic.

§ 25. INTRODUCTORY STATEMENTS CONCERNING TYPOLOGY. 81

When the art of writing came into more general use, the events of the day also were soon drawn into the circle of rhythmical narration. The subjects presented were more the humorous and instructive and less the heroic. Subsequently the singing tone disappeared in recitation, which little by little passed over into simple *declamation*.

Meanwhile the old march and dance melodies were not neglected; the latter were developed in forms more and more complex, as the worship of the gods, the festivals, etc., became with the increasing refinement of customs more and more important. But, with the contemporaneous perfection of musical instruments, and especially with the development of the drama, purely lyrical vocal music was also further advanced. This found a peculiar development in the solo (monody) of the drama. The regular dance of the chorus was wanting; consequently a strict division of the composition was not necessary. This monody was sung by artists who made it their especial study; consequently the poet composer could allow himself the completest liberty. The competition among the poets of this epoch was great, so that they soon began to strive simply for effect, the attractions of pure art being no longer so powerful as at an earlier day. A people with corrupted taste finds pleasure in trills, coloratures, etc., and in dissonances, after which the effect of harmony is so much the greater. An even, uninterrupted succession of measures was no longer pleasing; therefore the dochmii, and later the inverted dochmii, amphidochmii, etc., arose. In like manner the regularity of the periodology was often broken down, that the beauty of order, arising from chaos, might be so much the more apparent, as also for various other reasons.

The last period of poetry has been reached. A rich literature has been collected, in which the later poets glean without creative power of their own. Religious worship, with its solemn music, its dancing choruses, etc., has disappeared in the wild tumult of wars and under the influence of a destructive philosophy. But the texts of the poets have been saved from the great flood.

The more complex rhythmical compositions of the old poets are no longer at all understood; and so a return is made to the simply constructed national songs of an earlier day. But the melodies themselves are wanting, and the poems are consequently only declaimed. The poet composes slavishly according to models of short and long syllables, and makes verses mechanically without reference to their being sung. He falls into a dry schematism, and in order to show something of art, becomes rigorous in the forms of the measures. But that he fails to understand the rhythm is shown, for instance, by his false use of the caesura. This is the point of view of a Horace, a Catullus, and in general of the whole later time.

Let us now review the genesis of the poetic types as shown in the following table.

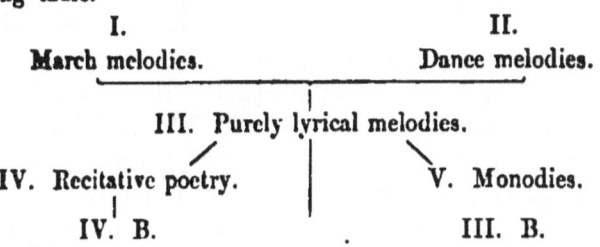

2. If the poetic productions of Greek literature now existing should be considered only in the order of the times in which they were written, we should come to the opposite conclusion. Recitative poetry, powerfully developed in the great national epics (Homer, Hesiod, Arctinus, Stasinus, etc.), comes first. Then purely lyrical poetry appears with Callinus, Archilochus, etc. The first march melodies were written by Tyrtaeus for the Spartans. And about the same time we hear of the first choric compositions (i. e. dance melodies), those namely of Alcman and Stesichorus. We should assume, therefore, the following development:

     I. Recitative poetry.
    II. Purely lyric poetry.
III. March melodies.   IV. Choric song.
           (Dance melodies.)

But this view is entirely unscientific, since it *does not explain* the facts. The epics appear first in literature only because their contents were deemed worthy of preservation. There were dance melodies *before* these, but the poems accompanying them were insignificant and so were lost. Only when the choric dance was developed in more perfect forms did writers of greater talent betake themselves to choric composition, and then their poems were preserved. So we can only conjecture what the original dance melodies were from the forms which have come from them into recitative and lyric poetry. For this reason recitative poetry must be considered first, and the discussion of the dance melodies, the artistically arranged song of the chorus, reserved to the very last.

§ 26. The Recitative Type.

1. It must be carefully borne in mind that recited poetry was developed from song. The simplest way in which sentences are united in a musical period is that two should correspond to one another as antecedent and consequent, the melody of the second completing or resolving that of the first, or, in other words, *answering* to it. The rhythmical sense of the Greeks inclined either to give both sentences the same length, or to shorten the second by a measure. They also frequently shortened the final measure of a sentence (κατάληξις). The two sentences are separated by a slight pause, which appears either as *diaeresis* (διαίρεσις, § 19, 2, II.) or as *caesura* (τομή, § 19, 2, III.). At the end of the second sentence there is then stronger punctuation, or at least an approach to a close in the thought. The whole is called a verse (§ 19, 2, I.).

The Greeks constructed their verses mainly of two tetrapodies, or of a tetrapody with following tripody, or of two tripodies.

If the verse consists of two tetrapodies, the first generally ends with full measure, while the second suffers catalexis; or the second sentence suffers syncope in the next to the last measure.

2. The characteristics, then, of recitative poetry are briefly:

I. *The verses consist each of two sentences, generally separated by caesura or diaeresis.*

II. *There is no union of the verses or sentences into strophes.*

3. The following are the different kinds of verses which were developed in Greek recitative poetry.

I. The *dactylic hexameter*, briefly *hexameter*, the metre of epic and also of gnomic and didactic poetry. — It has the *caesura*, for which see § 19, 2, III., where also examples are given.

But, since Homeric poetry was rather sung than merely recited, there are many verses with word-caesura wanting, especially if a proper name constitutes the third measure.

ὣς ἐφάμην, ὁ δέ μ᾽ οἰμώξας ἠμείβετο μύθῳ·
διογενὲς Λαερτιάδη, πολυμήχαν᾽ Ὀδυσσεῦ.

Od. XI. 59, 60.

If the end of the words in these verses is marked by a dot, the absence of the caesura in the third measure is seen at once, as follows:

§ 26. THE RECITATIVE TYPE.

$$-.\cup\cup|-.\cup.\cup.|--\|-.-|-\cup\cup.|--.\|$$
$$-\cup\cup|-.\quad-|-\cup\cup\|-.\cup\cup|-\cup.\cup|--.\|$$

In later poetry, particularly among the Romans, since the delivery was declamatory, stricter regard was paid to grammatical construction. The word-caesura was therefore seldom omitted, and almost only in proper names.

REM. I. All other caesuras than those given in § 19, 2, III. are purely formal conceptions, and are altogether without value. See Lehrs, *De Aristarchi studiis Homericis*, 2 ed. p. 394 sq.

REM. II. Equally valueless is a knowledge of the different names of the hexameter according to the number of light or heavy dactyls in it. In the genuine old poetry more light dactyls were used in lively description, more heavy ones in grave, but unconsciously; and the poet was far from refining upon their use.

II. The *trochaic tetrameter*, i. e. two trochaic tetrapodies with *diaeresis*.

Τοῖος ἀνθρώποισι θυμός, Γλαῦκε, Λεπτίνεω πάι,
γίγνεται θνητοῖς, ὁκοίην Ζεὺς ἐπ' ἡμέρην ἄγῃ,
καὶ φρονεῦσι τοῖ', ὁκοίοις ἐγκυρέωσιν ἔργμασιν.   ARCH.

$$-\cup|->|-\cup|->,\|-\cup|-\cup|-\cup|-\wedge\|$$
$$-\cup|->|-\cup|->,\|-\cup|-\cup|-\cup|-\wedge\|$$
$$-\cup|-\cup|-\cup|->,\|-\cup|-\cup|-\cup|-\wedge\|$$

As may be seen from this example, the first sentence originally allowed many more irrational syllables than the second, where the voice passes on more lightly to the close.

The trochaic tetrameter first occurs in the iambographers (Archilochus), then as metre of the dialogue in the drama, from which it was later more and more excluded by the iambic trimeter. On the naming of these two kinds of verse, cf. § 10, VII.

III. The *iambic trimeter*, occurring first in the iambographers but later the prevailing verse in the dialogue of the drama, consists of six iambic measures, which, as is shown by the admission of the irrational syllable into the even measures only, are united into three dipodies:

$$\check{>}:\overset{\cdot}{-}\cup\overset{\cdot}{-}\check{>}|\overset{\cdot}{-}\cup\overset{\cdot}{-}\check{>}|\overset{\cdot}{-}\cup\overset{\cdot}{-}\wedge\|.$$

This mode of writing has exactly the same value and significance as the other:

$$\check{>}:\overset{\cdot}{-}\cup|\overset{\cdot}{-}\check{>}|\overset{\cdot}{-}\cup|\overset{\cdot}{-}\check{>}|\overset{\cdot}{-}\cup|\overset{\cdot}{-}\wedge\|.$$

§ 26. THE RECITATIVE TYPE.   85

So the verse is called either "trimeter" or "hexapody." Cf. § 10, VII.

The trimeter, differently from the remaining verses that were recited, is not to be divided into two rhythmical sentences. This is proved beyond question by its relations in lyric strophes. Here it always answers to genuine hexapodies like

$$\cup \vdots \llcorner \mid \llcorner \mid \_ \cup \mid \_ \cup \mid \llcorner \mid \_ \wedge \|,$$

or

$$\cup \vdots \_ \cup \mid \_ \cup \mid \_ \cup \mid \_ \cup \mid \llcorner \mid \_ \wedge \|, \text{ etc.},$$

never to a verse that is unmistakably divided into tetrapody + dipody. (Cf. Book V.) Its length, moreover, is in strict accordance with the rules stated in § 21.

It is not to be denied, however, that in declamation the verse is very easily divided into two parts by a short pause, generally

$$\gtrless \vdots \_ \cup \mid \_ \gtrless, \mid \_ \cup \mid \_ \gtrless \mid \_ \cup \mid \_ \wedge \|,$$

less often

$$\gtrless \vdots \_ \cup \mid \_, \gtrless \mid \_ \cup \mid \_ \gtrless \mid \_ \cup \mid \_ \wedge \|.$$

But this division is in no sense necessary (though it does harmonize with the rhythm, $\gtrless \vdots \dot{\_} \cup \mid \_, \gtrless, \mid \dot{\_} \cup \mid \_ \gtrless \mid \_ \cup \mid \_ \wedge \|$), and, consequently, the omission of the pause is quite as frequent here as that of the word-caesura in the hexameter. In the trimeter, however, such a caesura might have been expected, since this was in the strict sense recited poetry.

The relation in the first ten verses of the *Antigone* is as follows:

*Ὦ κοινὸν αὐτάδελφον Ἰσμήνης κάρα,
ἆρ' οἶσθ' ὅτι Ζεὺς τῶν ἀπ' Οἰδίπου κακῶν
ὁποῖον οὐχὶ νῷν ἔτι ζώσαιν τελεῖ;
οὐδὲν γὰρ ἔστ' ἀλγεινὸν οὐδ' ἄτης ἄτερ
5   οὔτ' αἰσχρὸν οὔτ' ἄτιμόν ἐσθ', ὁποῖον οὐ
τῶν σῶν τε κἀμῶν οὐκ ὄπωπ' ἐγὼ κακῶν.
καὶ νῦν τί τοῦτ' αὖ φασι πανδήμῳ πόλει
κήρυγμα θεῖναι τὸν στρατηγὸν ἀρτίως;
ἔχεις τι κεἰσήκουσας; ἤ σε λανθάνει
10 πρὸς τοὺς φίλους στείχοντα τῶν ἐχθρῶν κακά;

$\gtrless \vdots \_ \cup \mid \_ \gtrless, \mid \_ \cup \mid \_ \gtrless \mid \_ \cup \mid \_ \wedge \|$ in 2, 3, 6, (7), 8.
$\gtrless \vdots \_ \cup \mid \_, \gtrless \mid \_ \cup \mid \_ \gtrless \mid \_ \cup \mid \_ \wedge \|$ in 4, 5, (7), 10.
$\gtrless \vdots \_ \cup \mid \_ \gtrless \mid \_ \cup \mid \_ \gtrless \mid \_ \cup \mid \_ \wedge \|$ in 1, 9.

This will serve as a type of the general case, though commonly the first sort of verse occurs in greater proportion than here.

§ 26. THE RECITATIVE TYPE.

It would seem, however, that in recitation there was early a tendency to put the two chief ictuses upon the first and fourth measures, giving the verse the appearance of being divided into two tripodies:

$$\acute{\smile} \vdots \_ \smile | \_ \acute{\smile} | \_, \smile, | \acute{\vdots} \acute{\smile} | \_ \smile | \_ \wedge \|.$$

This, however, cannot have been the original method, and is in conflict with the division of the verse into dipodies. Nevertheless, in recitation, the verse must often have been unconsciously divided into two such equal parts of three measures each. This is proved by the frequent close in the thought at the end of the third measure and the fact that the cyclic dactyl occurs oftenest in the fourth measure:

$$\smile \vdots \_ \smile | \_ \smile | \_ \smile, | \neg \smile \smile | \_ \smile | \_ \wedge \|.$$

In a much later time also it was thus declaimed, and so there arose the modern Alexandrine verse, § 21, 1, E.

IV. The *tetrameter scazon*, employed in particular by Ananius, consists of two trochaic tetrapodies with *diaeresis*; the second has halting close (§ 11, 6, I.):

"Ἔαρι μὲν χρόμιος ἄριστος, ἀνθίας δὲ χειμῶνι·
τῶν καλῶν δ' ὄψων ἄριστον καρὶς ἐκ συκέης φύλλου. ANAN.

$$\smile \smile \smile | \_ \smile | \smile \smile \smile | \_ \smile, \| \_ \smile | \_ \smile | \llcorner | \_ \smile \|$$
$$\_ \smile | \_ > | \_ \smile | \_ \smile, \| \_ \smile | \_ > | \llcorner | \_ \smile \|.$$

V. The *choliambus, trimeter scazon* (§ 11, 6, I.), consisting of two iambic tripodies, the second with halting close.

Ἐμοὶ γὰρ οὐκ ἔδωκας οὔτε πω χλαῖναν
δασεῖαν, οὐ χειμῶνι φάρμακον ῥίγευς
οὔτ' ἀσκέρῃσι τοὺς πόδας δασείῃσιν
ἔκρυψας, ὡς μή μοι χίμετλα ῥήγνυται. HIPPON.

$$\smile \vdots \_ \smile | \_ \smile | \_ \smile, | \_ \smile | \llcorner | \_ \smile \|$$
$$\smile \vdots \_ \smile | \_ > | \_ \smile, | \_ \smile | \llcorner | \_ \smile \|$$
$$> \vdots \_ \smile | \_ \smile | \_, \smile | \_ \smile | \llcorner | \_ \smile \|$$
$$\smile \vdots \_ \smile | \_ > | \_, \smile | \_ \smile | \llcorner | \_ \smile \|.$$

VI. The verse named by the old writers on metric ἑξάμετρον περιττοσυλλαβές, ἡρῷον ηὐξημένον, consists of a logaoedic tetrapody of three cyclic dactyls and an irrational choree as final measure, — followed by a falling choreic tetrapody. It always has diaeresis, and occurs only in the comic writers.

§ 26. THE RECITATIVE TYPE. 87

αὐτομάτη δὲ φέρει τιθύμαλλον καὶ σφακὸν πρὸς αὐτὸ
ἀσφάραγον κύτισόν τε· νάπαισιν δ' ἀνθέρικος ἀνηβᾷ
καὶ φλόμον ἄφθονον ὥστε παρεῖναι πᾶσι τοῖς ἀργοῦσιν.
                                                                CRATIN.

⏑‿⏑ | ‿⏑⏑ | ‿⏑⏑ | _ >, ‖ _ ⏑ | _ ⏑ | ⌊ | _ Λ ‖
‿⏑⏑ | ‿⏑⏑ | ‿⏑⏑ | _ >, ‖ _ ⏑ | ⏑⏑⏑ | ⌊ | _ Λ ‖, etc.

VII. The *metrum Cratineum* consists of a first Glyconic and a common choreic tetrapody, generally with diaeresis indicated by the close of a word. It is one of the sorts of verses with which the poet addresses the public in the parabasis of comedy.

Εὖιε κισσοχαῖτ' ἄναξ χαῖρ', ἔφασκ' Ἐκφαντίδης. CRATIN.

‿⏑⏑ | _ ⏑ | _ ⏑ | ⌊, ‖ _ ⏑ | _ > | _ ⏑ | _ Λ ‖.

πάντα φορητὰ πάντα τολμητὰ τῷδε τῷ χορῷ. Id.

‿⏑⏑ | _ ⏑ | _ ⏑ | ⌊ ‖ _ ⏑ | _ ⏑ | _ ⏑ | _ Λ ‖.

VIII. The *metrum Eupolideum* is like the *metrum Cratineum* in every respect, except that the first sentence is a *third* Glyconic. Its use is the same.

παντοίοις γε μὴν κεφαλὴν ἀνθέμοις ἐρέπτομαι,
λειρίοις, ῥόδοις, κρίνεσιν κόσμοσανδάλοις ἴοις,
καὶ σισυμβρίοις, ἀνεμωνῶν κάλυξί τ' ἠριναῖς. CRATIN.

_ ⏑ | _ ⏑ | ‿⏑⏑ | ⌊, ‖ _ ⏑ | _ ⏑ | _ ⏑ | _ Λ ‖
_ ⏑ | _ ⏑ | ‿⏑⏑ | ⌊, ‖ _ ⏑ | _ ⏑ | _ ⏑ | _ Λ ‖
_ ⏑ | _ ⏑ | ‿⏑⏑ | ⌊ ‖ _ ⏑ | _ ⏑ | _ ⏑ | _ Λ ‖.

IX. The *first Priapeus*, so called because it was especially used in Priapean satyric songs, belongs here as metre of the old parabasis. The other two Priapei, given below, have quite the same use. It consists of two first Glyconics, one catalectic and one falling. Diaeresis is generally indicated by the close of a word.

ἀλλὰ δίαιταν ἢν ἔχουσ' οἱ κόλακες πρὸς ὑμᾶς
λέξομεν· ἀλλ' ἀκούσαθ' ὥς ἐσμεν ἅπαντα κομψοὶ
ἄνδρες· ὅτοισι πρῶτα μὲν παῖς ἀκόλουθός ἐστιν
ἀλλότριος τὰ πολλά, μικρὸν δὲ τὸ κάμνον αὐτοῦ.
                                                                EUP. Col.

‿⏑⏑ | _ ⏑ | _ ⏑ | ⌊, ‖ ‿⏑⏑ | _ ⏑ | ⌊ | _ Λ ‖,
less frequently

‿⏑⏑ | _ ⏑ | _ ⏑ | ⌊ ‖ ‿⏑⏑ | _ ⏑ | ⌊ | _ Λ ‖.

X. The *second Priapeus* consists of two second Glyconics, one catalectic and one falling.

ἠρίστησα μὲν ἰτρίου λεπτοῦ μικρὸν ἀποκλάς. CRATIN.

_ ≤ | _ ∪ ∪ | _ ∪ | ⌴, ‖ _ ≤ | _ ∪ ∪ | ⌴ | _ ∧ ‖.

XI. The *third Priapeus* consists of a catalectic third and a falling second Glyconic.

οὐ βέβηλος ἃ τελεταὶ τοῦ νέου Διονύσου. EUPHORIO.

_ ∪ | _ ∪ | _ ∪ ∪ | ⌴, ‖ _ ∪ | _ ∪ ∪ | ⌴ | _ ∧ ‖.

XII. Finally for the classic period the *anapaestic tetrameter* is to be noticed, which like the Priapei was used in the parabasis. It consists of a full and a falling anapaestic tetrapody. The verse has caesura.

εὐφημεῖν χρὴ κἀξίστασθαι τοῖς ἡμετέροισι χοροῖσιν,
ὅστις ἄπειρος τοιῶνδε λόγων, ἢ γνώμῃ μὴ καθαρεύει,
ἢ γενναίων ὄργια Μουσῶν μήτ᾽ εἶδεν μήτ᾽ ἐχόρευσεν.

AR. RAN.

_ ⋮ _ _ _ | _ _ | _ _ | _, _ ‖ _ ∪ ∪ | _ ∪ ∪ | ⌴ | _ π̄ ‖
_ ⋮ ∪ ∪ _ | _ _ | _ ∪ ∪ | _, _ ‖ _ _ | _ ∪ ∪ | ⌴ | _ π̄ ‖
_ ⋮ _ _ _ | _ _ | ∪ ∪ _ | _, _ ‖ _ _ | _ ∪ ∪ | ⌴ | _ π̄ ‖.

The name is derived from the fact that the measures were united two and two into an $^8/_8$ measure.

_ ⋮ _ _ _ _ | _ _ _, _ ‖ _ ∪ ∪ _ ∪ ∪ | ⌴ _ π̄ ‖.

XIII. In the Alexandrian time, further, two ionic dipodies were united without anacrusis and with great license (especially in the occurrence of anaclasis) into the so-called *Sotadeum*.

ἥβην τ᾽ ἐρατήν, καὶ καλὸν ἡλίου πρόσωπον.

_ _ ∪ ∪ | _ _ _ ∪ ∪, ‖ _ ∪ _ ∪ | _ _ π̄ ‖.

ῥῆσιν δ᾽ ἀγαθὴν σὺ δεδομένην φύλασσε σαυτῷ.

_ _ ∪ ∪ | _ ∪ ∪ ∪ ∪ ‖ _ ∪ _ ∪ | _ _ π̄ ‖.

οὐ κρίνει δικαίως τὰ κατ᾽ ἄνθρωπον ἕκαστον.

_ > _ ∪ | _ _ ∪ ∪, ‖ _ _ ∪ ∪ | _ _ π̄ ‖.

XIV. The *Galliambic*, an enthusiastic metre found especially in the poems sung to Cybele by her priests (the γαλλοί), consists of two ionic dipodies with anacrusis. The pure form is:

∪ ∪ ⋮ _ _ ∪ ∪ | _ _, ∪ ∪ ‖ _ _ ∪ ∪ | ⌴ π̄ ‖.

προφανῶς τοῦτο διδάσκων ἀποδύσῃ βιοτήν.

The anacrusis is frequently contracted, less often the arsis of the second measure:

§ 27. THE LYRIC TYPE.

$$\_\stackrel{.}{.}\_\cup\cup\cup\cup|\_\_,\_\|\_\cup\cup\cup\cup|\_\overline{\wedge}\,\|.$$

αἷς ἔντεα παταγεῖται καὶ χάλκεα κρόταλα.

The form with dichorees (which may be resolved) is more frequent:

$$\cup\cup\stackrel{.}{.}\cup\cup\cup\_\cup|\_\_,\cup\cup\|\_\cup\cup\cup\cup|\_\overline{\wedge}\,\|.$$

ubi capita Maenades vi jaciunt hederigerae.

Catullus has left us a poem in this metre (*carm.* 63) which is, of course, designed for recitation. He has used a stereotyped form, and has deviated from it only in a few verses. This form can be gathered from the first five verses of the poem:

> *Super alta vectus Attis celeri rate maria*
> *Phrygium ut nemus citato cupide pede tetigit*
> *adiitque opaca silvis redimita loca deae,*
> *stimulatus ibi furenti rabie, vagus animis,*
> *devolvit ile acuto sibi pondere silicis.*

This is the metrical model; but the Romans certainly recited quite differently, viz.:

$$\check{\omega}\stackrel{.}{.}\_\cup|\_\cup|\_|\_,\omega\|\_\cup|\cup\cup\cup|\_\wedge\|.$$

XV. Finally a verse of Anacreon may be mentioned, which also belongs to the present type, though it was sung:

$$\cup\stackrel{.}{.}\cup\cup\cup|\_|\overline{\cup\cup}|\_\|\overline{\cup\cup}|\_\cup|\_|\_\wedge\|.$$

ἀναπέτομαι δὴ πρὸς Ὄλυμπον πτερύγεσσι κούφαις
διὰ τὸν ἔρωτ'· οὐ γὰρ ἐμοὶ παῖς ἐθέλει συνηβᾶν.

4. It is worthy of notice that no verses in quinquepartite measure occur in recitative poetry. Paeonics, like bacchii, are hard to declaim, and are used, therefore, without exception (as also the dochmii) only in poems designed to be sung.

§ 27. The Lyric Type.

I. Free Metrical Forms.

1. Before taking up the lyric type proper, a metrical license which was developed in it must be considered.

To recitative poetry there properly belong only the dactylic hexameter, trochaic tetrameter, and iambic trimeter. The remaining verses enumerated in the preceding paragraph were borrowed from lyric poetry at a later stage of its development, with exception of the anapaestic tetrameter, which was originally a march-melody. The verses borrowed from lyric poetry are logaoedic; and logaoedic verses are distinguished by variety in the form of their measures, which can be attained only by a freer treatment of the quantity of syllables.

It has already been remarked in § 20, 2, that the verses of lyric poetry proper, consisting in general of only one sentence, seldom had the chief ictus on the first measure. To give the following verses e. g. this intonation:

Ποικιλόθρον' ἀθάνατ' Ἀφρόδιτα,
παῖ Διὸς δολόπλοκε, λίσσομαί σε,
μή μ' ἄσαισι μήτ' ὀνίαισι δάμνα, πότνια, θῦμον,
$\dot{\cup}\mid\_\cup\mid\smile\cup\mid\_\cup\mid\_\cup\|$, etc.

would be altogether unnatural. In the melody also all effect would have been lost, if the verse had begun with an especially strong ictus and closed feebly. The rhythmical sentence becomes a unit through its one chief ictus, let it stand where it may, exactly as the grammatical sentence may have its chief ictus at the most different places.

The following musical sentence e. g. may be used for the above strophe:

Ποι - κι - λό - θρον' ἀ - θά - ναт' Ἀ - φρό - δι - τα,

and so on.

The first measure appears almost like anacrusis. It is metrically, therefore, used very freely. In the old lyric poets it may be not only a choree proper ($\dot{\_} \cup$), but also an irrational choree ($\dot{\_} >$), an inverted choree ($\cup \_$, certainly not an iambus, $\cup \dot{\_}$), or even a shortened choree ($\cup \cup$). — This has been named the *basis*, a name which will be retained. But it must be noted that the basis forms an inherent part of the rhythm and is not simply introductory to it. The ancients themselves understood by βάσις, *measure*, so that with them βάσις = πούς, in general.

The second Glyconic, for example, had four different forms by change in the basis, viz.:

$\_\cup\mid\smile\cup\mid\_\cup\mid\_\wedge\|$ οὔτε μὴν ἀπαλὴν κάσιν. Αν. *fr.* 12.
$\_>\mid\smile\cup\mid\_\cup\mid\_\wedge\|$ στίλβων καὶ γεγανωμένος. Id. *fr.* 13.
$\cup\_\mid\smile\cup\mid\_\cup\mid\_\wedge\|$ ἔρως παρθένιος πόθῳ. Id. *fr.* 13.
$\cup\cup\mid\smile\cup\mid\_\cup\mid\_\wedge\|$ ἄγε δὴ χέλυ δῖά μοι. Sapph. *fr.* 45.

I. FREE METRICAL FORMS.

This basis is found also in the other logaoedic verses of the old lyric poets, even with preceding anacrusis. The following examples from Alcaeus will illustrate:

Ἀσυνέτημι τῶν ἀνέμων στάσιν·
τὸ μὲν γὰρ ἔνθεν κῦμα κυλίνδεται,
τὸ δ' ἔνθεν· ἄμμες δ' ἂν τὸ μέσσον
νᾶι φορήμεθα σὺν μελαίνᾳ.

∪ : ∪ ∪ | _ ∪ | ‿∪ | _ ∪ | _ ∧ ||
∪ : _ ∪ | _ > | ‿∪ | _ ∪ | _ ∧ ||
∪ : _ ∪ | _ ∪ | _ ∪ | _ ∪ ||
‿∪ | ‿∪ | _ ∪ | _ ∪ ||

Ἦλθες ἐκ περάτων γᾶς ἐλεφαντίνας
λάβαν τῶ ξίφεος χρυσοδέταν ἔχων
ἐπειδὴ μέγαν ἆθλον Βαβυλωνίοις
συμμάχεις τελέσας, ῥύσαό τ' ἐκ πόνων,
κτένναις ἄνδρα μαχαίταν βασιληίων
παλαίσταν ἀπολείποντα μόνον μίαν
παχέων ἀπὸ πέμπων.

_ ∪ | ‿∪ | ∟ || ‿∪ | _ ∪ | _ ∧ ||
∪ _ | ‿∪ | ∟ || ‿∪ | _ ∪ | _ ∧ ||
∪ _ | ‿∪ | ∟ || ‿∪ | _ ∪ | _ ∧ ||
_ ∪ | ‿∪ | ∟ || ‿∪ | _ ∪ | _ ∧ ||
_ > | ‿∪ | ∟ || ‿∪ | _ ∪ | _ ∧ ||
∪ _ | ‿∪ | ∟ || ‿∪ | _ ∪ | _ ∧ ||
∪ ∪ | ‿∪ | ∟ || _ .....

2. When logaoedic verses began to be used also in recitation, the basis remained. But a recited verse, in which the element of melody is lacking, must follow the rhythm more strictly, or it will else appear like a sentence of prose. Therefore equality in the measures, at least, must be preserved: a measure of two shorts (∪ ∪, *pyrrhic*) is no longer admissible. The tribrach, however, is admitted, but seldom.

Both sentences of the Eupolidean verse (§ 26, 3, VIII.), as well as of the second and third Priapean verses (ib. X., XI.), begin with such a basis; but in the Cratinean verses (ib. VII.) only the second sentence does this, since the first begins with a cyclic dactyl, which must be kept as characteristic measure of logaoedic verses. On this ground the first Priapeus has no basis.

The following, therefore, in which all the possible forms of the basis are given, is a more accurate statement of the different recitative metres than was given in § 26.

§ 27. THE LYRIC TYPE.

Metrum Cratineum:

⏖∪ | −∪ | −∪ | ⌊ ‖ − ∪ | − ⏑̄ | − ∪ | − ∧ ‖
        − >
        ∪ −
        ∪ ∪ ∪

Metrum Eupolideum:

− ∪ | − ⏑̄ | ⏖∪ | ⌊ ‖ − ∪ | − ⏑̄ | − ∪ | − ∧ ‖
− >   − >
∪ −   ∪ −
∪ ∪ ∪   ∪ ∪ ∪

Priapeus secundus:

− ∪ | ⏖∪ | − ∪ | ⌊ ‖ − ∪ | ⏖∪ | ⌊ | − ∧ ‖
− >   − >
∪ −   ∪ −
∪ ∪ ∪   ∪ ∪ ∪

Priapeus tertius:

− ∪ | − ⏑̄ | ⏖∪ | ⌊ ‖ − ∪ | ⏖∪ | ⌊ | − ∧ ‖
− >   − >
∪ −   ∪ −
∪ ∪ ∪   ∪ ∪ ∪

ὦ θεώμενοι, κατερῶ πρὸς ὑμᾶς ἐλευθέρως
τἀληθῆ, νὴ τὸν Διόνυσον τὸν ἐκθρέψαντά με.

AR. *Nub.* 518 *sq.*

− ∪ | − ∪ | ⏖∪ | ⌊, ‖ − ∪ | − ∪ | − ∪ | − ∧ ‖
− > | − > | ⏖∪ | ⌊ ‖ − ∪ | − > | − ∪ | − ∧ ‖.

3. In choric poetry, which was accompanied by dancing, the basis is not admissible. For here the measures must have an exact length, or the dance will be but a planless moving of the chorus to and fro. The *pyrrhic* therefore, first of all, is not allowable under any circumstances. The strict dance-rhythm, moreover, demands also a strict melody according exactly in strophe and antistrophe. Therefore the measures must accord metrically. The irrational measures may indeed correspond to the rational (− ⏑̄); and two shorts may stand as equal to the simple long (− ⌣⌣ and − ⁀⁀), since, in singing, two short notes which fall to two syllables in the strophe can without difficulty be transferred to a long syllable in the antistrophe (just as every circumflexed syllable in prose has two notes). But it is impossible for a proper and an inverted choree to correspond metrically. For how could $\overset{>}{\text{♩}}\,\text{♪}$ and $\overset{>}{\text{♪}}\,\text{♩}$ admit the same melody? Consequently in choric

II. THE EPODES. 93

poetry a metrical correspondence like ⌣ ⌒ is altogether inadmissible, and the very few places where it occurs are in corrupt passages, which are, therefore, to be emended.

But valid objections could not be made to a correspondence like ⌣ ⌢⌢, since here not only the length of the measures is exactly preserved, but also the last two eighth-notes can easily be united into a single syllable. And so in fact an inverted choree corresponds to a tribrach several times in the choruses of Pindar and Euripides. For an example see § 17, 4, I.

With this exception, ⌣ — at the beginning of a logaoedic verse is generally to be divided ⌣ ⋮ ∟ |. Examples occur in § 22, 11, B and C.

§ 28. The Lyric Type (*continued*).

II. THE EPODES (οἱ ἐπῳδοί).

1. In recitative poetry, which appropriated to itself the simplest forms, occurs the most primitive sort of rhythmical period, the recitative verse; this consists of two sentences which either have equal length, or the second of which is catalectic or "falling," or is even shortened by an entire measure. In the oldest lyric poetry, as cultivated in particular by Archilochus, a step is taken toward a further development. The verse is no longer an independent period, notwithstanding the pause that closes it and the fact that it may consist of two sentences; but a new verse follows, sometimes in-quite a different rhythm, which is either to round off the melody of the first, or to constitute a contrast to it. In this way the two are united into an organic whole, which has a fixed melody that returns with every repetition of the two rhythms.

2. In considering the best known epodic "strophes" which have been preserved, we naturally begin with the "distichon," which consists of two dactylic verses, the "heroic" and the "elegiac" hexameter (*versus elegiacus*). The latter is usually, but erroneously, called *pentameter*. An example has already been given in § 11, 6, III.

The distichon was a melody used chiefly to express sorrow or lamentation. Not only the so-called elegies, however, were written in this rhythm, but also many of the martial songs of Callinus, Tyrtaeus, Archilochus, and Theognis. Later it was used more and more in gnomic poems, composed first by Theognis and then by Solon and many others. Finally, it was frequently employed in humorous love-songs, as later in

§ 28. THE LYRIC TYPE.

the *Amores* of Ovid. These poems, nevertheless, always improperly retained the name of "elegies."

3. There were other melodies also, which were used for comic effect, in particular those in which the difference of the verses in metre, or a marked disparity in their length, expressed the intended contrast in a lively manner. In these the longer verse may follow the shorter, by which a comic effect is produced. The hearer expects after the first short verse a still shorter one to follow, a satisfactory close being commonly attained in this way. But, on the contrary, the second is made much the longer. Such successions of verses are really a continuing series of comic effects of the unexpected sort. (Cic. de Or. II. § 255: *Sed scitis esse notissimum ridiculi genus, cum aliud exspectamus, aliud dicitur.*)

Since the rich epodic literature of the Greeks has been lost with the exception of a few fragments, the epodes of Horace must be used in illustration. The forms he has employed are the following:

I. The *iambic group*, consisting of an iambic hexapody and an iambic tetrapody.

$$\check{\circ} \vdots \_ \cup | \_ \check{\circ} | \_ \cup | \_ \check{\circ} | \_ \cup | \_ \wedge \|$$
$$\cup \vdots \_ \cup | \_ \check{\circ} | \_ \cup | \_ \wedge \|$$

Ep. 2.
Beatus ille, qui procul negotiis,
ut prisca gens mortalium . . .

II. The *first Pythiambic group*, consisting of a dactylic verse of two tripodies (hexameter) and of an iambic tetrapody.

$$\_ \infty | \_ \infty | \_, \infty \| \_ \infty | \_ \cup \cup | \_ \_ \|$$
$$\check{\circ} \vdots \_ \cup | \_ \check{\circ} | \_ \cup | \_ \wedge \|$$

Ep. 15.
Nox erat et caelo fulgebat luna sereno
inter minora sidera.

III. The *second Pythiambic group*, consisting of an iambic trimeter following the dactylic hexameter.

$$\_ \infty | \_ \infty | \_, \infty \| \_ \infty | \_ \cup \cup | \_ \_ \|$$
$$\check{\circ} \vdots \_ \cup | \_ \check{\circ} | \_ \cup | \_ \check{\circ} | \_ \cup | \_ \wedge \|$$

Ep. 16.
Altera jam teritur bellis civilibus aetas,
suis et ipsa Roma viribus ruit.

IV. The *Alcmanian group*, consisting of a dactylic hexameter followed by a dactylic tetrameter.

$$-\overline{\smile}\,|\,-\overline{\smile}\,|\,-,\overline{\smile}\,\|\,-\overline{\smile}\,|\,-\smile\smile\,|\,-\,-\,\|$$
$$-\overline{\smile}\,|\,-\overline{\smile}\,|\,-\smile\smile\,|\,-\,-\,\|$$

Ep. 12.

Quid tibi vis mulier nigris dignissima barris?
munera cur mihi quidve tabellas . . .

V. Horace has not used groups of two verses each in which the longer follows the shorter, but by uniting two such has formed four-lined groups of this kind. Cf. § 29, 3, II. and V.

4. By a further development, three verses are united in a group according to the following law: the group begins with a long verse, followed by a second that is shorter and in different measure. The third verse reconciles this opposition, either returning to the measure of the first verse or having a greater length. There are three kinds:

I. The *first Archilochian group*, consisting of a dactylic hexameter, an iambic tetrapody, and a catalectic dactylic trimeter.

$$-\overline{\smile}\,|\,-\overline{\smile}\,|\,-\overline{\smile}\,\|\,-\overline{\smile}\,|\,-\smile\smile\,|\,-\,-\,\|$$
$$\check{\smile}\,\vdots\,-\smile\,|\,-\check{\smile}\,|\,-\smile\,|\,-\wedge\,\|$$
$$-\smile\smile\,|\,-\smile\smile\,|\,-\overline{\wedge}\,\|$$

Ep. 13.

Horrida tempestas caelum contraxit et imbres
nivesque deducunt Jovem;
nunc mare nunc siluae . . .

II. The *second Archilochian group*, consisting of an iambic hexapody, a catalectic dactylic trimeter, and an iambic tetrapody.

$$\check{\smile}\,\vdots\,-\smile\,|\,-\check{\smile}\,|\,-\smile\,|\,-\check{\smile}\,|\,-\smile\,|\,-\wedge\,\|$$
$$-\smile\smile\,|\,-\smile\smile\,|\,-\wedge\,\|$$
$$\check{\smile}\,\vdots\,-\smile\,|\,-\check{\smile}\,|\,-\smile\,|\,-\wedge\,\|$$

Ep. 11.

Pecti, nihil me sicut antea juvat
scribere versiculos
amore perculsum gravi.

III. The *third Archilochian group*, consisting, *in the original form*, of a dactylic tetrapody with the last measure always a dactyl, a trochaic tripody, and a falling iambic hexapody.

§ 29. THE LYRIC TYPE.

$$\_ \overline{\smile} \mid \_ \overline{\smile} \mid \_ \overline{\smile} \mid \_ \cup \cup \parallel$$
$$\_ \cup \mid \_ \cup \mid \_ \cup \parallel$$
$$\breve{\diamond} \vdots \_ \cup \mid \_ \breve{\diamond} \mid \_ \cup \mid \_ \cup \mid \_ \mid \_ \wedge \parallel$$

ARCHIL. *fr.*

τοῖος γὰρ φιλότητος ἔρως ὑπὸ
καρδίην ἐλυσθεὶς
πολλὴν κατ' ἀχλὺν ὀμμάτων ἔχευεν.

For the remodelling of this group by Horace, see § 29, 3, III.

IV. A peculiar sort of three-lined epode has been preserved in Aristophanes, *Ran.* VI. (416–418):

$$\breve{\diamond} \vdots \_ \cup \mid \_ \cup \mid \_ \mid \_ \wedge \parallel$$
$$\breve{\diamond} \vdots \_ \cup \mid \_ \cup \mid \_ \mid \_ \wedge \parallel$$
$$\breve{\diamond} \vdots \_ \cup \mid \_ \breve{\diamond} \mid \_ \cup \mid \_ \breve{\diamond} \mid \_ \cup \mid \_ \wedge \parallel$$

Βούλεσθε δῆτα κοινῇ
σκώψωμεν Ἀρχέδημον;
ὃς ἑπτέτης ὢν οὐκ ἔφυσε φράτερας.

§ 29. The Lyric Type (*continued*).

III. FOUR-LINED GROUPS.

1. It is not by mere chance, that four-lined groups are the prevailing form in Greek poetry that was designed to be sung. This is notably the case also in English. By such a grouping symmetry could be attained along with variety; and thus the whole made a satisfactory impression, while the melody still possessed in itself enough of variety not to be tiresome by continued repetition.

In Aeolic (Alcaeus, Anacreon, Sappho, etc.) and Ionic lyric poetry four-lined groups were developed in great variety. But since little that is entire has been preserved, it must suffice to become acquainted with these groups as found in Horace. — What Horace has independently originated or changed will be pointed out and briefly discussed.

2. *First form of construction*: the same verse occurs four times without change.

Whether Horace has here followed the model of Greek poets cannot be certainly determined, but this is probable.

The repetition of exactly the same verse approaches the usage of recitative poetry, to which there is here a further correspondence in that

III. FOUR-LINED GROUPS.

the verses are independent periods consisting of two or three sentences each.

There are two varieties of this group.

I. The *lesser Asclepiadean group*, consisting of four *lesser Asclepiadean* verses.

The *versus Asclepiadeus minor* consists of two catalectic Pherecratean verses, a second and a first, with diaeresis:

_ ⌒ | ⌣ ⌣ | ⌊ , ‖ ⌣ ⌣ | _ ⌣ | _ ⋀ ‖.

Horace is peculiar in always beginning the first Pherecratean with an irrational measure, so that his strophe reads:

_ > | ⌣ ⌣ | ⌊ , ‖ ⌣ ⌣ | _ ⌣ | _ ⋀ ‖
_ > | ⌣ ⌣ | ⌊ , ‖ ⌣ ⌣ | _ ⌣ | _ ⋀ ‖
_ > | ⌣ ⌣ | ⌊ , ‖ ⌣ ⌣ | _ ⌣ | _ ⋀ ‖
_ > | ⌣ ⌣ | ⌊ , ‖ ⌣ ⌣ | _ ⌣ | _ ⋀ ‖

This regularity results from Horace's ignorance of the rhythm. He must, of course, have felt the rhythm as well as we, but he made a concession, in this constant use of the apparent spondee, to the metrical theorists of his day, who concerned themselves wholly with longs and shorts. The Latin language, moreover, is rich in long syllables, but relatively poor in short ones.

In order to give a clearer idea of the force of the four-lined group, certain principles and the use of certain geometrical figures must be introduced from Book V. on "Eurhythmy."

The *Asclepiadean* was originally a period consisting of two logaoedic tripodies corresponding to each other. This is indicated by

Later two of these periods were united in a group, indicated by

in which the curve at the left shows how the entire verses, which are now only subordinate periods or groups, correspond; the curves at the right, how the first and second sentences in the first verse correspond respectively to the first and second sentences in the second. These two

§ 29. THE LYRIC TYPE.

verses, though metrically exactly equal, were not here independent periods, but were closely united into a single group, the melody of the first verse not ending with the key-note. Perhaps also the melody of the second was not identical with that of the first, but only analogous. Four verses being thus united, the scheme of the entire group would be

Concerning this scheme cf. § 34, 3, 4.
The melody might also be arranged

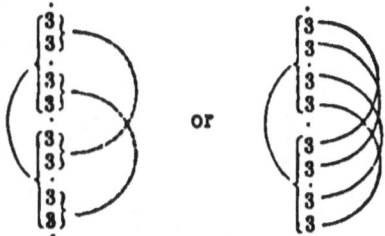

i. e. the first two verses corresponded to the last two.
An example is found in Hor. carm. III. 30:

> *Exegi monumentum aere perennius*
> *regalique situ pyramidum altius,*
> *quod non imber edax, non Aquilo impotens*
> *possit diruere aut Innumerabilis* . . . .

It is worthy of note here that the groups are not separated by punctuation. But still such a division into four-lined groups should be made, because in all the odes of Horace the total number of verses is divisible by four, with a few exceptions where interpolation is obvious.

II. The *greater Asclepiadean group*, consisting of four *greater Asclepiadean verses*. The *versus Asclepiadeus major* is composed of a catalectic second *Pherecratean*, a catalectic *Adonic*, and a catalectic first *Pherecratean*:

$$\_ \cup | \_ \cup \cup | \_, \| \_ \cup \cup | \_, \| \_ \cup \cup | \_ \cup | \_ \wedge \|,$$

with diaeresis in both places. In Horace the first measure is always irrational (cf. under I.), so that his strophe has the form:

III. FOUR-LINED GROUPS.

_ > | ⏑⏑ | ⎿, ‖ ⏑⏑ | ⎿, ‖ ⏑⏑ | _ ⏑ | _ ∧ ‖
_ > | ⏑⏑ | ⎿, ‖ ⏑⏑ | ⎿, ‖ ⏑⏑ | _ ⏑ | _ ∧ ‖
_ > | ⏑⏑ | ⎿, ‖ ⏑⏑ | ⎿, ‖ ⏑⏑.| _ ⏑ | _ ∧ ‖
_ > | ⏑⏑ | ⎿, ‖ ⏑⏑ | ⎿, ‖ ⏑⏑ | _ ⏑ | _ ∧ ‖

The division of the greater Asclepiadean verse is:

$\left.\begin{array}{c}\dot{3}\\2\\3\end{array}\right)$

i. e. the first and third sentences correspond, while the middle one has a series of tones of its own. Cf. § 34, 6.

Since here, as in the preceding case (I.), the verses are no longer independent periods, but have become subordinate members in the greater whole, the division of the entire group is:

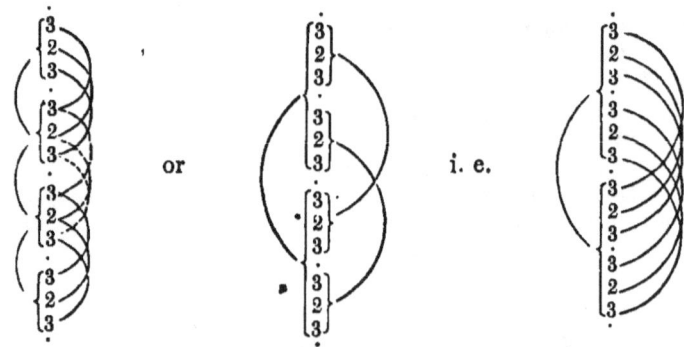

HOR. *carm.* I. 11.

Tu ne quaesieris, scire nefas, quem mihi, quem tibi
finem di dederint, Leuconoë, nec Babylonios
tentaris numeros. Ut melius, quidquid erit, pati!
seu plures hiemes seu tribuit Jupiter ultimam . . . .

3. *Second form of construction:* an epodic group is repeated. Here Horace seems to be for the most part the originator, since among the Greeks these epodic groups were not united.

I. The *dactylic Archilochian group:* the repeated group consists of a dactylic hexameter and a dactylic trimeter.

_ ⏒ | _ ⏒ | _, ⏒ ‖ _ ⏒ | _ ⏑⏑ | _ _ ‖
_ ⏑⏑| _ ⏑⏑ | _ ⋏ ‖
_ ⏒ | _ ⏒ | _, ⏒ ‖ _ ⏒ | _ ⏑⏑ | _ _ ‖
_ ⏑⏑| _ ⏑⏑ | _ ⋏ ⟧

§ 29. THE LYRIC TYPE.

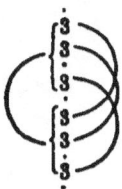

A palinodic period, cf. § 34, 3.

HOR. *carm.* IV. 7.

Diffugere nives, redeunt jam gramina campis
arboribusque comae;
mutat terra vices et decrescentia ripas
flumina praetereunt.

II. The *greater Sapphic group:* a group is repeated of which the first verse is a falling logaoedic *tetrapody*, the second a third *Priapeus*. Horace has here also always used the irrational measure where it is allowed, so that his group has the form:

HOR. *carm.* I. 8.

Lydia, dic, per omnes
te deos oro, Sybarin cur properes amando
perdere; cur apricum
oderit campum, patiens pulveris atque solis?

III. The *logaoedic Archilochian group*, as used by Horace, is likewise four-lined. Cf. carefully § 28, 4, III. He has united the second of the three verses in the *third Archilochian group* to the first, since neither *syllaba anceps* nor *hiatus* occurs between the two. The two-lined epodic group so arising is repeated:

III. FOUR-LINED GROUPS.

Hor. *Carm.* I. 4.

Solvitur acris hiems grata vice veris et Favoni,
trahuntque siccas machinae carinas;
ac neque jam stabulis gaudet pecus aut arator igni,
nec prata canis albicant pruinis.

Horace must have read the dactyls as cyclic, for it is impossible that he should have united a purely dactylic and a purely choreic sentence into one verse. What he has done here was done by the Romans very commonly even in hexameter, so that their sole point of agreement with the Greeks was the scheme of the syllables. The forms of this scheme were no longer sung, but only recited; and in declamation the difference between long and short syllables is not so great. Only he who feels poetry and song inseparable, and thus grasps the thought of the forms, recites with metrical accuracy.

IV. The *four-lined Alcmanian group* consists of two Alcmanian epodic groups united. Cf. § 28, 3, IV.

$$\_\infty \mid \_\infty \mid \_, \infty \parallel \_\infty \mid \_\cup\cup \mid \_\_ \parallel$$
$$\_\infty \mid \_\infty \mid \_\cup\cup \mid \_\_ \parallel$$
$$\_\infty \mid \_\infty \mid \_, \infty \parallel \_\infty \mid \_\cup\cup \mid \_\_ \parallel$$
$$\_\infty \mid \_\infty \mid \_\cup\cup \mid \_\_ \rrbracket$$

Hor. *Carm.* I. 7.

Laudabunt alii claram Rhodon aut Mytilenen
aut Epheson bimarisve Corinthi
moenia vel Baccho Thebas vel Apolline Delphos
insignes aut Thessala Tempe.

V. The *interchanging Asclepiadean group:* a group is repeated consisting of a second Glyconic and the lesser Asclepiadean. Here also Horace has regularly used the irrational measure when allowed.

§ 29. THE LYRIC TYPE.

$$\_ > | \smile\smile | \_\smile | \_ \wedge \|$$
$$\_ > | \smile\smile | \llcorner, \| \smile\smile | \_\smile | \_ \wedge \|$$
$$\_ > | \smile\smile | \_\smile | \_ \wedge \|$$
$$\_ > | \smile\smile | \llcorner, \| \smile\smile | \_\smile | \_ \wedge \rrbracket$$

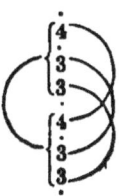

Hor. *Carm.* I. 3.

Sic te diva potens Cypri,
sic fratres Helenae, lucida sidera,
ventorumque regat pater
obstrictis aliis praeter Iapyga.

4. *Third form of construction:* two independent groups, which constitute a sort of antithesis to each other, are united.

This is an important advance toward greater variety.

I. The *contrasted Asclepiadean group:* the first period consists of two lesser Asclepiadean verses, the second of two second Glyconic verses, of which the first is falling. The form in Horace is:

$$\_ > | \smile\smile | \llcorner, \| \smile\smile | \_\smile | \_ \wedge \|$$
$$\_ > | \smile\smile | \llcorner, \| \smile\smile | \_\smile | \_ \wedge \rrbracket$$
$$\_ > | \smile\smile | \llcorner. | \_ \wedge \|$$
$$\_ > | \smile\smile | \_\smile | \_ \wedge \rrbracket$$

I. $\begin{pmatrix} 3 \\ 3 \\ \cdot \\ 3 \\ 3 \end{pmatrix}$ II. $\begin{pmatrix} 4 \\ \cdot \\ 4 \end{pmatrix}$

Hor. *Carm.* I. 5.

Quis multa gracilis te puer in rosa
perfusus liquidis urget odoribus,
grato, Pyrrha, sub antro?
cui flavam religas comam . . . ?

II. The *Alcaïc group:* the first period consists of two *Alcaïci hendecasyllabi*, the other of an *Alcaïcus enneasyllabus* and an *Alcaïcus decasyllabus*.

$$\overset{\smile}{\_\_} | \_\smile | \_\overset{\smile}{\_\_}, | \smile\smile | \_\smile | \_ \wedge \|$$
$$\overset{\smile}{\_\_} | \_\smile | \_\overset{\smile}{\_\_}, | \smile\smile | \_\smile | \_ \wedge \rrbracket$$
$$\overset{\smile}{\_\_} | \_\smile | \_\overset{\smile}{\_\_} | \_\smile | \_\smile \|$$
$$\smile\smile | \smile\smile | \_\smile | \_\smile \rrbracket$$

I. $\begin{pmatrix} 5 \\ 5 \end{pmatrix}$

II. $\begin{pmatrix} 4 \\ 4 \end{pmatrix}$

III. FOUR-LINED GROUPS.

Hor. *Carm.* I. 9.

Vides ut alta stet nive candidum
Soracte, nec jam sustineant onus
silvae laborantes geluque
flumina constiterint acuto.

Horace has introduced diaeresis, which has nothing to do with the rhythm. It does not occur in Alcaeus, as the following strophe shows:

χείμωνι μοχθεῦντες μεγάλῳ μάλα·
περ μὲν γὰρ ἄντλος ἰστοπέδαν ἔχει,
λαῖφος δὲ πᾶν ζάδηλον ἤδη
καὶ λάκιδες μεγάλαι κατ' αὖτο.

III. The *ionic group*: the first period consists of two ionic dipodies, the second of two ionic tripodies.

```
∪∪ : _ _ ∪∪ | _ _ ⊼ ||             I.  2)
∪∪ : _ _ ∪∪ | _ _ ⊼ ]]                 2
∪∪ : _ _ ∪∪ | _ _ ∪∪ | _ _ ⊼ ||    II. 3)
∪∪ : _ _ ∪∪ | _ _ ∪∪ | _ _ ⊼ ]]        3
```

Hor. *Carm.* III. 12.

Miserarum est neque amori
dare ludum, neque dulci
mala vino lavere, aut exanimari
metuentis patruae verbera linguae.

5. *Fourth form of construction:* a period of three equal verses is closed by a fourth as a sort of postlude (ἐπῳδικόν), which may also be united to the third verse without pause. Cf. § 35, I.

I. The *Asclepiadean Glyconic group:* three lesser Asclepiadean verses with closing Glyconic.

```
_ > | ⌣∪ | ∟, || ⌣∪ | _ ∪ | _ ∧ ||     ⎧3
_ > | ⌣∪ | ∟, ||  ∪∪ | _ ∪ | _ ∧ ||    ⎪3
_ > | ⌣∪ | ∟, || ⌣∪ | _ ∪ | _ ∧ ||     ⎨3
    _ > | ⌣∪ | _ ∪ | _ ∧]]              ⎩3
```

4 = ἐπῳδικόν.

§ 29. THE LYRIC TYPE.

Hor. *Carm.* I. 24.

Quis desiderio sit pudor aut modus
tam cari capitis? Praecipe lugubres
cantus, Melpomene, cui liquidam pater
vocem cum cithara dedit.

II. The *common Sapphic group*: the *Sapphicus minor* (Σαπφικὸν ἑνδεκασύλλαβον) three times, with closing Adonic. The form in Horace is:

$$\_\cup|\_>|\_,\cup\cup|\_\cup|\_\cup\|$$
$$\_\cup|\_>|\_,\cup\cup|\_\cup|\_\cup\|$$
$$\_\cup|\_>|\_,\cup\cup|\_\cup|\_\cup\|\_\cup\cup|\_\cup|$$

$$\left.\begin{array}{c}5\\5\\5\end{array}\right\}$$
$$2 = \text{ἐπῳδικόν}.$$

Hor. *Carm.* I. 2.

Jam satis terris nivis atque dirae
grandinis misit pater et rubente
dextera sacras jaculatus arces terruit urbem.

Here also the second measure is always irrational. The caesura, which always occurs, has not the least to do with the rhythm, but rather disturbs it when observed, since the cyclic dactyl is thereby dismembered. The verses in Sappho, since they are not divided into two sentences, are naturally without this caesura, and the second measure is not always irrational.

Ποικιλόθρον' ἀθάνατ' Ἀφρόδιτα,
παῖ Διὸς δολόπλοκε, λίσσομαί σε,
μή μ' ἄσαισι μητ' ὀνίαισι δάμνα, πότνια, θῦμον,

that is

$$\_\cup|\_\stackrel{\smile}{\_}|\_\cup\cup|\_\cup|\_\cup\|, \text{ etc.}$$

That the last sentence is not to be written separately is shown by various examples both in Sappho and Horace (though they are comparatively fewer in the latter), in which, if the last sentence should be written separately, the third verse would end in the middle of a word.

Φαίνεταί μοι κῆνος ἴσος θέοισιν
ἔμμεν ὤνηρ, ὅστις ἐναντίος τοι
ἰζάνει, καὶ πλασίον ἆδυ φωνείσας ὑπακούει.

Iliae dum se nimium querenti
jactat ultorem, vagus et sinistra
labitur ripa Jove non probante uxorius amnis.

Hor. *Carm.* I. 2, v. 19.

IV. LYRIC SYSTEMS. 105

Here it is obvious that the last verse is not to be written, —

*labitur ripa Jove non probante u-
xorius amnis.*

6. It is here proper to recapitulate the facts which show that the odes of Horace were intended only for declamation and were written after given metrical models, the poet not being governed by a melody whose demands he endeavored to meet.

I. The irrational choree is treated as a distinct form of measure, since only by exception the rational choree takes its place. Cf. 2, I. and II.; 3, V.; and 5, II.

II. Horace used all dactyls as cyclic, as is to be seen from his construction of the *logaoedic Archilochian group* (3, III.).

III. In the *Alcaic group* (4, II.) he uses diaeresis, and in the *common Sapphic group* (5, II.) caesura, both without regard to the rhythm of the verse.

§ 30. The Lyric Type (*concluded*).

IV. LYRIC SYSTEMS.

1. We saw in § 26 how two rhythmical sentences are united into the simplest period, the recitative verse; then in § 28, how from two independent verses, which make a sort of contrast to one another, a unified rhythmical group arises. In the same paragraph it was shown how three verses, standing in a beautiful relation to one another, may be united into a carefully rounded whole. Finally, it was seen in § 29 how four verses are united into a group, the division of which is dependent upon determined laws and therefore has a fixed character.

The lyric systems to which we now proceed may be characterized as a succession of verses which neither of themselves constitute rhythmical periods (since they do not consist of an antecedent and consequent sentence forming an antithesis to one another, as is the case in recitative verses), nor appear as well-rounded units when united in longer series. These systems are successions of verses in the same measure, consisting generally (originally always) of a single sentence. Though sometimes arranged in four-lined groups, the four verses stand in no relation of antithesis to one another, since they are all constructed alike. They are just as clearly distinguished also from the first form of construction of the four-lined strophes (§ 29, 2), since the verses have no antitheses within themselves.

This regular movement is often varied by giving the verses (or sentences) a different metrical form. But in doing this no fixed principle is observed. Even where four-lined groups seem to be formed, no exact metrical correspondence, in case there is any difference at all in their metrical forms, prevails among them. If, for example, two metrical forms, *a* and *b*, interchange, the first system (the first apparent *group*) may have in the first verse the form *a*, while the second has the form *b*, etc. It is, therefore, clear that these systems did not have exactly the same melody; they are rather compositions in which a musical theme was sometimes repeated, sometimes varied, but on no fixed principle.

These systems or parts of them are, moreover, often closed by sentences of fixed form, especially by falling sentences or by those of a less number of measures. These final sentences are sometimes a sort of postlude (ἐπῳδικόν), sometimes they constitute real antitheses. But even in the last case no strongly periodic relation arises, since only the last verse (or sentence) of a series has its antithesis, while each of the verses (sentences) would have one, if the construction were periodic. This is in fact, it will be remembered, the case in the epodic groups.

Finally, the verses may be more closely connected with one another, and sink into merely subordinate sentences not separated by verse-pauses, a pause occurring only at the end of a group of several such sentences. This, however, does not give rise to a verse in the proper sense. For such a union of sentences into a *line* (στίχος) has no rhythmical division within itself (is not a μέτρον), and several such lines united to one another constitute no period.

In every case, therefore, the *system* is distinguished from the *group* by having no strictly regulated antitheses. If several sentences unite without pauses, they do not constitute true verses, but only *lines*, which it is not possible to group into periods.

In the lyric system, therefore, the sentence is really the highest rhythmical unit.

In consequence of this, these systems cannot be used either in the choruses of the dramas or as march-melodies, since they are altogether unadapted for dancing and marching. Neither are they found in the monodies of Attic tragedy on account of their uniformity, nor in the κομμοί (§ 33, 4, A, V.), since it is impossible for excitement, deep passion, or sharp contrasts to be expressed by them. They are used,

IV. LYRIC SYSTEMS.   107

consistently with their nature, only in simple songs for the people like those of Anacreon and his imitators, and then in comic songs of Attic comedy. Some of the lyric systems, however, are very similar to genuine lyric groups, e. g. those given below in 4, I. and II.

The following are the different forms of construction of the lyric systems.

2. FIRST FORM OF CONSTRUCTION: a succession of verses consisting of only one sentence, either of like form or of different but not regularly changing forms.

I. The *hemiambics*, iambic falling tetrapodies, the metre of several of the songs formerly ascribed to Anacreon.

$$\angle : \_ \cup | \_ \cup | \_ | \_ \wedge \|$$

Anacreont. 19.

Ἡ γῆ μέλαινα πίνει,
πίνει δὲ δένδρε' αὖ γῆν. .
πίνει θάλασσα δ' αὔρας,
ὁ δ' ἥλιος θάλασσαν,
τὸν δ' ἥλιον σελήνη. .
τί μοι μάχεσθ', ἑταῖροι,
καὐτῷ θέλοντι πίνειν;

II. The *Anacreontics*, ionic dipodies with or without anaclasis.

A. The verses with dichorees in unbroken succession:

$$\cup \cup : \_ \cup \_ \cup | \_ \_ \overline{\wedge} \|$$

Anacreont. 48.

Δότε μοι λύρην Ὁμήρου
φονίης ἄνευθε χορδῆς.
φέρε μοι κύπελλα θεσμῶν
φέρε μοι νόμους κεράσσω,
μεθύων ὅπως χορεύσω,
ὑπὸ σώφρονος δὲ λύσσης,
μετὰ βαρβίτων ἀείδων,
τὸ παροίνιον βοήσω.
δότε μοι λύρην Ὁμήρου
φονίης ἄνευθε χορδῆς.

B. The pure forms and those with a dichoree irregularly interchanged:

§ 30. THE LYRIC TYPE.

∪∪ : — ∪ — ∪ | — — ⊼ ‖
∪∪ : — > — ∪ | — — ⊼ ‖
∪∪ : — — ∪∪ | — — ⊼ ‖

Anacreont. 37.

Ἴδε πῶς φανέντος ἦρος
Χάριτες ῥόδα βρύουσιν·
ἴδε πῶς κῦμα θαλάσσης
ἀπαλύνεται γαλήνῃ·
ἴδε πῶς νῆσσα κολυμβᾷ·
ἴδε πῶς γέρανος ὁδεύει.
ἀφελῶς δ᾽ ἔλαμψε Τίταν·
νεφελῶν σκιαὶ δονοῦνται.
τὰ βροτῶν δ᾽ ἔλαμψεν ἔργα.
καρποῖς γαῖα προκύπτει.
Βρομίου στραφὲν τὸ νᾶμα
κατὰ φύλλον κατὰ κλῶνα
καθελὼν ἤνθισε καρπός.

∪∪ : — ∪ — ∪ | — — ⊼ ‖
∪∪ : — ∪ — ∪ | — — ⊼ ‖
∪∪ : — — ∪∪ | — — ⊼ ‖
∪∪ : — ∪ — ∪ | — — ⊼ ‖
∪∪ : — — ∪∪ | — — ⊼ ‖
∪∪ : — ∪ ∪ ∪∪ | — — ⊼ ‖
∪∪ : — ∪ — ∪ | — — ⊼ ‖
∪∪ : — ∪ — ∪ | — — ⊼ ‖
∪∪ : — ∪ — ∪ | — — ⊼ ‖
— : — — ∪ ∪ | — — ⊼ ‖
∪∪ : — ∪ — ∪ | — — ⊼ ‖
∪∪ : — — ∪∪ | — — ⊼ ‖
∪∪ : — — ∪∪ | — — ⊼ ‖

3. SECOND FORM OF CONSTRUCTION: a division into four-lined groups is indicated by the punctuation; but that these are not genuine groups in which the same melody is exactly repeated, but are rather systems in which the singer himself changes the melody from one system to another, is shown, exactly as in the Anacreontics, by their irregularity in the interchange of metrical forms where such interchange occurs.

IV. LYRIC SYSTEMS.

I. *Four-lined hemiambic systems:*

Anacreont. 13.

Οἱ μὲν καλὴν Κυβήβην
τὸν ἡμίθηλυν Ἄττιν
ἐν οὔρεσιν βοῶντα
λέγουσιν ἐκμανῆναι.

οἱ δὲ Κλάρου παρ' ὄχθαις
δαφνηφόροιο Φοίβου
λαλὸν πιόντες ὕδωρ
μεμηνότες βοῶσιν.

ἐγὼ δὲ τοῦ Λυαίου
καὶ τοῦ μύρου κορεσθεὶς
καὶ τῆς ἐμῆς ἑταίρης
θέλω θέλω μανῆναι.

II. *Four-lined Anacreontic systems:*

Anacreon.

Πολιοὶ μὲν ἡμὶν ἤδη
κρόταφοι κάρη τε λευκόν,
χαρίεσσα δ' οὐκέθ' ἥβη
πάρα, γηραλέοι δ' ὀδόντες.

γλυκεροῦ δ' οὐκέτι πολλὸς
βιότου χρόνος λέλειπται·
διὰ ταῦτ' ἀνασταλύζω
θαμὰ Τάρταρον δεδοικώς.

Ἀίδεω γάρ ἐστι δεινὸς
μυχός, ἀργαλέη δ' ἐς αὐτὸν
κάθοδος· καὶ γὰρ ἕτοιμον
καταβάντι μὴ ἀναβῆναι.

∪∪ː＿∪＿∪｜＿＿⊼‖
∪∪ː＿∪＿∪｜＿＿⊼‖
∪∪ː＿∪＿∪｜＿＿⊼‖
∪∪ː＿∪＿∪｜＿＿⊼‖

§ 30. THE LYRIC TYPE.

$$\smile\smile : \_\_\smile\smile | \_\_ \overline{\wedge} \|$$
$$\smile\smile : \_\smile\_\smile | \_\_ \overline{\wedge} \|$$
$$\smile\smile : \_\smile\_\smile | \_\_ \overline{\wedge} \|$$
$$\smile\smile : \_\smile\_\smile | \_\_ \overline{\wedge} \|$$

$$\smile\smile : \_\smile\_\smile | \_\_ \overline{\wedge} \|$$
$$\smile\smile : \_\smile\_\smile | \_\_ \overline{\wedge} \|$$
$$\smile\smile : \_\_\smile\smile | \_\_ \overline{\wedge} \|$$
$$\smile\smile : \_\smile\_\smile | \_\_ \overline{\wedge} \|$$

It is clear that the first verse in the second system has not the same melody with the corresponding verse in the first and third; likewise that the third verse in the third system has not the same melody with the third verse in the first and second: these verses do not correspond metrically.

4. THIRD FORM OF CONSTRUCTION: verses of equal length, but of different metrical form, occur in a fixed order, so that there result systems of four or six verses; these, however, are distinguished from the groups of § 29 by the fact that their verses are always composed of a single sentence.

The first sentences of the system are distinguished from those that follow by being metrically (but not rhythmically) longer. Generally they either have anacrusis, or else end *full*, while the sentences at the close are catalectic or falling.

I. Three full trochaic tetrapodies united with one catalectic trochaic tetrapody in a four-lined system:

$$\_\smile | \_\overset{\smile}{\smile} | \_\smile | \_\smile \|$$
$$\_\smile | \_\overset{\smile}{\smile} | \_\smile | \_\smile \|$$
$$\_\smile | \_\overset{\smile}{\smile} | \_\smile | \_\smile \|$$
$$\_\smile | \_\overset{\smile}{\smile} | \_\smile | \_\overline{\wedge} \|$$

Anacreon.

Πῶλε Θρηκίη, τί δή με
λοξὸν ὄμμασι βλέπουσα
νηλεῶς φεύγεις, δοκέεις δὲ
μ' οὐδὲν εἰδέναι σοφόν;

II. A catalectic and a falling first Glyconic used alternately, and united in a four-lined system:

$$\widetilde{\smile\smile} | \_\smile | \_\smile | \_\wedge \|$$
$$\widetilde{\smile\smile} | \_\smile | \_ | \_\wedge \|$$
$$\widetilde{\smile\smile} | \_\smile | \_\smile | \_\wedge \|$$
$$\widetilde{\smile\smile} | \_\smile | \_ | \_\wedge \|$$

IV. LYRIC SYSTEMS. 111

Anacreont. 66.

'Ηδυμελὴς 'Ανακρέων,
ἡδυμελὴς δὲ Σαπφώ·
Πινδαρικὸν δέ μοι μέλος
συγκεράσας τις ἐγχέοι.

III. Five hemiambics and a falling first Glyconic united in a six-lined system:

∪ ⋮ ‒ ∪ | ‒ ∪ | ⌊ | ‒ ∧ ‖
∪ ⋮ ‒ ∪ | ‒ ∪ | ⌊ | ‒ ∧ ‖
∪ ⋮ ‒ ∪ | ‒ ∪ | ⌊ | ‒ ∧ ‖
∪ ⋮ ‒ ∪ | ‒ ∪ | ⌊ | ‒ ∧ ‖
∪ ⋮ ‒ ∪ | ‒ ∪ | ⌊ | ‒ ∧ ‖
‾∪ ∪ | ‒ ∪ | ⌊ | ‒ ∧ ‖

Anacreont. 38.

Ἐγὼ γέρων μέν εἰμι,
νέων πλέον δὲ πίνω·
κἂν μὲν δέῃ χορεύειν,
Σειληνὸν ἐν μέσοισι
μιμούμενος χορεύσω,
σκῆπτρον ἔχων τὸν ἀσκόν.

5. FOURTH FORM OF CONSTRUCTION: several sentences ending full are united in one verse and closed by a catalectic or a falling sentence; — or catalectic sentences are in this way closed by a falling sentence. The final sentence may of itself constitute a verse; so likewise the preceding sentences may be divided into verses, the last of which is sometimes united with the final sentence in one verse. The final sentence further may, in place of being catalectic or falling, be shortened by one or two measures.

We give, in what follows, systems from Aristophanes arranged according to their length.

I. *Eq.* VII. (973 – 976.)

‒ ◡ | ‾∪∪ | ‒ ∪ | ⌊ ‖ ‒ ◡ | ‾∪∪ | ‒ ∪ | ⌊ ‖ ‒ ◡ | ‾∪∪ | ‒ ∪ | ‒ ∧ ‖
‒ ◡ | ‾∪∪ | ⌊ | ‒ ∧ ⁞

Ἥδιστον φάος ἡμέρας ἔσται τοῖσι παροῦσι πᾶσιν καὶ τοῖς ἀφικνουμένοις,
ἢν Κλέων ἀπόληται.

§ 30. THE LYRIC TYPE.

II. *Eq.* VIII. (1111-1120).

[metrical scansion]

Ὦ Δῆμε, καλήν γ' ἔχεις ἀρχήν, ὅτε πάντες ἄνθρωποι δεδίασί σ' ὥσπερ
ἄνδρα τύραννον.
ἀλλ' εὐπαράγωγος εἶ, θωπευόμενός τε χαίρεις κἀξαπατώμενος, πρὸς τόν τε
λέγοντ' ἀεὶ κέχηνας· ὁ νοῦς δέ σου παρὼν ἀποδημεῖ.

III. *Ran.* VIII. (534-541).

[metrical scansion]

Ταῦτα μὲν πρὸς ἀνδρός ἐστι νοῦν ἔχοντος καὶ φρένας καὶ πολλὰ περι-
πεπλευκότος,
μετακυλίνδειν αὑτὸν αἰεὶ πρὸς τὸν εὖ πράσσοντα τοῖχον μᾶλλον ἢ γεγραμ-
μένην
εἰκόν' ἑστάναι, λαβόνθ' ἓν σχῆμα. τὸ δὲ μεταστρέφεσθαι πρὸς τὸ μαλ-
θακώτερον
δεξιοῦ πρὸς ἀνδρός ἐστι καὶ φύσει Θηραμένους.

IV. *Ach.* IX. (836-841).

[metrical scansion]

Εὐδαιμονεῖ γ' ἄνθρωπος· οὐκ ἤκουσας οἷ προβαίνει
τὸ πρᾶγμα τοῦ βουλεύματος; καρπώσεται γὰρ ἁνὴρ
ἐν τἀγορᾷ καθήμενος·
κἂν εἰσίῃ τις Κτησίας
ἢ συκοφάντης ἄλλος, οἰμώζων καθεδεῖται.

§ 31. The March Type.

1. The characteristics of the march type are so accurately and sharply defined, both metrically and rhythmically, that their recognition is easy. They are the following:

I. The measure of the march type is without exception the anapaest, the ethical force and metrical form of which have already been considered, § 10, II. and § 11, 6, II.

II. All anapaestic sentences are tetrapodies. If the text and the melody have less than four measures, there is a pause in the singing until the four measures are made complete.

III. All verses which have their four measures expressed in words are catalectic. The last measure is completed by the anacrusis of the next verse, until a verse follows of different metrical form, namely a paroemiac, by which the group is closed (§ 11, 6, II).

If a verse consists of two or three measures, the pause in the singing (see II.) lasts until the thesis of the fourth measure is reached, its arsis being furnished by the anacrusis of the next verse.

IV. From III. there naturally arises this metrical principle, that these verses, each of four measures, must end with a full word, the final vowel of which may be elided; and that no hiatus is allowed between the close of one verse and the beginning of the next. This is just the rule which regulates the caesura, § 19, 2, III.

The apparent dipodies and tripodies that occur are of course not subject to this rule, since there is a long pause between them and the following verse.

2. All these peculiarities stand in the closest relation to the purpose of the march melodies themselves. If, namely, the soldier is to march to the song, the following conditions must be met:

1) The song must be divided into exactly equal measures, to the ictuses of which he is to tread.

2) These measures must be distinctly divided into equal halves, thesis and arsis, both having a strong ictus. But the one ictus must exceed the other in weight, in order that the soldier as he marches may, in observance of them, tread somewhat more heavily with the one foot, somewhat more lightly with the other, and may always easily know from the melody itself with which foot he is to tread at any particular ictus. So the measure is the anapaest, not the dactyl.

§ 31. THE MARCH TYPE.

3) It is not, however, absolutely necessary that all measures should have two strong ictuses; it is sometimes sufficient for a measure to have only one ictus, as e. g. — ⏀. For once having the right movement, the soldier can make no mistake, if only the chief ictus is clearly marked by the melody. Verses, therefore, like the following frequently occur:

$$\_ \vdots \_ \cup \cup \mid \_ \cup \cup \mid \sqcup \mid \bar{\wedge}.$$

4) The sentences must all uniformly consist of four measures, that the equal division may be sustained: 2 eighth-notes + 2 eighth-notes = 1 measure; 1 measure + 1 measure = half of the sentence; 2 measures + 2 measures = the whole sentence. Only in this way would the movement remain uniform throughout.

5) There can be no pauses after the verses *at will;* for if this were done, the time could not be kept, and regular marching would be at an end.

6) But it is impossible, on account of lack of breath, to sing and march at once for any great length of time. Therefore apparent dipodies follow the tetrapodies in long march melodies, where there is a pause in the singing for two full measures, the marching continuing. Or the march song consists entirely of apparent tripodies, after which there is a pause of a full measure, as is to be seen in the following enumeration.

3. The different march melodies are:

I. The *paroemiac*, the anapaestic tripody. The following march song (ἐμβατήριον) of Tyrtaeus, in which the older form of the anapaests without resolution of the thesis prevails, is composed of paroemiacs:

$$\infty \vdots \_ \infty \mid \_ \infty \mid \_ \_ \mid \bar{\wedge}$$

Ἄγετ', ὦ Σπάρτας εὐάνδρου
κοῦροι πατέρων πολιατᾶν,
λαιᾷ μὲν ἴτυν προβάλεσθε,
δόρυ δ' εὐτόλμως πάλλοντες
μὴ φειδεσθαι τᾶς ζωᾶς·
οὐ γὰρ πάτριον τᾷ Σπάρτᾳ.

II. Another march melody of Tyrtaeus, likewise of anapaests in the older form, consists of regularly interchanging acatalectic tetrapodies and so-called paroemiacs. Such a combination is to be regarded a period (verse) of two sentences, and has been named the *anapaestic tetrameter.*

$$\infty \vdots \_ \infty \mid \_ \infty \mid \_ \infty \mid \_, \infty \parallel \_ \infty \mid \_ \infty \mid \_ \_ \mid \bar{\wedge},$$

Ἄγετ' ὦ Σπάρτας ἔνοπλοι κοῦροι, ποτὶ τὰν Ἄρεος κίνασιν.

§ 31. THE MARCH TYPE. 115

Probably four such verses were united in a group, after which a long pause occurred of about four measures. In the Attic comedy the anapaestic tetrameter plays a chief rôle in the parabasis proper, where it was seldom wanting. Resolution of the thesis occurs here.

ὦ μέγα σεμναὶ Νεφέλαι, φανερῶς ἠκούσατέ μου καλέσαντος.
ἤσθου φωνῆς ἅμα καὶ βροντῆς μυκησαμένης θεοσέπτου;

AR. *Nub.* 291 *sq.*

_ ⋮ ◡ ◡ _ | _ ◡ ◡ | _ ◡ ◡ | _, _ ‖ _ ◡ ◡ | _ ◡ ◡ | _ _ | ⊼
_ ‖ _ _ | _ ◡ ◡ | _ _ | _, _ ‖ _ ◡ ◡ | _ ◡ ◡ | _ _ | ⊼

III. In the parodos and exodos of Attic tragedy, if anapaests occur, the succession of common tetrapodies is usually broken at intervals by a single apparent dipody and is finally closed by a *paroemiac*. This is such a melody as was probably often sung by soldiers on the march. A somewhat long pause is made after the *paroemiac*, perhaps of exactly four measures. A corresponding close in the thought is always marked by the punctuation. An example occurs in the *Persae* of Aeschylus (v. 55 *sq.*):

τὸ μαχαιροφόρον τ' ἔθνος ἐκ πάσης
'Ασίας ἕπεται
δειναῖς βασιλέως ὑπὸ πομπαῖς.
τοιόνδ' ἄνθος Περσίδος αἴας
οἴχεται ἀνδρῶν,
οὓς περὶ πᾶσα χθὼν 'Ασιᾶτις
θρέψασα πόθῳ στένεται μαλερῷ
τοκέες δ' ἄλοχοί θ' ἡμερολεγδὸν
τείνοντα χρόνον τρομέονται.

◡ ◡ ⋮ _ ◡ ◡ | _ ◡ ◡ | _ _ | _,
◡ ◡ ‖ _ ◡ ◡ | _ ⊼ | ⊼ | ⊼,
_ ‖ _ ◡ ◡ | _ ◡ ◡ | _ _ | ⊼ ⇑
_ ⋮ _ _ | _ _ | ◡ ◡ _ | _,
_ ‖ ◡ ◡ _ | _ ⊼ | ⊼ | ⊼,
_ ‖ ◡ ◡ _ | _ _ | ◡ ◡ _ | _, etc.

In comedy a part of the parabasis (in the broader sense) was composed of these tetrapodies, and was called πνῖγος or μακρόν, because it was all to be recited in one breath, except when the occasional apparent dipody allowed a short rest toward the end of the system; yet even this does not always occur.

IV. The ἐνόπλιος ("verse for the march under arms") or προσοδιακός ("verse for processions") is an apparent tripody. The anacrusis may be irrational.

Τὸν Ἑλλάδος ἀγαθέας
στραταγὸν ἀπ' εὐρυχόρου
Σπάρτας ὑμνήσομεν, ὦ
ἰήιε Παιάν.

> ⋮ _ ⌣ ⌣ | _ ⌣ ⌣ | ⌴ | ⊼,
> ‖ _ ⌣ ⌣ | _ ⌣ ⌣ | ⌴ | ⊼,
_ ‖ _ _ | _ ⌣ ⌣ | ⌴ | ⊼,
> ‖ _ ⌣ ⌣ | ⌴ | ⌴ | ⊼ ⇑.

4. Other melodies than the anapaestic might obviously be used as accompaniment to the march. If the melody were logaoedic, for example, only two things would be necessary, — to sing so rapidly that each measure would occupy the time of but one step, and to divide the measures into tetrapodies without intervening pauses. But such an accompaniment would be ill suited to the steady movement of marching, and it cannot be regarded a characteristic march melody. No discussion, of course, can here be made of marches the movements of which were involved, and which were in fact, according to the ancient view, rather dances than marches. We must seek for these rather in the choruses of the drama.

§ 32. The Choric Type.

1. Who knows whether in the popular song, —

Ὦ Λίνε πᾶσι θεοῖσιν
τετιμένε, σοὶ γὰρ ἔδωκαν
πρώτῳ μέλος ἀνθρώποισιν
φωναῖς λιγυραῖς ἀεῖσαι·
Φοῖβος δὲ κότῳ σ' ἀναιρεῖ,
Μοῦσαι δέ σε θρηνέουσιν, i. e.

⌣⌣ | ⌣⌣ | ⌴ | _ ∧ ‖
⌣ ⋮ ⌣⌣ | ⌣⌣ | ⌴ | _ ∧ ‖
> ⋮ ⌣⌣ | _ > | ⌴ | _ ∧ ‖
> ⋮ ⌣⌣ | _ > | ⌴ | _ ∧ ‖, etc., —

§ 32. THE CHORIC TYPE. 117

there has not been preserved one of the oldest dance melodies, such as Homer describes the Linus dance to have been (see § 6, 1)? We have a *systematic* succession of verses of equal length, to which the singers dance in a circle, — or rather march, but not with that firm tread of the warrior which has its fittest expression in anapaests.

2. But this circular dance is not necessarily continuous. After the singing of two sentences that correspond to each other the dancer may come to a standstill. This gives rise to the verse, the simplest period, beyond which recitative poetry did not go.

Again, during the singing of a second verse the singers may return in the *opposite* direction to their original position, the dance movements and the melody of the second verse exactly corresponding to those of the first.

3. Two verses so corresponding to one another constitute, next to the single verse, the simplest form of period adapted to orchestic melodies. But the dance may be further varied. The circular dance, first to the right and then to the left, just described may, of course, be repeated at pleasure; but after it has been executed once the dancers may also advance toward one another from both sides of the curve while a third verse is sung, and then, while a fourth verse is sung, separate from one another again, so that they come to their original places. In this case the strophe of the song must have four verses, as e. g. in the *contrasted Asclepiadean group* (§ 29, 4, I.), in which the accompanying movements of the dance would be

$$\_ > | \smile\smile | \llcorner, \| \smile\smile | \_\smile | \_ \wedge \|$$
$$\_ > | \smile\smile | \llcorner, \| \smile\smile | \_\smile | \_ \wedge \rrbracket$$
$$\_ > | \smile\smile | \llcorner | \_ \wedge \|$$
$$\_ > | \smile\smile | \_\smile | \_ \wedge \rrbracket$$

I. $\left(\begin{Bmatrix}3\\3\end{Bmatrix} \right.$ Circular dance to the right.

  $\left. \begin{Bmatrix}3\\3\end{Bmatrix} \right.$ Circular dance to the left.

II. $\begin{pmatrix}4\\4\end{pmatrix}$ Forward march.
      Return.

Without doubt the verses which correspond to one another must be throughout of equal length (i. e. must have the same number of measures and the same duration); for otherwise the dancer would not be able to return again to his original position.

§ 32. THE CHORIC TYPE.

4. It is not necessary that the dance be co-extensive with the song. It may continue through several verses, and then the dancer may come to a stand during a short postlude. In this way the *Asclepiadean Glyconic group* consists of three verses of six measures each, followed by a verse of four measures:

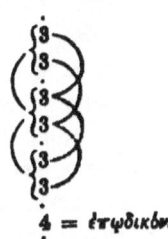

4 = ἐπῳδικόν.

The last verse is a *postlude*, ἐπῳδικόν, during which the dancer must have paused; for there is no corresponding verse during the singing of which the same movement in reversed order could have taken place, so that the dancer would arrive again at his original position. In the first three verses the dancer probably moved forward during the first sentence, backward during the second:

    3 Forward.
    3 Return.
    3 Forward.
    3 Return.
    3 Forward.
    3 Return.
    4 Halt.

In the same way a verse to which no other corresponded, and during the singing of which therefore the dancer stood still, could begin the strophe; this was called *prelude*, προῳδικόν.

But within a period also — we will take the smallest sort, the verse — there could be a sentence during the singing of which the dance ceased. This would be an *interlude*, μεσῳδικόν. Of this sort is the *greater Asclepiadean verse*:

_ ᷄ | ᴗ ᴗ | ᴸ, ‖ ᷄ ᴗ ᴗ | ᴸ, ‖ ᷄ ᴗ ᴗ | _ ᴗ | _ ∧ ‖

    3
    2 μεσῳδικόν.
    3

We distinguish, therefore, two sorts of sentences, those that correspond and those that do not, the latter under the names prelude, interlude, and postlude, or προῳδικόν, μεσῳδικόν, and ἐπῳδικόν.

§ 32. THE CHORIC TYPE. 119

5. The lyrical groups which have been discussed in § 29 will give us some idea of the simple dances described above. These groups arose as dance melodies. At a later day they were cultivated both in the old forms and in others also that were less strict. Then they were purely lyrical, i. e. were sung to the lyre without dance accompaniment. For the rhythm of the dance has also its place in the melody itself. Or is the mere melody of a dance, as we sometimes hear it at a concert, nothing without the accompanying dance? The melody, certainly, gets its peculiar character not only from the different sorts of measures with their various ictus-relations, but also from the grouping and arrangement of the sentences. There are many figure-dances in which the different movements are well expressed by the melody. And what appears at first sight to be simply accompaniment produces an effect as a musical form when given alone.

6. The choruses that at the religious festivals of the Greeks executed skilful marches and dances to the accompaniment of song, that celebrated the deeds of the gods, and in the drama, especially in tragedy, delivered splendid poetical and musical compositions, not standing still but with regular and symmetrical movements, — these choruses were composed of men who not only were acquainted with strict tactic order as soldiers, but also belonged to the better classes and were of refined and cultivated tastes. It is not possible that when such men danced and marched to the music of such songs the most beautiful symmetry and perfect order should not have prevailed in all their movements. Nay, we must suppose that this chorus-dance was developed to the highest degree of art, in which form alone it could have kept pace with the swift advance of poetry and music. Some of the movements were executed without change of position, but in these too a perfect symmetry must have prevailed.

And so in fact it was. The rhythmical division of the strophes that have been preserved gives the most certain evidence of this. And even in mere recitation these rhythmical forms are of the highest effect.

7. The chief laws which hold good in the rhythmical composition of choric strophes are the following:

I. *Every verse, as is the case also in lyrical strophes, ends with a pause during which song and dance cease, but which may have been filled out by brief instrumental music analogous to the interludes between the lines of church hymns as sung in Germany.*

II. *These verses, though themselves rhythmically divided, nevertheless become subordinate elements in the higher unity of the period, which may be composed of several of them.*

III. *There is an exact correspondence of the sentences in the period one to another; and it is always the case that only sentences of equal length correspond to one another.*

IV. *The pauses at the end of the verses correspond just as exactly as do the sentences, since they constitute important elements, and since otherwise the divisions of time would be unequal.*

V. *The sentences that correspond are grouped in different ways, but according to the strictest mathematical principles, so that different sorts of periods are distinguishable.*

VI. *Preludes, interludes, and postludes are allowed.*

According to this, the dance melodies of choric poetry are distinguished from march melodies especially by the fact that they allow movement only during the song, never during the arbitrary pauses. They do not allow it even during single parts of the song (prelude, etc.).

The more accurate exhibition of these relations, which signify the most perfect eurhythmy, will be found in the following book.

§ 33. Choric Strophes.

1. In lyrical poetry the strophe, and with it the same melody, is repeated on to the end of the poem. But in choric poetry, though its strophes are so great and varied in themselves, there is an important deviation from this simple rule of construction.

I. In the old encomiastic poetry generally two strophes of the same form are sung, *strophe* and *antistrophe* (στροφή and ἀντίστροφος); then follows a strophe of another form, which is not repeated and was called ἡ ἐπῳδός (not ὁ ἐπῳδός, the signification of which is given in § 28). This succession is then maintained to the end of the poem, i. e. *A A B, A A B,* etc. But there also occur in Pindar eulogistic songs of several strophes of the same form without epode.

II. In dramatic poetry, especially tragedy, a strophe and antistrophe are given only once; then follow a strophe and antistrophe of different form, and so on:

A A, B B, C C, D D, etc.

§ 33. CHORIC STROPHES.

But sometimes also strophes are found which are not repeated, namely:

1) a *proöde*, ἡ προῳδός, at the beginning of the poem:

   A, BB, CC, etc.

2) an *epode*, ἡ ἐπῳδός, after a strophe and its antistrophe:

   AA, B, CC, etc.

3) a *mesode*, ἡ μεσῳδός, between a strophe and its antistrophe:

   A, B, A, CC, etc.

2. By this change of strophes, often both rhythmically and metrically very different, choric poetry was able not only to serve as a basis for various and complex dance movements, but also to express beautifully the change and progress of the thought.

But still greater variety was obtained. The strophe might be separated from its antistrophe not only by a mesode, but also by several other strophes; anapaestic systems also, which were not regularly sung but only recited in a singing tone, might intervene. Here again there prevailed the most beautiful order, as we shall be able to see from the following examples in Aeschylus and Euripides.

Ag. VII (1448 sq.).

A. συ. συ. A. συ. B. συ. συ. B. συ. συ. C. συ. συ. C. συ.

Cho. III (315 sq.).

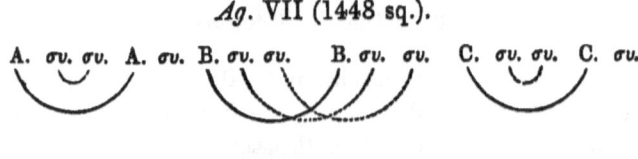

A. B. A. συ. C. B. C. συ. D. E. D. συ. F. E. F. G.H.H.G. I.I. K.K.συ.

El. II (167 sq.).

A. B. A. B.

Cho. V (738 sq.).

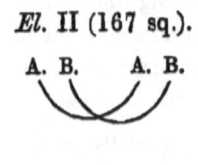

A. συ. A. B. C. B. D. συ. D.

3. Of course the choruses of the dramas need not consist of a long series of strophes and antistrophes; it is easy to find many consisting of a single strophe and antistrophe only, to which there is often added an epode.

4. The following names of the different choruses of the drama on the Attic stage should be noted:

A. In *tragedy* there are:

I. The *parodos*, ἡ πάροδος, the first song of the chorus, sung while it is taking its place and arranging itself in the orchestra. Sometimes preceded by anapaests during which the chorus marches in.

II. *Stasima*, στάσιμα, songs sung from the position which the chorus has taken in the parodos.

III. The *exodos*, ἡ ἔξοδος, sung while the chorus arranges itself to leave the orchestra. The march itself may then again proceed during the recitation of anapaests.

IV. *Dance-songs*, ὑπορχήματα, melodies with livelier dance movements than the stasima.

V. Κομμοί, songs of which the parts were sung alternately by the chorus and the actor.

VI. Songs of individual actors, *monodies*, μονῳδίαι, called ἀπὸ σκηνῆς.

In the last two sorts, since they lack a regular choric dance accompaniment, a strict division of the composition, like that in the chorus proper, was not necessary. Cf. § 25, 1, *med.* The third volume of the *Kunstformen*, namely *Die Monodien und Wechselgesänge der Attischen Tragödie*, gives an exact and complete statement of the principles governing their composition.

B. The *parabasis* of Attic *comedy*, in which the chorus addresses the spectators, consists when complete of seven parts:

κομμάτιον, παράβασις, μακρόν, στροφή, ἐπίρρημα, ἀντίστροφος, ἀντεπίρρημα.

I. The κομμάτιον consists of different verses, equal or unequal in length.

II. The παράβασις proper always consists of verses of the same length, usually of anapaestic tetrameters.

III. The μακρόν or πνῖγος always consists of anapaestic dimeters, concerning which cf. § 31, 3, III.

§ 33. CHORIC STROPHES.

IV. and VI. στροφή and ἀντίστροφος, named also ᾠδή and ἀντῳδή, are a regular lyrical song.

V. and VII. The ἐπίρρημα and ἀντεπίρρημα generally consist of trochaic tetrameters, and were delivered, along with I., II., and III., by the leader of the chorus (κορυφαῖος).

Moreover, songs and dance melodies occur in Attic comedy in various other places.

Fifth Book.

EURHYTHMY.

§ 34. The Periods according to their Grouping.

1. The simplest grouping is when two rhythmical sentences of equal length correspond to each other. This is the *stichic period:*

$$\|$$

χωρῶμεν ἐς πολυρρόδους
λειμῶνας ἀνθεμώδεις. *Ran.*VII.*str.*(448, 449).

$$> \vdots \_\cup|\_\cup|\_\cup|\_\wedge\| \qquad \tfrac{4}{4})$$
$$> \vdots \_\cup|\_\cup|\llcorner|\_\wedge\rrbracket \qquad$$

The same period occurs in the following, translated from the German:

    Annie of Tharaw, my true-love of old,
    She is my wife, and my goods, and my gold.
                                Longfellow.

$$\_\cup\cup|\_\cup\cup|\_\cup\cup|\_\wedge\wedge\| \qquad \tfrac{4}{4})$$
$$\_\cup\cup|\_\cup\cup|\_\cup\cup|\_\wedge\wedge\|$$

2. A *repeated stichic period* arises when more than two sentences of the same length correspond to one another:

$$\| \qquad \| \text{ etc.}$$

Cf. the lyric systems.

§ 34. THE PERIODS ACCORDING TO THEIR GROUPING. 125

Μακάριός γ' ἀνὴρ ἔχων
ξύνεσιν ἠκριβωμένην.
πάρα δὲ πολλοῖσιν μαθεῖν.
     Ran. XX. (1482 – 1484).

∪∪∪ | _ ∪ | _ ∪ | _ ∧ ‖
∪∪∪ | _ ∪ | _ ∪ | _ ∧ ‖
∪∪∪ | _ > | _ ∪ | _ ∧ ⫼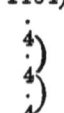

Illustrated by the following strophe from Longfellow:

  Maiden ! with the meek brown eyes,
  In whose orbs a shadow lies
  Like the dusk in evening skies !

_ ∪ | _ ∪ | _ ∪ | _ ∧ ‖
_ ∪ | _ ∪ | _ ∪ | _ ∧ ‖
_ ∪ | _ ∪ | _ ∪ | _ ∧ ⫼

3. A *palinodic period* arises when not a single sentence, but a combination of several sentences (i. e. a "group"), is repeated once in the same order:

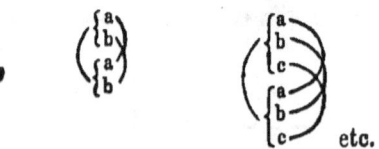 etc.

Φύονται δὲ καὶ νέοις ἐν ἀνδράσι πολιαὶ
θαμὰ καὶ παρὰ τὸν ἁλικίας ἐοικότα χρόνον.
     PIND. *Ol.* IV. *ep.*

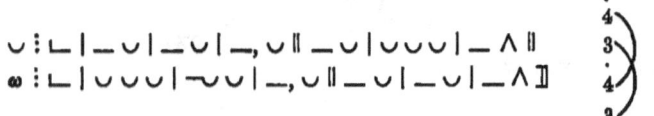

  Now let us sing, long live the king,
   And Gilpin, long live he;
  And, when he next doth ride abroad,
   May I be there to see !

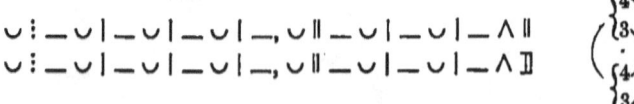

126 § 34. THE PERIODS ACCORDING TO THEIR GROUPING.

4. A *repeated palinodic period* is formed by the repetition of a group several times:

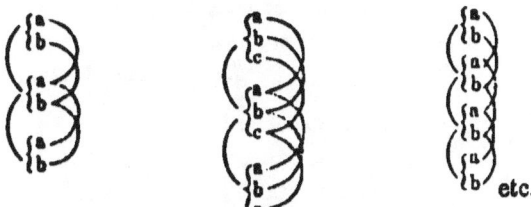

Ὁρᾷς τὸν θρασύν, τὸν εὐκάρδιον,
τὸν ἐν δαΐοις ἄτρεστον μάχαις,
ἐν ἀφόβοις με θηρσὶ δεινὸν χέρας;
SOPH. *Aj.* III. *str.* β´ (364–366).

```
∪ : _ _ ∪ | _ , ∪ ‖ _ _ ∪ | _ ∧ ‖     { do.
                                       { do.
∪ : _ _ ∪ | _ , ∪ ‖ _ _ ∪ | _ ∧ ‖     { do.
                                       { do.
∪ : ∪ ∪ _ ∪ | _ ∪ , ‖ _ _ ∪ | _ ∧ ]   { do.
                                       { do.
```

(By "do" is meant *dochmius*.)

    Our hills have dark and strong defiles,
      With many an icy bed;
    Heap there the rocks for funeral piles,
      Above the invader's head!
    Or let the seas, that guard our Isles,
      Give burial to his dead!
              Mrs. Hemans.

```
∪ : _ ∪ | _ ∪ | _ ∪ | _ , ∪ | ‿∪ | _ ∪ | _ ∧ ‖
∪ : _ ∪ | _ ∪ | ‿∪ | _ , ∪ | _ ∪ | _ ∪ | _ ∧ ‖
∪ : _ ∪ | _ ∪ | _ ∪ | _ , ∪ | ‿∪ | _ ∪ | _ ∧ ]
```

5. An *antithetic period* is formed by the inverted repetition of single sentences:

§ 84. THE PERIODS ACCORDING TO THEIR GROUPING. 127

'Ιαλτὸς ἐκ δόμων ἔβην
χοᾶν προπουπὸς ὀξύχειρι σὺν κόπῳ·
πρέπει παρηὶς φοινίοις ἀμυγμοῖς,
ὄνυχος ἄλοκι νεοτόμῳ.

AESCH. *Cho.* I. *str. a'* (22 – 25).

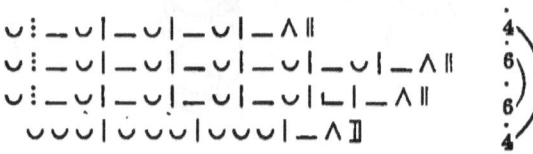

Through the bright battle-clime,
Where laurel boughs make dim the Grecian streams,
And reeds are whispering of heroic themes,
By temples of old time ...

Mrs. Hemans.

6. A *mesodic period* arises from the inverted arrangement of the sentences about an interlude (§ 32, 4).

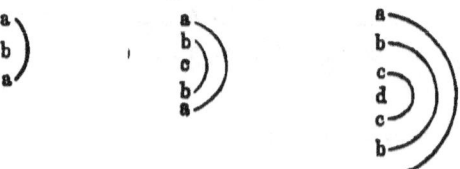

Tu ne quaesieris, scire nefas, quem mihi, quem tibi.

_ > | ⏑ ⏑ | ⌊, ‖ ⏑ ⏑ | ⌊, ‖ ⏑ ⏑ | _ ⏑ | _ ∧ ‖   3)
                                                  2)
                                                  3)

'Αμηχανῶ φροντίδος στερηθεὶς
εὐπάλαμον μέριμναν,
ὅπα τράπωμαι, πίτνοντος οἴκου.

AESCH. *Ag.* VII. *str. γ'* (1530 – 1532).

∪ : _ ∪ | ⌊ | _ ∪ | _ ∪ | ⌊ | _ ∧ ‖   6)
⏑ ∪ | _ ∪ | ⌊ | _ ∧ .‖   4)
∪ : _ ∪ | ⌊ | _ ∪ | _ ∪ | ⌊ | _ ∧ ‖   6)

Σέβας δ' ἄμαχον ἀδάματον ἀπόλεμον τὸ πρὶν
δι' ὤτων φρενός τε δαμίας
περαῖνον νῦν ἀφίσταται·
φοβεῖται δέ τις· τὸ δ' εὐτυχεῖν
τόδ' ἐν βροτοῖς θεός τε καὶ θεοῦ πλέον.

Id. *Cho.* I. *ant. β'* (54 – 60).

128 § 34. THE PERIODS ACCORDING TO THEIR GROUPING.

```
∪ː_∪|∪∪∪|∪∪∪|∪∪∪|_∪|_∧‖      6
∪ː∟|_∪|_∪|_∪|_∧‖              5
∪ː∟|∟|_∪|_∪|_∧‖               5
∪ː∟|_∪|_∪|_∪|_∧‖              5
∪ː_∪|_∪|_∪|_∪|_∪|_∧⟧          6
```

7. The *palinodic antithetic period.*

If we suppose a series of sentences, e. g. *a b c d e*, divided into several groups each of which constitutes by itself a small musical division, e. g. *ab, cd, e*, or also *abc, de*, and if we then suppose these groups repeated antithetically, we have

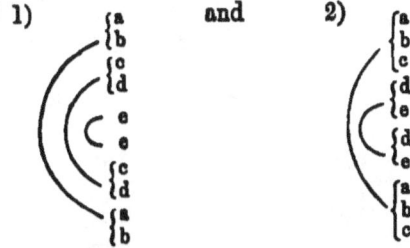

This is a palinodic antithetic period. It is strongly antithetic, since the groups which are regarded as units (and may consist of a single sentence, e. g. *e* in the first combination) are repeated in inverted order. But it is palinodic in that the single sentences in the group are repeated in the same order.

The series *a b c d e* admits of sixteen different combinations, of which the first two, the last two, and the tenth are given below. The two extremes would be, first, a period in which each sentence is regarded as a group in itself (this is consequently a purely antithetic period); and secondly, a period in which the five sentences together constitute a single group (a purely palinodic period). In the second, third, fourth, and fifth forms of the period two sentences are combined into a group, and the rest are taken singly; and in the sixth, seventh, and eighth, three sentences are combined and the other two taken singly. In the ninth, tenth, and eleventh forms of the period there are three groups, of which two consist of two sentences each and the other of a single sentence; in the twelfth and thirteenth two groups, of which one consists of four sentences and the other of the single sentence that remains; and in the fourteenth and fifteenth two groups, consisting one of two and the other of three sentences.

§ 34. THE PERIODS ACCORDING TO THEIR GROUPING.

1) *a, b, c, d, e.*   2) *ab, c, d, e.*   3) *a, bc, d, e.*
4) *a, b, cd, e.*   5) *a, b, c, de.*   6) *abc, d, e.*
7) *a, bcd, e.*   8) *a, b, cde.*   9) *ab, cd, e.*
10) *a, bc, de.*   11) *ab, c, de.*   12) *abcd, e.*
13) *a, bcde.*   14) *abc, de.*   15) *ab, cde.*
16) *abcde.*

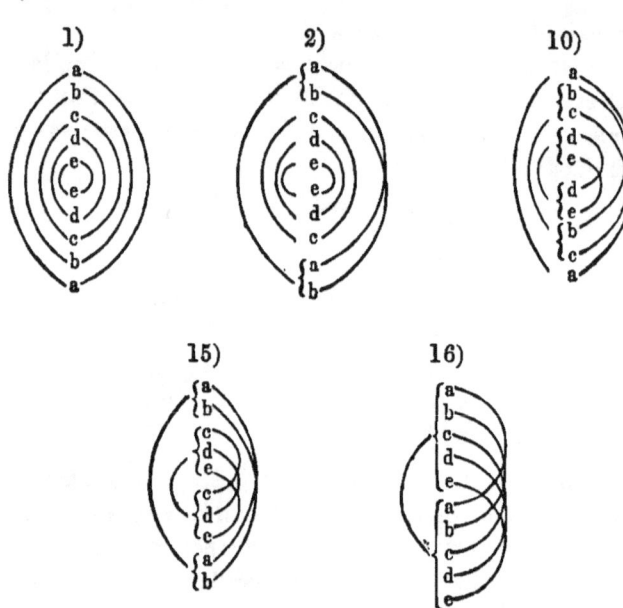

The following examples will illustrate:

*Ἡι σὺ πιστεύων ἀμέργει τῶν ξένων τοὺς καρπίμους
πρῶτος ὤν· ὁ δ' Ἱπποδάμου λείβεται θεώμενος.
ἀλλ' ἐφάνη γὰρ ἀνὴρ ἕτερος πολὺ
σοῦ μιαρώτερος, ὥστε με χαίρειν,
ὅς σε παύσει καὶ πάρεισι, δῆλός ἐστιν αὐτόθεν,
πανουργίᾳ τε καὶ θράσει καὶ κοβαλικεύμασιν.*

AR. *Eq.* I. (324–332).

```
_ ∪ | _ > | _ ∪ | _ >, ‖ _ ∪ | _ > | _ ∪ | _ ∧ ‖
_ ∪ | _ ∪ | _ ∪ | _ >, ‖ _ ∪ | _ ∪ | _ ∪ | _ ∧ ‖
_ ∪ ∪ | _ ∪ ∪ | _ ∪ ∪ | _ ∪ ∪ ‖
_ ∪ ∪ | _ ∪ ∪ | _ ∪ ∪ | _ _ ‖
_ ∪ | _ > | _ ∪ | _ ∪, ‖ _ ∪ | _ ∪ | _ ∪ | _ ∧ ‖
∪ ⋮ _ ∪ | _ ∪ | _ ∪ | ⌐, ‖ _ ∪ | _ ∪ | _ ∪ | _ ∧ ]
```

130 § 34. THE PERIODS ACCORDING TO THEIR GROUPING.

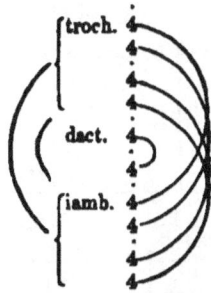

X. Εὐδαιμονικῶς γ' ὁ πρεσβύτης, ὅσα γ' ὧδ' ἰδεῖν, τὰ νῦν τάδε πράττει.
T. τί δῆτ', ἐπειδὰν νυμφίον μ' ὁρᾶτε λαμπρὸν ὄντα;
X. ζηλωτὸς ἔσει, γέρων, αὖθις νέος ὢν πάλιν, μύρῳ κατάλειπτος.
Id. *Pax.* VI. (856 – 862).

> : ‿‿ | _ > | _ ‿ ‖ ‿‿ | _ ‿ | _ ‿ ‖ ‿‿ | ∟ | _ ∧ ‖
‿ : _ ‿ | _ ‿ | _ > | _, ‿ ‖ _ ‿ | _ ‿ | ∟ | _ ∧ ‖
> : ‿‿ | _ > | _ ‿ ‖ ‿‿ | _ ‿ | _ ‿ ‖ ‿‿ | ∟ | _ ∧ ‖

Very beautiful palinodic antithetic periods occur in *Ant.* V. β', VII. β', VIII. α'.

This sort of period was developed in Greek poetry and music into exceedingly complex forms, as two examples from the *Bacchae* of Euripides will show.

Πόθι Νύσης ἄρα τᾶς θηροτρόφου θυρσοφορεῖς
θιάσους, ὦ Διόνυσ', ἢ κορυφαῖς Κωρυκίαις;
τάχα δ' ἐν τοῖς πολυδένδρεσσιν Ὀλύμπου
θαλάμοις, ἔνθα ποτ' Ὀρφεὺς κιθαρίζων
σύναγεν δένδρεα μούσαις, σύναγεν θῆρας ἀγρώτας. μάκαρ ὦ Πιερία,
σέβεταί σ' Εὔιος, ἥξει τε χορεύσων ἅμα βακχεύμασι, τόν τ' ὠκυρόαν
διαβὰς Ἀξιὸν εἱλισσομένας Μαινάδας ἄξει,
Λυδίαν τε, τὸν εὐδαιμονίας ὀλβοδόταν
πατέρα τε, τὸν ἔκλυον εὔιππον χώραν
ὕδασιν καλλίστοισι λιπαίνειν. *Bacch.* III. *ep.* (557 – 575).

§ 34. THE PERIODS ACCORDING TO THEIR GROUPING. 131

```
⏑⏑ ⋮ _ _ ⏑⏑ | _ _ ⏑⏑ ‖ _ _ ⏑⏑ | ⌊ ⏄ ‖
⏑⏑ ⋮ _ _ ⏑⏑ | _ _ ⏑⏑ ‖ _ _ ⏑⏑ | ⌊ ⏄ ‖
⏑⏑ ⋮ _ _ ⏑⏑ | _ _ ⏑⏑ | _ _ ⏄ ‖
⏑⏑ ⋮ _ _ ⏑⏑ | _ _ ⏑⏑ | _ _ ⏄ ‖
⏑⏑ ⋮ _ _ ⏑⏑ | _ _ ⏑⏑ ‖ _ _ ⏑⏑ | _ _ ⏑⏑ ‖ _ _ ⏑⏑ | ⌊ ⏄ ‖
⏑⏑ ⋮ _ _ ⏑⏑ | _ _ ⏑⏑ ‖ _ _ ⏑⏑ | _ _ ⏑⏑ ‖ _ _ ⏑⏑ | ⌊ ⏄ ‖
⏑⏑ ⋮ _ _ ⏑⏑ | _ _ ⏑⏑ ‖ _ _ ⏑⏑ | _ _ ⏄ ‖
⏑⏑ ⋮ ⌊ ⏑⏑ | _ _ ⏑⏑ ‖ _ _ ⏑⏑ | ⌊ ⏄ ‖
⏑⏑ ⋮ ⏑ ⏑ ⏑⏑⏑⏑ | _ _ _ | _ _ ⏄ ‖
⏑⏑ ⋮ _ _ _ | ⌊ ⏑⏑ | _ _ ⏄ ⟧
```

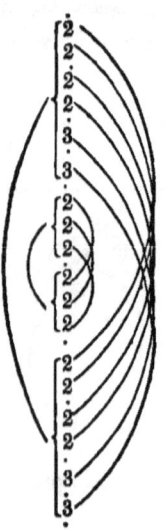

Ἀνοιστρήσατέ νιν ἐπὶ τὸν ἐν γυναικομίμῳ στολᾷ
Μαινάδων [δὴ] κατάσκοπον λυσσώδη.
μάτηρ πρῶτά νιν λευκᾶς ἀπὸ πέτρας
εὔσκοπος ὄψεται
δοκεύοντα, Μαινάσιν δ' ἀπύσει·
τίς ὅδ' ὀρειδρόμων μαστὴρ Καδμείων
ἐς ὄρος ἐς ὄρος ἔμολεν ἔμολ' ὦ Βάκχαι;
τίς ἄρα νιν ἔτεκεν;
οὐ γὰρ ἐξ αἵματος γυναικῶν ἔφυ·
λεαίνας δὲ γέγον' ὅδ' ἢ Γοργόνων Λιβυσσᾶν γένος.
Bacch. VI. *str.* (979 – 991).

§ 34. THE PERIODS ACCORDING TO THEIR GROUPING.

⏑ː ⎯⎯ ⏑ | ⏑ ⏑, ⏑ ‖ ⏑ ⏑ ⎯ ⏑ | ⎯ ⏑ ‖ ⎯⎯ ⏑ | ⎯ ∧ ‖
⎯ ⏑ | ⎣ | ⎯ ⏑ | ⎯ ⏑ ‖ ⎯⎯ > | ⎯ ∧ ‖
> ː ⎯⎯ ⏑ | ⎯, > ‖ ⎯ ⏑ ⏑ ⏑ | ⎯ ∧ ‖
> ː ⏑ ⏑ ⎯ ⏑ | ⎯ ∧ ‖
⏑ ː ⎯⎯ ⏑ | ⎯ ⏑ ‖ ⎯⎯ > | ⎯ ∧ ‖
⏑ ː ⏑ ⏑ ⎯ ⏑ | ⎯, > ‖ ⎯⎯ > | ⎯ ∧ ‖
⏑ ː ⏑ ⏑ ⏑ ⏑ ⏑ ⏑ | ⏑ ⏑ ⏑, ‖ ⏑ ⏑ ⎯ > | ⎯ ∧ ‖
⏑ ː ⏑ ⏑ ⏑ ⏑ ⏑ | ⎯ ∧ ‖
⎯ ⏑ | ⎣ | ⎯ ⏑ | ⎯, ⏑ ‖ ⎯⎯ ⏑ | ⎯ ∧ ‖
⏑ ː ⎯⎯ ⏑ | ⏑ ⏑, ⏑ ‖ ⎯⎯ ⏑ | ⎯, ⏑ ‖ ⎯⎯ ⏑ | ⎯ ∧ ‖

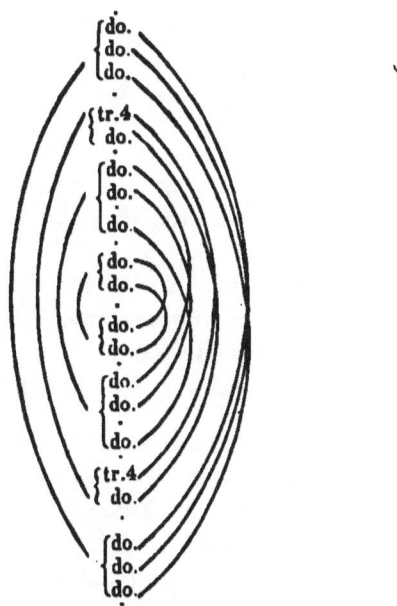

(By " do." is meant the *dochmius*; by " tr." the *trochee*.)

It is worthy of note that these magnificent periods, both from the *Bacchae* of Euripides, are examples of the livelier dance melodies described in § 33, 4, the hyporchemata. In all hyporchemata the periods are complex and in none does a repeated period occur, so that these livelier dance melodies are recognizable directly from the rhythmical schemes themselves. An exhaustive statement of the facts is made for the first time in the *Compositionslehre*, § 32, and the *Monodien*, § 6, 3. If the rhythmical scheme of the period leaves the matter at all in doubt, the contents of the song, or, to put it differently, the nature of the

§ 34. THE PERIODS ACCORDING TO THEIR GROUPING. 133

thought expressed by the words, will furnish a means of determination; in hyporchemata this calls always for a livelier dance movement. Cf. the two cases quoted above.

8. The *palinodic mesodic period* arises when an interlude occurs in a palinodic or palinodic-antithetic period.

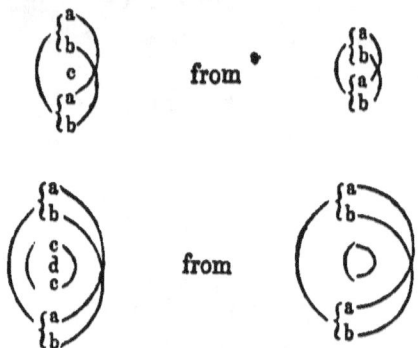

Εἰ δὲ κυρεῖ τις πέλας οἰωνοπόλων
ἔγγαιος οἶκτον ἀίων,
δοξάσει τιν' ἀκούειν ὄπα τᾶς
Τηρείας, μήτιδος οἰκτρᾶς, ἀλόχου,
κιρκηλάτας ἀηδόνος.
     AESCH. *Suppl.* I. *str.* β´ (57 – 62).

```
: ⏑⏑ | ⌣ | ⏑⏑ | ⌣ | ⏑⏑ | ⌣ ∧ ‖      (6
> : ⎯ ⏑ | ⎯ ⏑ | ⎯ ⏑ | ⎯ ∧ ‖           (4
: ⎯ ⏑ | ⏑⏑ | ⌣ | ⏑⏑ | ⎯ ∧ ‖            5
: ⏑⏑ | ⌣ | ⏑⏑ | ⌣ | ⏑⏑ | ⎯ ∧ ‖      (6
> : ⎯ ⏑ | ⎯ ⏑ | ⎯ ⏑ | ⎯ ∧ ]]          (4
```

Observe the exact agreement of the corresponding members, which here determines the nature of the period at the very first glance.

A. Ἰὼ Ζεῦ τίς ἂν πῶς πόρος κακῶν
γένοιτο καὶ λύσις τύχας ἃ πάρεστι κοιράνοις;
B. ἔξεισί τις; ἢ τέμω τρίχα,
καὶ μέλανα στόλον πέπλων
ἀμφιβαλώμεθ' ἤδη;
A. δῆλα μέν, φίλοι, δῆλά γ' ἀλλ' ὅμως
θεοῖσιν εὐχώμεσθα· θεῶν γὰρ δύναμις μεγίστα.
     EUR. *Alc.* II. *str.* (213 – 219).

§ 35. Preludes and Postludes.

1. To the eight sorts of periods just described, which are the only ones that occur in strictly choric poetry, preludes and postludes may be joined. Cf. § 32, 4, and 7, VI.

Periods, therefore, like the following are allowed, in which πρ. (προῳδικόν) indicates the prelude, ἐπ. (ἐπῳδικόν), the postlude.

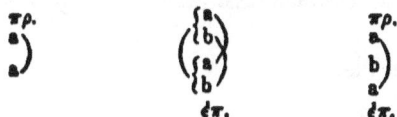

Φρόντισον, καὶ γενοῦ πανδίκως
εὐσεβὴς πρόξενος·
τὰν φυγάδα μὴ προδῷς,
τὰν ἔκαθεν ἐκβολαῖς
δυσθέοις ὁρμέναν.

AESCH. Suppl. III. str. α' (418 – 422).

"Ἄλευσον ἀνδρῶν ὕβριν εὖ στυγήσας·
λίμνᾳ δ' ἔμβαλε πορφυροειδεῖ
τὰν μελανόζυγ' ἄταν.

Ib. IV. str. α' (529 – 531).

§ 35. PRELUDES AND POSTLUDES. 135

$\cup \vdots \_\cup |\llcorner| \neg\cup\cup |\_\cup |\llcorner| \_\wedge \|$ $\left.\begin{array}{l}\dot{6}\\ \dot{6}\end{array}\right)$
$\llcorner|\llcorner| \neg\cup\cup |\neg\cup\cup |\llcorner| \_\wedge \|$
$\neg\cup\cup |\_\cup |\llcorner| \_\wedge \rrbracket$ $\dot{4} = \text{έπ.}$

Τί μέμονας τέκνον;
μήτι σε θυμοπληθὴς θορίμαργος ἄτα φερέτω· κακοῦ δ'
ἔκβαλ' ἔρωτος ἀρχάν.
Id. Sept. V. str. a' (686 – 688).

$\cup \vdots \cup\cup \_\cup |\_\wedge \|$
$> \vdots \cup\cup\_\cup |\_>, \|\cup\cup\_\cup|\_>, \|\cup\cup\_\cup|\_\wedge\|$
$\neg\cup\cup|\_\cup|\llcorner|\_\wedge\rrbracket$

$\dot{\text{do}}.= \pi\rho.$
$\left.\begin{array}{l}\dot{\text{do}}.\\ \text{do}.\\ \text{do}.\end{array}\right\}$
$\dot{\text{log}}.\ 4 = \text{έπ.}$

2. Preludes and postludes, however, are admitted only as follows:

I. *The prelude and postlude must each consist of a single rhythmical sentence.*

Periods, therefore, like

$\left.\begin{array}{l}a\\ b\end{array}\right\} = \pi\rho.$ $\left(\begin{array}{l}\{c\\ \{d\end{array}\right)$

$\left(\begin{array}{l}\{c\\ \{d\\ \{c\\ \{d\end{array}\right)$ $\left(\begin{array}{l}\{c\\ \{d\end{array}\right)$

                    $\left.\begin{array}{l}a\\ b\end{array}\right\} = \text{έπ.}$

do not occur. The choric song does not serve as an accompaniment to the dance only; it is as well a melody the relation of whose parts must be characterized in the musical composition also by perfect proportion and symmetry. If, now, two rhythmical members appear to introduce or close a period, they form by themselves, if of equal length, a stichic period; the first sentence is then the musical antecedent, and the second is the consequent which brings the first to a satisfactory close. In such a case, therefore, it would be wrong to write the series *aa bc bc*

$\left.\begin{array}{l}a\\ a\end{array}\right\} = \pi\rho.$

$\left(\begin{array}{l}\{b\\ \{c\\ \{b\\ \{c\end{array}\right)$

There are rather two periods here, one stichic and one palinodic:

1) $\begin{Bmatrix} a \\ b \end{Bmatrix}$ 2) $\begin{Bmatrix} b \\ b \\ c \end{Bmatrix}$

If, on the other hand, there should appear to be two sentences of different lengths, they could not, of course, form a period; but, quite as certainly, they could not sustain the relation of a prelude or postlude to the period to which they appeared to be joined.

II. PRELUDES *stand only at the beginning of choric strophes, and do not introduce periods within them, except in the* κομμοί (§ 33, 4, A, V.).

The prelude is an invitation, so to speak, to begin the dance, and at the same time is an introduction to the following music, which is made more impressive by the contrast. The melody would be divided by preludes within the strophes into widely separated parts, which is allowed only when, as in alternate songs, the strophes distributed among the different singers are really divided into independent parts.

III. *The preludes and postludes must not together exceed in length the total length of the corresponding members.*

The following, therefore, would not be true periods:

$5 = \pi\rho.$ $6 = \pi\rho.$ dact. $4 = \ell\pi.$
$\begin{Bmatrix} 2 \\ 3 \end{Bmatrix}$ $\begin{Bmatrix} 2 \\ 3 \\ 2 \\ 3 \end{Bmatrix}$ troch. $\begin{Bmatrix} 4 \\ 4 \end{Bmatrix}$
$4 = \ell\pi.$ dact. $3 = \ell\pi.$
      $5 = \ell\pi.$

It is obvious that in such cases as these the character of the rhythmical period would be completely obliterated.

For a fuller treatment of preludes and postludes, see *Compositionslehre*, § 36, 10 – 12.

§ 36. Position of the Verse-Pauses.

1. The verse, which we have found above (§ 32, 2) to be the simplest form of the period, becomes itself a subordinate member in the higher unity of the rhythmical period. Yet not only the sentences of which verses consist are to be taken into consideration as corresponding quantities, but also the pauses which close the verses. The portions of time, therefore, during which song and dance cease, and which may be filled out only by an interlude at most, must correspond just as exactly as

§ 36. POSITION OF THE VERSE-PAUSES.   137

the rhythmical sentences themselves. Even in mere rhythmical recitation these pauses, which serve as a rest to the voice, come out sharply, and must be observed.

The rules for the proper placing of the verse-pauses are given below. Examples will be found in the preceding paragraphs, and in the lyric parts of the *Antigone* and the *Medea*, which are given at the end of the book. It is superfluous to enumerate the possible wrong places for the pauses. The rules now to be given will be found to be verified by the whole choric literature.

2. *Every period ends with a full verse.*

There are but two exceptions to this rule, both in Pindar. One of the instances is, —

Οὐλυμπίᾳ Πυθοῖ τε νικώντεσσιν. ὁ δ' ὄλβιος, ὃν φᾶμαι κατέχοντ' ἀγαθαί.

PIND. *Ol.* VII. *ant.* α'.

>⁚∪|⏑⏑‖∪|⏑⏑]⏑∪∪|⏑∪∪|⏑⏑‖⏑∪∪|⏑∪∪|
⏑⏤]

I. $\begin{smallmatrix}2\\2\end{smallmatrix}\Big)$

II. $\begin{smallmatrix}3\\3\end{smallmatrix}\Big)$

In no case may a period begin within a verse whose first part belongs to some other period, as

I. $\left(\begin{smallmatrix}\{a\\b\end{smallmatrix}\atop\begin{smallmatrix}\{a\\b\end{smallmatrix}\right)$

II. $\begin{smallmatrix}c\\c\end{smallmatrix}\Big)$

Moreover, it cannot even be completely contained within such a verse.

I. $\left(\begin{smallmatrix}\{a\\b\end{smallmatrix}\atop\begin{smallmatrix}\{a\\b\end{smallmatrix}\right)$

II. $\begin{smallmatrix}c\\c\end{smallmatrix}\Big)$

3. *The two members of the stichic period may or may not, at pleasure, be separated by a verse-pause.*

§ 36. POSITION OF THE VERSE-PAUSES.

4. *In the repeated stichic period, if a pause occurs at all, it must occur throughout.*

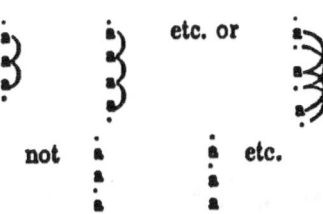

5. *In the palinodic period the pauses must correspond palinodically.* That is, if an antecedent member has a pause, its corresponding consequent must also have it; if it is lacking in the one case, it must be lacking in the other also.

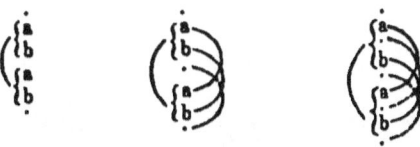

Moreover, the pauses between the two groups may in no case be lacking when the sentences within the groups are separated by pauses.

We could not, therefore, have:

In such a case as this we should no longer be able to regard the sentences *a* and *b* as united into a group, since the two parts of the group are more widely separated from one another by the verse-pause than are the two groups themselves, which have no verse-pause between them.

It should further be noticed that almost always, even in the period of four members, the two groups are separated by a verse-pause. In longer periods this becomes necessary.

6. *In the repeated palinodic period the pauses also must be repeated palinodically.*

While, therefore, e. g.

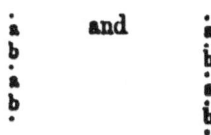

§ 36. POSITION OF THE VERSE-PAUSES. 139

are proper periods, on the other hand the repeated period

is not a true one. There must either be no pause in the last group, or else a corresponding pause must occur also in the first two groups.

7. *In no case in a repeated period may the last group be incomplete.* Such a period, therefore, as the following is impossible:

The proper grouping of the strophe of Pind. *Nem.* VII., which has been supposed to contradict this, is as follows:

I.   ◡ ⁝ ⌊ ⏐ ⏑◡ ⏐ ＿◡ ⏐ ⌊ ‖ ＿◡ ⏐ ＿◡ ⏐ ＿ ∧ ‖
⏑◡ ⏐ ＿◡ ⏐ ◡◡◡ ⏐ ＿◡ ‖ ⌊ ⏐ ⏑◡ ⏐ ＿◡ ⏐ ⌊ ‖ ＿◡ ⏐
＿·◡ ⏐ ＿ ∧ ⟧

II.   ⏑◡ ⏐ ＿◡ ⏐ ⌊ ⏐ ＿◡ ‖ ＿◡ ⏐ ＿◡ ⏐ ＿ ∧ ‖
◡ ⁝ ＿◡ ⏐ ⌊ ⏐ ＿◡ ‖ ◡◡◡ ⏐ ⏑◡ ⏐ ＿◡ ⏐ ＿◡ ‖
5   ◡ ⁝ ⏑◡ ⏐ ⌊ ⏐ ＿◡ ⏐ ＿◡ ⏐ ◡◡◡ ⏐ ＿ ∧ ⟧

III. > ⁝ ⏑◡ ⏐ ＿◡ ⏐ ⌊ ‖ ◡◡◡ ⏐ ◡◡◡ ⏐ ＿◡ ⏐ ＿ ∧ ‖
> ⁝ ⌣ω ⏐ ＿◡ ⏐ ⌊ ‖ ◡◡◡ ⏐ ＿◡ ⏐ ＿ ∧ ‖
> ⁝ ⏑◡ ⏐ ＿◡ ⏐ ⌊ ‖ ＿ ⁈ ⏐ ⏑◡ ⏐ ＿◡ ⏐ ＿◡ ⟧

I. $\begin{Bmatrix}4\\3\\4\\4\\3\end{Bmatrix}$ II. $\begin{matrix}4\\3\\3\\4\\6\ \text{ἐπ.}\end{matrix}$ III. $\begin{Bmatrix}3\\4\\6\\3\\4\end{Bmatrix}$

8. *In the antithetic period the pauses must correspond antithetically.* That is, if a pause follows an antecedent member, it must precede the corresponding consequent, and *vice versâ*.

Antithetic periods may be divided into two classes, those with and those without middle-pauses.

§ 36. POSITION OF THE VERSE-PAUSES.

In a period of six members the different arrangements of the pauses that are possible are the following.

A. Periods without middle-pause.

Γλαυκοὶ δὲ δράκοντες, ἐπεὶ κτίσθη νέον
πύργον ἐσαλλόμενοι τρεῖς, οἱ δύο μὲν κάπετον,
αὖθι δ᾽ ἀτυζομένῳ ψυχὰς βάλον.
                                   PIND. Ol. VIII. ep. β'.

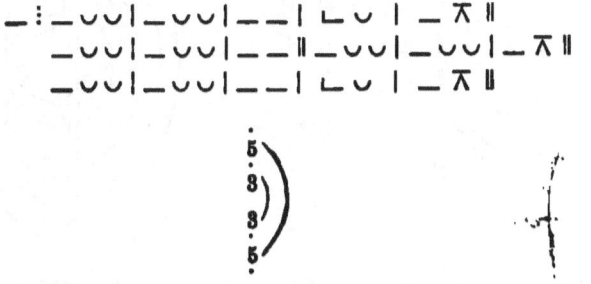

B. Periods with middle-pause.

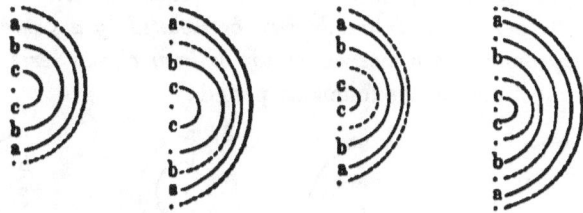

An example is found in § 34, 5, *et al.*

9. *In the palinodic antithetic period the pauses closing the groups correspond antithetically, the pauses within the groups palinodically. All groups must be separated from one another by pauses.*

As illustrations two combinations of the period of ten members, namely 2) and 15) of the enumeration in § 34, 7, are selected.

§ 36. POSITION OF THE VERSE-PAUSES. 141

2)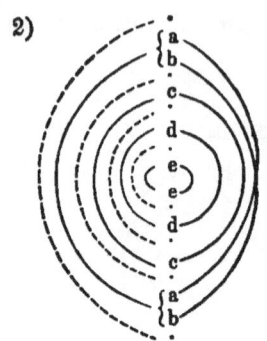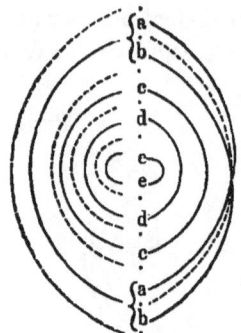

Then the same with middle-pauses.

15) 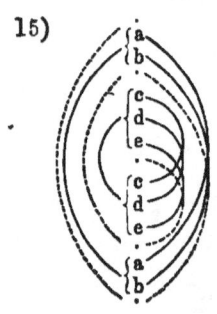 etc. to the form in which all the sentences are isolated, viz.: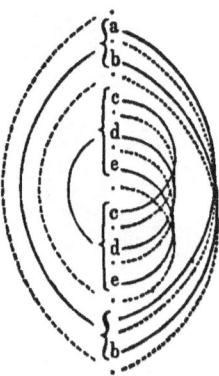

Excellent examples occur in § 34, 7, of periods of ten, eight, eighteen, and twenty members respectively.

10. *In the mesodic period, which in other respects follows the laws of the antithetic period, the interlude may be isolated by a pause on each side, or may stand within a verse, or may begin or close a verse.*

This is illustrated in the following period:

1) 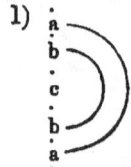 2) 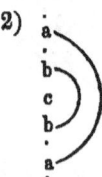 3)  4)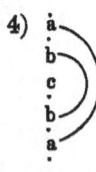

The fundamental principle of rhythm is movement. Since, now, the movement of the dance stops during the interlude, it is indifferent whether these orchestic pauses be lengthened by a pause in the singing or not.

§ 36. POSITION OF THE VERSE-PAUSES.

But also in the song all four forms have their force, and make satisfactory impression even in recitation, as is clearly seen from the following examples.

1)   Ἀμηχανῶ φροντίδος στερηθεὶς
     εὐπάλαμον μέριμναν,
     ὅπα τράπωμαι, πίτνοντος οἴκου.
                                        AESCH. *Ag.* VII. *str.* γ´ (1530–1532).

$$\cup \vdots \_ \cup | \_ | \_ \cup | \_ \cup | \_ | \_ \wedge \| \qquad 6$$
$$\_ \cup \cup | \_ \cup | \_ | \_ \wedge \| \qquad 4$$
$$\cup \vdots \_ \cup | \_ | \_ \cup | \_ \cup | \_ | \_ \wedge]\!] \qquad 6$$

This form of the period seems the most natural.

2) Ἐπισκοπεῖν δὲ πανταχῇ κυκλοῦσαν ὄμμα χρὴ χοροῦ κατάστασιν.
                                        AR. *Thesm.* VIII. α´ (958, 959).

$$\cup \vdots \_ \cup | \_ \cup | \_ \cup | \_, \cup \| \_ \cup | \_ \cup, \| \_ \cup | \_ \cup | \_ \cup | \_ \wedge \|$$

$$\begin{matrix} 4 \\ 2 \\ 4 \end{matrix}\Big)$$

Likewise in the *greater Asclepiadean*:

Μηδὲν ἄλλο φυτεύσῃς πρότερον δένδρεον ἀμπέλω.   ALC.

$$\_ \cup | \_ \cup \cup | \_ \| \_ \cup \cup | \_, \| \_ \cup \cup | \_ \cup | \_ \wedge \| \qquad \begin{matrix}3\\2\\3\end{matrix}\Big)$$

Here it is easy to see from the chief ictus with which each sentence begins, that the verse is divided into three parts; and from the length of these sentences, that the first corresponds to the third, while the second occupies an independent place and is consequently interlude.

3)   Μᾶτερ ὦ χρυσοστεφάνων ἀέθλων Οὐλυμπία,
     δέσποιν᾽ ἀλαθείας· ἵνα μάντιες ἄνδρες . . .
                                        PIND. *Ol.* VIII. *str.* α´.

$$\_ \cup | \_ \_ | \_ \cup \cup | \_ \cup \cup | \_ \_ \| \_ \cup | \_ \wedge \| \qquad 5$$
$$\_ \vdots \_ \cup | \_ \_ | \_ \cup \cup | \_ \cup \cup | \_ \_]\!] \qquad \begin{matrix}2\\5\end{matrix}$$

If the first verse is intoned properly, that is, if it is given two chief ictuses, its division into two sentences becomes apparent to the ear. Then, when the second verse is recited to its close, it is perceived that it corresponds to the first sentence of the preceding verse. We then

§ 36. POSITION OF THE VERSE-PAUSES. 143

see that the second sentence of the first verse stands alone, and is consequently interlude.

4)   Βουλᾶν τε καὶ πολέμων
         ἔχοισα κλαῖδας ὑπερτάτας.
                      PIND. *Pyth.* VIII. *str. a'*.

$$> : \_ \cup | \smile \cup | \_ \wedge \|$$
$$\cup : \_ \cup | \_ \ \| \smile \cup | \_ \cup | \_ \wedge \]$$
$$\left. \begin{array}{c} 3 \\ 2 \\ 3 \end{array} \right)$$

It is seen from the length of the sentences that the second sentence in the second verse corresponds to the first verse : consequently the first sentence of the second verse stands unconnected and must be interlude.

In the palinodic mesodic period, on the other hand, there must be some pause at the interlude, since otherwise the groups would not be distinctly separated, such separation being required by the palinodic principle.

11. *Prelude and postlude may, at pleasure, be immediately connected without a pause with another sentence or may be separated from it by a pause.*

The reason has been given above (10) in treating of the interlude. Periods like the following, therefore, may occur:

1) $\left. \begin{array}{l} a = \pi\rho. \\ b \\ b \end{array} \right)$ 2) $\left. \begin{array}{l} a = \pi\rho. \\ b \\ b \end{array} \right)$ 3) $\left. \begin{array}{l} a \\ b \\ b \\ a \\ c = \epsilon\pi. \end{array} \right)$ 4) $\left. \begin{array}{l} a \\ b \\ b \\ a \\ c = \epsilon\pi. \end{array} \right)$

For example:

1) Ὅς τᾶς ὀφιώδεος υἱόν ποτε Γοργόνος ἦ πόλλ' ἀμφὶ κρουνοῖς
   Πάγασον ζεῦξαι ποθέων ἔπαθεν. PIND. *Ol.* XIII. *ep. γ'.*

$$> : \smile \cup | \smile \cup | \ \_ \ \| \smile \cup | \smile \cup | \_ >, \| \_ \cup | \_ \cup \|$$
$$\_ \cup | \_, > | \smile \cup | \smile \cup | \_ \wedge \]$$

$$\left. \begin{array}{l} 3 = \pi\rho. \\ 3 \\ 2 \\ 2 \\ 3 \end{array} \right)$$

2) Παλαίχθονος   paeon. = πρ.
   τέκος, κλῦθί μου πρόφρονι καρδίᾳ, $\left. \begin{array}{l} \text{do.} \\ \text{do.} \\ \text{do.} \end{array} \right)$
   Πελασγῶν ἄναξ.
         AESCH. *Suppl.* II. *str. a'* (347, 348).

144 § 37. METRICAL AGREEMENT OF CORRESPONDING MEMBERS.

3) Ἔπειτ' ἐπεμνησάμην ἀμειλίχων
πόνων, μεγαίρω δὲ δυσφιλὲς γαμήλευμ', ἀπεύχετον δόμοις.
   Id. *Choeph.* IV. *str.* γ' (623 – 625).

∪ : _ ∪ | ⌐ | _ ∪ | _ ∪ | _ ∪ | _ ∧ ‖
∪ : _ ∪ | ⌐ | _ ∪ | _ ∪ | _ ∪ | ⌐ ‖ _ ∪ | _ ∪ | _ ∪ | _ ∧]

6)
6)
4 = ἐπ.

4) Τὸ πᾶν ἀτίμως ἔλεξας, οἴμοι.
   πατρὸς δ' ἀτίμωσιν ἄρα τίσει
   ἕκατι μὲν δαιμόνων
   ἕκατι δ' ἀμᾶν χερῶν.
5 ἔπειτ' ἐγὼ νοσφίσας ὀλοίμαν.
   Ib. III. *str.* ζ' (434 – 438).

∪ : _ ∪ | ⌐ | _ ∪ | _ ∪ | ⌐ | _ ∧ ‖
∪ : _ ∪ | ⌐ | _ ∪ | _ ∪ | ⌐ | _ ∧ ‖
∪ : _ ∪ | ⌐ | _ ∪ | _ ∧ ‖
∪ : _ ∪ | ⌐ | _ ∪ | _ ∧ ‖
5 ∪ : _ ∪ | ⌐ | _ ∪ | _ ∪ | ⌐ | _ ∧]

6 = τρ.
6
4)
4)
6

§ 37. Metrical Agreement of the Corresponding Members.

1. Notwithstanding these strict rules for the position of the pauses, cases frequently occur in which we are not at all able to determine with certainty, from the length of the rhythmical sentences and the position of the pauses, what sort of a period we have.

E. g. the series

may be regarded either a palinodic-mesodic, or an antithetic period with postlude:

§ 37. METRICAL AGREEMENT OF CORRESPONDING MEMBERS. 145

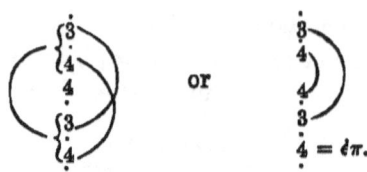

The confusion becomes still greater when the sentences are of the same length. This occurs very frequently. So the series

may be regarded not only as two distinct stichic periods, but also as a palinodic, and as an antithetic period.

But the limit has not yet been reached. This series may be still further combined in these two ways:

Here we reach the limit. In the case of such a series as this we shall generally be right if we choose that combination which is the most natural. This would here be the palinodic. For if the sentences have the same length, but are partly separated by a pause, groups are formed; and it would not be proper to classify periods as antithetic in which the beginning of one verse corresponded to the close of the other, unless this appeared from the different length of the sentences, as e. g. in the following:

$$\left.\begin{matrix}\dot4\\\dot5\\\dot5\\\dot4\end{matrix}\right)\!\Big)$$

But in innumerable cases there will still be doubt. In such cases the doubt is almost always solved with certainty *by the metrical form of*

146 § 37. METRICAL AGREEMENT OF CORRESPONDING MEMBERS.

the sentences. To illustrate, let us take four tetrapodies of different characteristic forms. These forms show us at once how to combine.

1) _ ⌣ | _ ⌣ | _ ⌣ | _ ⋀ ‖   4̣⎫
    ⌣⌣ | _ ⌣ | ⌴ | _ ⋀ ‖   4̣⎟
    ⌣⌣ | _ ⌣ | ⌴ | _ ⋀ ‖   4̣⎬
    _ ⌣ | _ ⌣ | _ ⌣ | _ ⋀ ⫶   4̣⎭

2) _ ⌣ | _ ⌣ | _ ⌣ | _ ⋀ ‖   I. 4̣⎫   II. 4̣⎫
    _ ⌣ | _ ⌣ | _ ⌣ | _ ⋀ ⫶   4̣⎭   4̣⎭
    ⌣⌣ | _ ⌣ | ⌴ | _ ⋀ ‖
    ⌣⌣ | _ ⌣ | ⌴ | _ ⋀ ⫶

3) _ ⌣ | _ ⌣ | _ ⌣ | _ ⋀ ‖   ⎛4̣⎞
    ⌣⌣ | _ ⌣ | ⌴ | _ ⋀ ‖   ⎜4̣⎟
    _ ⌣ | _ ⌣ | _ ⌣ | _ ⋀ ‖   ⎜4̣⎟
    ⌣⌣ | _ ⌣ | ⌴ | _ ⋀ ⫶   ⎝4̣⎠

The sentences of the same or similar forms correspond to one another. The melodies, of course, corresponded to these metrical forms.

2. The importance of this rule will be seen from the examples which follow, taken from Aristophanes and Euripides, in whose dramas occur many noble periods of sentences of equal lengths. Examples have been chosen in which two (*ab*), three (*abc*), or four (*abcd*) characteristic forms occur.

A. *Two Characteristic Forms.*

X. Ζηλῶ σε τῆς εὐβουλίας, μᾶλλον δὲ τῆς εὐωχίας, ἄνθρωπε, τῆς παρούσης.
Δ. τί δῆτ᾽, ἐπειδὰν τὰς κίχλας
ὀπτωμένας ἴδητε;
X. οἶμαί σε καὶ τοῦτ᾽ εὖ λέγειν.
Δ. τὸ πῦρ ὑποσκάλευε.
X. ἤκουσας ὡς μαγειρικῶς κομψῶς τε καὶ δειπνητικῶς αὐτῷ διακονεῖται;
   Ar. *Ach.* XII. *str.* (1008–1017).

> ⫶ _ ⌣ | _ > | _ ⌣ | _ , > ‖ _ ⌣ | _ > | _ ⌣ | _ , > ‖ _ ⌣ | _ ⌣ |
⌣ ⫶ _ ⌣ | _ > | _ ⌣ | _ ⋀ ‖   ⌴ | _ ⋀ ‖
> ⫶ _ ⌣ | _ ⌣ | ⌴ | _ ⋀ ‖
> ⫶ _ ⌣ | _ > | _ ⌣ | _ ⋀ ‖
⌣ ⫶ _ ⌣ | _ ⌣ | ⌴ | _ ⋀ ‖
> ⫶ _ ⌣ | _ ⌣ | _ ⌣ | _ , > ‖ _ ⌣ | _ > | _ ⌣ | _ , > ‖ _ ⌣ | _ ⌣ |
                                                          ⌴ | _ ⋀ ⫶

§ 37. METRICAL AGREEMENT OF CORRESPONDING MEMBERS. 147

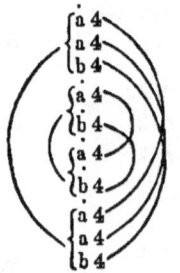

a = catalectic or acatalectic.

b = falling.

"Ἀγ' εἶα νῦν τῶν σκωμμάτων ἀπαλλαγέντες ἤδη
ὑμεῖς ἐπ' ἄλλ' εἶδος τρέπεσθ', ἐγὼ δ' ἰὼν ἤδη λάθρᾳ
βουλήσομαι τοῦ δεσπότου λαβών τιν' ἄρτον καὶ κρέας
μασώμενος τὸ λόιπὸν οὕτω τῷ κόπῳ ξυνεῖναι.
AR. *Plut.* I. *ep.* (316 – 321).

∪ ⁝ _ ∪ | _ > | _ ∪ | _, ∪ ‖ _ ∪ | _ ∪ | ∟ | _ ∧ ‖
> ⁝ _ ∪ | _ > | _ ∪ | _, ∪ ‖ _ ∪ | _ > | _ ∪ | _ ∧ ‖
> ⁝ _ ∪ | _ > | _ ∪ | _, ∪ ‖ _ ∪ | _ > | _ ∪ | _ ∧ ‖
∪ ⁝ _ ∪ | _ ∪ | _ ∪ | _ >, ‖ _ ∪ | _ ∪ | ∟ | _ ∧ ⟧

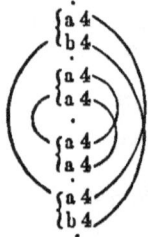

a = catalectic or acatalectic.

b = falling.

Ἀλλ', ὦ Χαριτιμίδη
καὶ Σμίκυθε καὶ Δράκης, ἔπου κατεπείγων,
σαυτῷ προσέχων, ὅπως μηδὲν παραχορδιεῖς
ὧν δεῖ σ' ἀποδεῖξαι·
5 ὅπως δὲ τὸ σύμβολον
λοβόντες ἔπειτα πλησίοι καθεδούμεθ', ὡς
ἂν χειροτονῶμεν
ἅπανθ' ὅποσ' ἂν δέῃ
τὰς ἡμετέρας φίλας.
10 καί τοι τί λέγω; φίλους γὰρ χρῆν μ' ὀνομάζειν.
AR. *Eccl.* I. *str.* (293 – 299).

> ⁚ ⌣∪ | _ ∪ | _ ∧ ‖
> ⁚ ⌣∪ | _ ∪ | _ , ∪ ‖ ⌣∪ | ⌊ | _ ∧ ‖
> ⁚ ⌣∪ | _ ∪ | _ , > ‖ ⌣∪ | _ ∪ | _ ∧ ‖
> ⁚ ⌣∪ | ⌊ | _ ∧ ‖
5   ∪ ⁚ ⌣∪ | _ ∪ | _ ∧ ‖
∪ ⁚ ⌣∪ | _ ∪ | _ ∪ ‖ ⌣∪ | _ ∪ | _ ∧ ‖
> ⁚ ⌣∪ | ⌊ | _ ∧ ‖
∪ ⁚ ⌣∪ | _ ∪ | _ ∧ ‖
> ⁚ ⌣∪ | _ ∪ | _ ∧ ‖
10 > ⁚ ⌣∪ | _ ∪ | _ , > ‖ ⌣∪ | ⌊ | _ ∧ ⫽

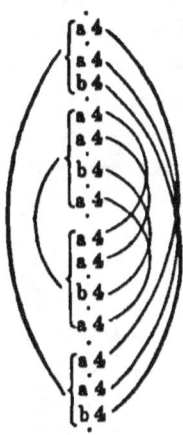

B. *Three Characteristic Forms.*

Νῦν δή σε πάντα δεῖ κάλων ἐξιέναι σεαυτοῦ
καὶ λῆμα θούριον φορεῖν καὶ λόγους ἀφύκτους
ὅτοισι τόνδ᾽ ὑπερβαλεῖ. ποικίλος γὰρ ἀνὴρ
κἀκ τῶν ἀμηχάνων πόρους εὐμηχάνους πορίζει.

Αr. *Eq.* V. *str.* (756 – 759).

> ⁚ _ ∪ | _ ∪ | _ ∪ | _ , > ‖ _ ∪ | _ ∪ | ⌊ | _ ∧ ‖
> ⁚ _ ∪ | _ ∪ | _ ∪ ⌊ , ‖ _ ∪ | _ ∪ | ⌊ | _ ∧ ‖
∪ ⁚ _ ∪ | _ ∪ | _ ∪ ⌊ , ‖ _ ∪ | _ ∪ | ⌊ | _ ∧ ‖
> ⁚ _ ∪ | _ ∪ | _ ∪ | _ , > ‖ _ ∪ | _ ∪ | ⌊ | _ ∧ ⫽

§ 37. METRICAL AGREEMENT OF CORRESPONDING MEMBERS. 149

C. *Four Characteristic Forms.*

Ζηλῶ γε τῆς εὐτυχίας
τὸν πρέσβυν, οἳ μετέστη
ξηρῶν τρόπων καὶ βιοτῆς·
ἕτερα δὲ νῦν ἀντιμαθὼν
5 ἢ μέγα τι μεταπεσεῖται
Ἐπὶ τὸ τρυφᾶν καὶ μαλακόν.
τάχα δ᾽ ἂν ἴσως οὐκ ἐθέλοι.
Τὸ γὰρ ἀποστῆναι χαλεπὸν
φύσεος, ἣν ἔχοι τις ἀεί.
10 Καίτοι πολλοὶ ταῦτ᾽ ἔπαθον·
ξυνόντες γνώμαις ἑτέρων
μεταβάλλοντο τοὺς τρόπους.

AR. *Vesp.* XIV. *str.* (1450-1461).

a = catalectic, and with the second measure syncopated.
b = falling.
c = catalectic, and without syncope.
d = catalectic, and with the first measure syncopated.

Δ. Βρεκεκεκὲξ κοὰξ κοάξ.
τουτὶ παρ᾽ ὑμῶν λαμβάνω.
Β. δεινά τἄρα πεισόμεσθα.
Δ. δεινότερα δ᾽ ἔγωγ᾽, ἐλαύνων
5 εἰ διαρραγήσομαι.
Β. βρεκεκεκὲξ κοὰξ κοάξ.

150 § 37. METRICAL AGREEMENT OF CORRESPONDING MEMBERS.

Δ. οἰμώζετ᾽· οὐ γάρ μοι μέλει.
Β. ἀλλὰ μὴν κεκραξόμεσθά γ᾽,
ὁπόσον ἡ φάρυγξ ἂν ἡμῶν
10   χανδάνῃ, δι᾽ ἡμέρας
βρεκεκεκὲξ κοὰξ κοάξ.
Δ. βρεκεκεκὲξ κοὰξ κοάξ.
τούτῳ γὰρ οὐ νικήσετε.
Ar. Ran. I. (251-263).

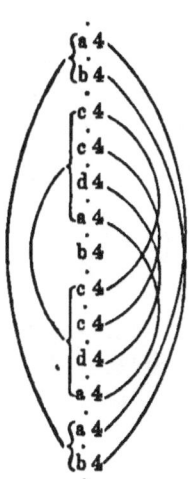

Πᾷ μοι γενναίων πατέρων
γενναίων τ᾽ ἐκ τοκάδων
πᾷ δή μοι νίσει σκοπέλους;
οὐ τᾷδ᾽ ὑπήνεμος αὔρα
5   καὶ ποιηρὰ βοτάνα,
δινᾶέν θ᾽ ὕδωρ ποταμῶν
ἐν πίστραις κεῖται πέλας ἄντρων, οὔ σοι βλαχαὶ τεκέων;
ψύττα, σὺ τάδ᾽ οὔ, κοὺ τάδε νεμεῖ,
οἵδ᾽ αὖ κλιτὺν δροσεράν;
10   ὦ ὕπαγ᾽ ὦ κεράστα
ἢ ῥίψω πέτρον κατὰ σοῦ
Κύκλωπος ἀγροβάτα
μηλοβάτα στασιωρόν.

Eur. Cycl. I. str. (41-53).

§ 37. METRICAL AGREEMENT OF CORRESPONDING MEMBERS. 151

```
         _> | _ > | ⌣⌣ | _ ⋀ ‖
         ⌊  | _ > | ⌣⌣ | _ ⋀ ‖
         _> | _ > | ⌣⌣ | _ ⋀ ‖
         >  _ ⌣ | ⌣⌣ |  ⌊  | _ ⋀ ‖
    5    ⌊  | _ > | ⌣⌣ | _ ⋀ ‖
         >  ⌊  | _ ⌣ | ⌣⌣ | _ ⋀ ‖
         _> | _ > | ⌣⌣ |  ⌊  ‖ _> | _ > | ⌣⌣ | _ ⋀ ‖
         > ⌣⌣⌣ | _ ⌐ | ⌣⌣⌣ | _ ⋀ ‖
         ⌊  | _ ⌐ | ⌣⌣ | _ ⋀ ‖
         ⌣⌣ | _ ⌣ |  ⌊  | _ ⋀ ‖
   10    _> | _ > | ⌣⌣ | _ ⋀ ‖
         ⌊  | _ > | ⌣⌣ | _ ⋀ ‖
         ⌣⌣ | ⌣⌣ |  ⌊  | _ ⋀ ‖
```

a 4
c 4
a 4
d 4
c 4
b 4
4
4
b 4
c 4
d 4
a 4
c 4
d 4

3. In the last example (cf. also *Compositionslehre*, § 32, 2) a falling verse corresponds as consequent to a catalectic as antecedent. This case is very frequent. Cf. the examples in § 34, 8. The converse does not occur so frequently. Other sentences dissimilar in form to one another often correspond. This is true especially in long repeated periods, which would be too uniform if the metrical constitution of the sentences remained always the same.

The laws governing the metrical correspondence of two of the commonest rhythmical sentences, the choreic hexapody and tetrapody, are developed in the *Compositionslehre*, § 18 and § 19. Logaoedic sentences of the same length with these show the same relations. The

§ 87. METRICAL AGREEMENT OF CORRESPONDING MEMBERS.

correspondence of short sentences, such as choreic and logaoedic dipodies and tripodies, is simple and easily understood, since these sentences have little that is characteristic. The dipody indeed, like the pentapody, does not often occur. In other sorts of measures very great differences of form in corresponding sentences are not often met with, except perhaps in Doric strophes; and, even in these, limits are carefully observed. For example, corresponding to the tripody _ ∪ ∪ |
_ ∪ ∪ | _ _ ‖ we find _ ∪ ∪ | _ ∪ ∪ | ⌐ ‖, but seldom ⌐ ∪ | ⌐ ∪ |
_ _ ‖, etc. Again, such a correspondence in the case of the tetrapody as ⌐ ∪ | _ _ | ⌐ ∪ | _ _ ‖ and _ ∪ ∪ | _ ∪ ∪ | _ ∪ ∪ | _ _ ‖ occurs but seldom. In the ionic measure, the forms of which are more or less various, there is less of exact metrical correspondence between the sentences than in other rhythms, because this measure has for the most part an enthusiastic character.

Only one thing further need be noticed, that frequently sentences correspond which are strikingly different in their metrical form, whereby a sharp contrast is expressed in the music and in the rhythm. When sentences with many of their measures contracted correspond to others with many of their measures resolved, such an effective contrast is produced. Such a contrast exists also when a series of choreic dactyls (§ 15) corresponds to a series of trochees of the ordinary form. E. g.

Τίπτε μοι τόδ' ἐμπέδως δεῖμα προστατήριον
καρδίας τερασκόπου ποτᾶται;
μαντιπολεῖ δ' ἀκέλευστος ἄμισθος ἀοιδά;
οὐδ' ἀποπτύσας δίκαν δυσκρίτων ὀνειράτων . . .

Aesch. *Ag.* IV. *str. α'* (975 – 981).

_ ∪ | _ ∪ | _ ∪ | ⌐, ‖ _ ∪ | _ ∪ | _ ∪ | _ ∧ ‖
_ ∪ | _ ∪ | _ ∪ | _ ∪ | ⌐ | _ ∧ ‖
_ ⏑⏑ | _ ⏑⏑ | _ ⏑⏑ | _ ⏑⏑ | ⌐ | _ ∧ ‖
_ ∪ | _ ∪ | _ ∪ | ⌐, ‖ _ ∪ | _ ∪ | _ ∪ | _ ∧ ‖

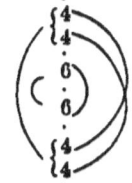

Here, as always, the metrical forms of the corresponding sentences are exactly adapted to the rhythmical expression of the thought contained in the words.

THE LYRIC PARTS

OF THE

MEDEA OF EURIPIDES

AND OF THE

ANTIGONE OF SOPHOCLES.

THE LYRIC PARTS OF THE MEDEA.

I.

THE PARODOS.

Proōde, 131-138; *Str.* and *Ant.*, 148-159 and 173-183; *Epod.* 204-212.

στρ.   Ἔκλυον φωνάν, ἔκλυον δὲ βοὰν
       τᾶς δυστάνου
           Καλχίδος, οὐδέ πω ἤπιος· ἀλλά,
           γεραιά, λέξον· ἐπ' ἀμφιπύλου γὰρ
5   ἔσω μελάθρου γόον ἔκλυον· οὐδὲ
           συνήδομαι, ὦ γύναι, ἄλγεσι δώματος,
       ἐπεί μοι φίλον κέκρανται.

σ.   Ἄιες, ὦ Ζεῦ καὶ γᾶ καὶ φῶς,
       ἰαχάν, οἵαν ἁ δύστανος
       μέλπει νύμφα;
           Τίς σοί ποτε τᾶς ἀπλάστου
5   κοίτας ἔρος, ὦ ματαία,
       σπεύσει θανάτου τελευτάν;
       μηδὲν τόδε λίσσου.
       εἰ δὲ σὸς πόσις
       καινὰ λέχη σεβίζει,
10   κείνῳ τόδε μὴ χαράσσου·
       Ζεύς σοι τόδε συνδικήσει.
           Μὴ λίαν τάκου
       δυρομένα σὸν εὐνέταν.

MEDEA I. (131–212).

Pr.

```
I.  ∪∪⁝ _ _ | _ ∪∪ | _ ∪∪ | _ ⊼ ‖
         ⊔ |  ⊔  |  ⊔  | _ ⊼ ]       I.  ⁝4⁾      II.  ⁝4,⁾
II.     _ ∪∪ | _ ∪∪ | _ ∪∪ | _ ∪            ⁝4⁾          4,⁾
    ∪‖ _ _  | _ ∪∪ | _ ∪∪ | _ ∪                           4,⁾
    ∪‖ _ ∪∪ | _ ∪∪ | _ ∪∪ | _ ∪                           4,⁾
    ∪‖ _ ∪∪ | _ ∪∪ | _ ∪∪ | _ ∪∪ ‖                        4,⁾        5
    ∪⁝  ⊔  | ⊔ ∪  | ⊔ ∪  | _ _ ]                      4 = ἐπ.
```

Str.

```
I.   _ ⁝ ∪ ∪ _ | _ _ | _ _ | _
     ∞‖ _ _  | _ _ | _ _ | _
     _‖ _ _  | _ ↑ | ↑↑ | ↑↑ ⇑
II.  >⁝ ⁓∪  | _ ∪ | ⌐ | _ ∧ ‖
     >⁝ ⁓∪  | _ ∪ | ⌐ | _ ∧ ‖           5
     >⁝ ⁓∪  | _ ∪ | ⌐ | _ ∧ ‖
     ℓ⁝ ⁓∪  |  ⌐  | _ ∧ ‖
        _ ∪  | _ ∪ | _ ∧ ‖
        ⁓∪   | _ ∪ | ⌐ | _ ∧ ‖
     >⁝ ⁓∪  | _ ∪ | ⌐ | _ ∧ ‖           10
     >⁝ ⁓∪̈  | _"∪ | ⌐ | _ ∧ ]
III.  _ ∪  |  ⌐  |  ⌐  | _ ∧ ‖
      ⁓∪ | _ ∪ | _ ℓ | _ ∧ ]
```

I. ⁝4⁾   II. 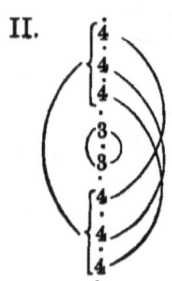   II. ⁝4⁾
   ⁝4⁾   ⁝4⁾
   ⁝δ⁾

ἀ.
       Πῶς ἂν ἐς ὄψιν τὰν ἀμετέραν
ἔλθοι μύθων τ' αὐθαδέντων
δέξαιτ' ὀμφάν,
       Εἴ πως βαρύθυμον ὀργὰν
5   καὶ λῆμα φρενῶν μεθείη.
μήτοι τό γ' ἐμὸν πρόθυμον
φίλοισιν ἀπέστω.
ἀλλὰ βᾶσά νιν
δεῦρο πόρευσον οἴκων
10 ἔξω, φίλα καὶ τάδ' αὔδα,
σπεύσασα πρίν τι κακῶσαι
       Τοὺς ἔσω· πένθος
γὰρ μεγάλως τόδ' ὁρμᾶται.

ἀπ.
       Ἀχὰν ἄιον πολύστονον
γόων, λιγυρὰ δ' ἄχεα μογερὰ
βοᾷ τὸν ἐν λέχει προδόταν κακόνυμφον·
       Θεοκλυτεῖ δ' ἄδικα παθοῦσα
5   τὰν Ζηνὸς ὁρκίαν Θέμιν,
ἅ νιν ἔβασεν Ἑλλάδ' ἐς ἀντίπορον
δι' ἅλα νύχιον ἐφ' ἁλμυρὰν
πόντου κλῇδ' ἀπέραντον.

Epod.

I.   ∟ | ∟ | _ ∪ | _ ∪ | _ ∪ | _ ∧ ‖
    ∪ ⋮ _ ∪ | ∪ ∪ ∪ | ∪ ∪ ∪ | ∪ ∪ ∧ ‖
    ∪ ⋮ _ ∪ | _ ∪ | ⌣ ∪ | ⌣ ∪ | ∟ | _ ∧]

II.   ∪ ∪ ∪ | _ ∪ | ∪ ∪ ∪ | _ ∪ ‖
    > ⋮ _ ∪ | _ ∪ | _ ∪ | _ ∧ ‖   5
    ⌣ ∪ | _ ∪ | ⌣ ∪ | ⌣ ∪ | _ ∧ ‖
    ∪ ⋮ ∪ ∪ ∪ | ∪ ∪ ∪ | _ ∪ | _ ∧ ‖
    _ > | ⌣ ∪ | ∟ | _ ∧]

I. $\begin{Bmatrix} 6 \\ 4 \\ 6 \end{Bmatrix}$ II. $\begin{Bmatrix} \begin{Bmatrix} 4 \\ 4 \end{Bmatrix} \\ 5 \\ \begin{Bmatrix} 4 \\ 4 \end{Bmatrix} \end{Bmatrix}$

Proöde.

Westphal (*Spec. Metrik*, p. 63) thinks that he finds in Per. II. two pentapodies, —

and   _ ∪ ∪ | _ ∪ ∪ | _ ∪ ∪ | _ ∪ ∪ | _ _ ‖

    _ ∪ ∪ | _ ∪ ∪ | _ ∪ ∪ | _ ∪ ∪ | _ ∪ ∪ ‖ −,

enclosing a dactylic hexameter of the form, —

    _ ∪ ∪ | _ ∪ ∪ | _ ∪ ∪ ‖ _ ∪ ∪ | _ ∪ ∪ | _ ∪ ∪ ‖,

and followed by an iambic pentapody. But such an arrangement were nothing more than a *quodlibet*. That we have tetrapodies here throughout is shown by the exact agreement of the members of Per. II. in the matter of the caesura (feminine caesura). The "versus nexi" are indicated in the text by being printed further to the right. Why the poet used here these "versus nexi" is clear when we recall that anapaests both precede and follow the proöde.

Str.

Per. I. For v. 3, an apparent spondaic dipody (marked in the scheme designed to show the eurhythmy δ), see *Monodien und Wechselgesänge*, p. 163. The rhythm of this period is anapaestic.

II.

First Stasimon (410 – 445).

σ. α'.   Ἄνω ποταμῶν ἱερῶν χωροῦσι παγαί, καὶ δίκα καὶ πάντα πάλιν
στρέφεται.
ἀνδράσι μὲν δόλιαι βουλαί, θεῶν δ'
οὐκέτι πίστις ἄραρε.   τὰν δ' ἐμὰν εὔκλειαν ἔχειν βιοτὰν στρέψουσι
φᾶμαι·
Ἔρχεται τιμὰ γυναικείῳ γένει·
5   Οὐκέτι δυσκέλαδος φάμα γυναῖκας ἕξει.

ἀ. α'.   Μοῦσαι δὲ παλαιγενέων λήξουσ' ἀοιδᾶν τὰν ἐμὰν ὑμνεῦσαι
ἀπιστοσύναν.
οὐ γὰρ ἐν ἁμετέρᾳ γνώμᾳ λύρας
ὤπασε θέσπιν ἀοιδὰν Φοῖβος, ἀγήτωρ μελέων· ἐπεὶ ἀντάχησ' ἂν
ὕμνον
Ἀρσένων γέννᾳ· μακρὸς δ' αἰὼν ἔχει
5   Πολλὰ μὲν ἁμετέραν ἀνδρῶν τε μοῖραν εἰπεῖν.

σ. β'.   Σὺ δ' ἐκ μὲν οἴκων πατρῴων ἔπλευσας
μαινομένᾳ κραδίᾳ, διδύμας ὁρίσασα πόντου
πέτρας· ἐπὶ δὲ ξένᾳ ναίεις χθονί, τᾶς ἀνάνδρου
Κοίτας ὀλέσασα λέκτρον,
5 τάλαινα, φυγὰς δὲ χώρας
ἄτιμος ἐλαύνει.

ἀ. β'.   Βέβακε δ' ὅρκων χάρις, οὐδ' ἔτ' αἰδὼς
Ἑλλάδι τᾷ μεγάλᾳ μένει, αἰθερία δ' ἀνέπτα.
σοὶ δ' οὔτε πατρὸς δόμοι, δύστανε, μεθορμίσασθαι
Μόχθων πάρα, τῶν δὲ λέκτρων
5 ἄλλα βασίλεια κρείσσων
δόμοισιν ἀνέστα.

Str. α'.

I. ≥ ⋮ _⌣⌣ | _⌣⌣ | _ _ | ⌊⌣ | _ _, ‖ ⌊⌣ | _ _ | _⌣⌣ |
　　　　　　　　　　　　　　　　　　　_⌣⌣ | _ ⊼ ‖
　　_⌣⌣ | _⌣⌣ | _ _ | ⌊⌣ | _ ⊼ ‖
　　_⌣⌣ | _⌣⌣ | _ ≥ | ⌊⌣ | _ _ ‖ _⌣⌣ | _⌣⌣ | _ _ |
　　　　　　　　　　　　　　　　　　　⌊⌣ | _ _]

II. ⌊⌣ | _ _ ‖ ⌊⌣ | _ _ ‖ ⌊⌣ | _ ⊼]
III. _⌣⌣ | _⌣⌣ | _, _ ‖ ⌊⌣ | ⌊⌣ | _ _]　　　　5

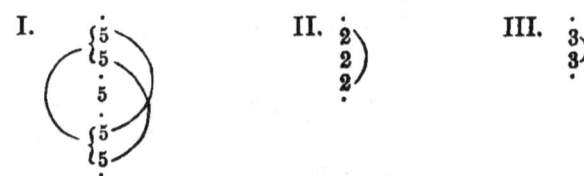

Str. β'.

I. ⌣ ⋮ _⌣ | ⌊ | ⌣⌣ | _⌣ | ⌊ | _ ∧ ‖
　　⌣⌣ | ⌣⌣ | _, ω ‖ ⌣⌣ | _⌣ | ⌊ | _ ∧ ‖
　　> ⋮ ⌣⌣ | _⌣ | _, > ‖ ⌣⌣ | _⌣ | ⌊ | _ ∧]

II. > ⋮ ⌣⌣ | _⌣ | ⌊ | _ ∧ ‖
　　ᶾ ⋮ ⌣⌣ | _⌣ | ⌊ | _ ∧ ‖　　　　　　　5
　　⌣ ⋮ ⌣⌣ | ⌊ | _ ∧]

I.　6̇ = πρ.

　　({3̇\
　　 {4\
　　 {3̇/
　　 {4/)

II.　4̇)
　　　4̇)
　　　3̇ = ἐπ.

The composition of str. α' is peculiar (in particular as regards the single long verse composed of two pentapodies), but nevertheless beautiful. It is quite analogous to that of the "Attic Scolium-strophe," discussed in the *Compositionslehre*, § 35, 4. The last tripody is of livelier form, in order to lead over easily to the logaoedics of str. β'. Precisely the same thing occurs in the next chorus.

III.

Second Stasimon (627 – 663).

σ. α'. Ἔρωτες ὑπὲρ μὲν ἄγαν ἐλθόντες οὐκ εὐδοξίαν
   οὐδ᾽ ἀρετὰν παρέδωκαν ἀνδράσιν· εἰ δ᾽ ἅλις ἔλθοι
   Κύπρις, οὐκ ἄλλα θεὸς εὔχαρις οὕτως.
   μήποτ᾽, ὦ δέσποιν᾽, ἐπ᾽ ἐμοὶ χρυσέων
5 Τόξων ἐφείης ἱμέρῳ χρίσασ᾽ ἄφυκτον οἰστόν.

ἀ. α'. Στέργοι δέ με σωφροσύνα δώρημα κάλλιστον θεῶν·
   μηδέ ποτ᾽ ἀμφιλόγους ὀργὰς ἀκόρεστά τε νείκη
   Θυμὸν ἐκπλήξασ᾽ ἑτέροις ἐπὶ λέκτροις
   προσβάλοι δεινὰ Κύπρις, ἀπτολέμους δ᾽
5 Εὐνὰς σεβίζουσ᾽ ὀξύφρων κρίνοι λέχη γυναικῶν.

σ. β'. Ὦ πατρίς, ὦ δῶμά τ᾽ ἐμόν, μὴ δῆτ᾽ ἄπολις γενοίμαν
   Τὸν ἀμηχανίας ἔχουσα δυσπέρατον αἰῶν᾽, οἰκτρότατον ἀχέων.
   θανάτῳ θανάτῳ πάρος δαμείην
   ἀμέραν τάνδ᾽ ἐξανύσασα· μόχθων δ᾽ οὐκ ἄλλος ὕπερθεν ἢ
5 γᾶς πατρίας στέρεσθαι.

ἀ. β'. Εἴδομεν, οὐκ ἐξ ἑτέρων μύθων ἔχομεν φράσασθαι·
   Σὲ γὰρ οὐ πόλις, οὐ φίλων τις ᾤκτισεν παθοῦσαν δεινότατα
                                                        παθέων.
   ἀχάριττος ὄλοιθ᾽, ὅτῳ πάρεστι
   μὴ φίλους τιμᾶν καθαρὰν ἀνοίξαντα κλῇδα φρενῶν· ἐμοὶ
5 μὲν φίλος οὔποτ᾽ ἔσται.

Str. α'.

I. ≥ː ‿◡◡ | ‿◡◡ | ‿, ‿ ‖ ‿◡ | ‿‿ | ‿◡ | ‿ ⊼ ‖
   ‿◡◡ | ‿◡◡ | ‿.≥.‖ ‿◡◡ | ‿◡◡ | ‿∗ | ‿ ⊼ ⫶

II. ‿◡ | ‿‿ | ‿◡◡ | ‿◡◡ | ‿‿ ‖
    ‿◡ | ‿‿ | ‿◡◡ | ‿◡◡ | ‿ ⊼ ⫶

III. ‿ː ‿◡ | ‿‿ | ‿◡ | ‿, ‿ ‖ ‿◡ | ‿◡ | ⊔ | ‿ ⊼ ⫶   5

Str. β'.

I. ⌣◡ | ‿◡ | ⌣◡ | ‿, > ‖ ⌣◡ | ‿◡ | ‿◡ | ‿ ⊼ ⫶

II. ω ː ⌣◡ | ‿◡ | ‿◡ | ‿◡ | ‿◡ ‖ ‿ > | ⌣◡ | ◡◡◡ | ‿ ∧ ‖
    ω ː ⌣◡ | ‿◡ | ‿◡ | ‿◡ ‖
    ‿◡ | ‿ > | ⌣◡ | ‿◡ | ‿ ‖ ‿ > | ⌣◡ | ‿◡ | ‿ ∧ ‖
    ⌣◡ | ‿◡ | ‿ | ‿ ∧ ⫶   5

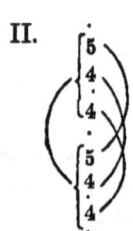

In str. α' occur in Doric melodies falling sentences. This is against ancient usage, though it occurs in Pindar, Nem. VIII. Ep. 6, which is to be written:

‿◡ | ‿‿ | ‿◡◡ | ⊔ ‖ ‿◡ | ‿ > ‖ ‿◡◡ | ‿◡◡ | ⊔ | ‿ ⊼ ⫶

IV.

Third Stasimon (824–865).

σ. α′
Ἐρεχθεΐδαι τὸ παλαιὸν ὄλβιοι
καὶ θεῶν παῖδες μακάρων, ἱερᾶς
χώρας ἀπορθήτου τ᾽ ἀποφερβόμενοι,
Κλεινᾶς, ἀεὶ διὰ λαμπροτάτου
5 βαίνοντες ἁβρῶς αἰθέρος ἔνθα ποθ᾽ ἁγνὰς
ἐννέα Πιερίδας Μούσας λέγουσι
ξανθὰν Ἁρμονίαν φυτεῦσαι·

ἀ. α′.
Τοῦ καλλινάου τ᾽ ἀπὸ Κηφισοῦ ῥοὰς
τὰν Κύπριν κλῄζουσιν ἀφυσσομέναν
χώραν καταπνεῦσαι μετρίαις ἀνέμων
Αὔραις· ἀεὶ δ᾽ ἐπιβαλλομέναν
5 χαίταισιν εὐώδη ῥοδέων πλόκον ἀνθέων
τᾷ σοφίᾳ παρέδρους πέμπειν ἔρωτας
παντοίας ἀρετᾶς ξυνεργούς.

σ. β′.
Πῶς οὖν ἱερῶν ποταμῶν ἢ πόλις ἢ φίλων
πόμπιμός σε χώρα
Τὰν παιδολέτειραν ἕξει,
τὰν οὐχ ὁσίαν μετ᾽ ἄλλων;
5 σκέψαι τεκέων πλαγάν,
σκέψαι φόνον οἷον αἴρει.
μὴ πρὸς γονάτων σε πάντως
πάντῃ σ᾽ ἱκετεύομεν,
τέκνα φονεύσῃς.

ἀ. β′.
Πόθεν θράσος ἢ φρενὸς ἢ χειρί, τέκνον, σέθεν
καρδίᾳ τε λήψει,
Δεινὰν προσάγουσα τόλμαν;
πῶς δ᾽ ὄμματα προσβαλοῦσα
5 τέκνοις ἄδακρυν μοῖραν
σχήσεις; φόνῳ οὐ δυνάσει,
παίδων ἱκετᾶν κτανόντων,
τέγξαι χέρα φοινίαν
τλάμονι θυμῷ.

Str. α'.

I. ≥ ⋮ _ ᴗ ᴗ | _ ᴗ ᴗ | ≥ _ | ⌊ ᴗ | _ ⊼ ‖
　　⌊ ᴗ | _ _ | _ ᴗ ᴗ | _ ᴗ ᴗ | _ ⊼ ‖
　_ ⋮ ⌊ ᴗ | _ _ | _ ᴗ ᴗ | _ ᴗ ᴗ | _ ⊼ ⟧

II. _ ⋮ ⌊ ᴗ | _ ᴗ ᴗ | _ ᴗ ᴗ | _ ⊼ ‖
　_ ⋮ ⌊ ᴗ | _ _ | _ ᴗ ᴗ | _ ᴗ ᴗ | _ _ ‖
　_ ᴗ ᴗ | _ ᴗ ᴗ | _ _ | ⌊ ᴗ | _ _ ‖
　_ _ | _ ᴗ ᴗ | ⌊ ᴗ | _ _ ⟧

I. 5)
    5)
    5)

II. 4)
    5)
    5)
    4)

Str. β'.

I. ≥ ⋮ ⌣ ᴗ ᴗ | ⌣ ᴗ ᴗ | ⌊, ‖ ⌣ ᴗ ᴗ | _ ᴗ | _ ∧ ‖
　_ ᴗ | _ ᴗ | ⌊ | _ ∧ ⟧

II. > ⋮ ⌣ ᴗ ᴗ | _ ᴗ | ⌊ | _ ∧ ‖
　> ⋮ ⌣ ᴗ ᴗ | _ ᴗ | ⌊ | _ ∧ ‖
　> ⋮ ⌣ ᴗ ᴗ | _ > | _ ∧ ‖
　> ⋮ ⌣ ᴗ ᴗ | _ ᴗ | ⌊ | _ ∧ ‖
　> ⋮ ⌣ ᴗ ᴗ | _ ᴗ | ⌊ | _ ∧ ‖
　> ⋮ ⌣ ᴗ ᴗ | _ ᴗ | _ ∧ ‖
　　⌣ ᴗ ᴗ | _ ᴗ ⟧

I. 3)
    3)
    4 = ἐπ.

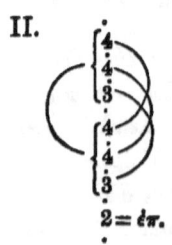

V.

Fourth Stasimon (976-1001).

σ. α'. Νῦν ἐλπίδες οὐκέτι μοι παίδων ζόας,
οὐκέτι· στείχουσι γὰρ ἐς φόνον ἤδη.
Δέξεται νύμφα χρυσέων ἀναδεσμῶν
δέξεται δύστανος ἄταν·
5 ξανθᾷ δ' ἀμφὶ κόμᾳ θήσει τὸν Ἅιδα
κόσμον αὐτὰ χεροῖν.

ἀ. α'. Πείσει χάρις ἀμβρόσιός τ' αὐγὰ πέπλον
χρυσότευκτόν τε στέφανον περιθέσθαι·
Νερτέροις ἤδη πάρα νυμφοκομήσει.
τοῖον εἰς ἕρκος πεσεῖται
5 καὶ μοῖραν θανάτου δύστανος· ἄταν δ'
οὐκ ὑπερφεύξεται.

σ. β'. Σὺ δ', ὦ τάλαν, ὦ κακόνυμφε κηδεμὼν τυράννων,
παισὶν οὐ κατειδὼς
ὄλεθρον βιοτᾷ προσάγεις, ἀλόχῳ τε σᾷ στυγερὸν θάνατον.
δύστανε μοίρας ὅσον παροίχει.

ἀ. β'. Μεταστένομαι δὲ σὸν ἄλγος, ὦ τάλαινα παίδων
μᾶτερ, ἃ φονεύσεις
τέκνα νυμφιδίων ἕνεκεν λεχέων, ἅ σοι προλιπὼν ἀνόμως
ἄλλᾳ ξυνοικεῖ πόσις συνεύνῳ.

Str. α'.

I. _ː_∪∪|_∪∪| __ | ⌐∪ |_⊼ ‖
    ⌐∪| __ |_∪∪|_∪∪|__]

II. ⌐∪| __ |_∪∪|_∪∪|__ ‖
    ⌐∪| __ | ⌐∪ | __ ‖
    __|_∪∪| __ | ⌐∪ |__ ‖   5
    ⌐∪| ⌐ | ⌐∪ |_⊼]

I. {5 5}

Str. β'.

∪ː⌣∪|⌣∪|_∪,‖_∪|_∪| ⌐ |_∧ ‖
    _∪|_∪| ⌐ |_∧ ‖
ω ː⌣∪|⌣∪|⌣∪|_,∪‖⌣∪|⌣∪|_∧ ‖
> ː_∪| ⌐ |_∪|_∪| ⌐ |_∧]

6 = ἐπ.

VI.

Kommatic song of the Chorus, with trimeters spoken in part by the sons of Medea (1251-1292).

σ.   Χ.   Ἰὼ Γᾶ τε καὶ παμφαὴς
ἀκτὶς Ἀελίου, κατίδετ' ἴδετε τὰν
ὀλομέναν γυναῖκα, πρὶν φοινίαν
τέκνοις προσβαλεῖν χέρ' αὐτοκτόνον·
5   Τᾶς σᾶς γὰρ ἀπὸ χρυσέας γονᾶς
ἔβλαστεν, θεοῦ δ' αἵματι πίτνειν
   Φόβος ὑπ' ἀνέρων.
ἀλλά νιν, ὦ φάος,
   Διογενές, κάτειργε, κατάπαυσον, ἔξελ' οἴκων φονίαν τάλαιναν τ'
                                                    Ἐρινὺν ὑπ' ἀλαστόρων.

ἀ.   Μάταν μόχθος ἔρρει τέκνων,
μάταν ἄρα γένος φίλιον ἔτεκες, ὦ
κυανεῶν λιποῦσα Συμπληγάδων
πετρᾶν ἀξενωτάταν εἰσβολάν.
5   Δειλαία, τί σοι φρενῶν βαρὺς
χόλος προσπίτνει καὶ δυσμενὴς
   Φόνος ἀμείβεται;
χαλεπὰ γὰρ βροτοῖς
   Ὁμογενῆ μιάσματ' ἐπὶ γαῖαν αὐτοφόνταις ξυνῳδὰ θεόθεν πίτνοντ'
                                                    ἐπὶ δόμοις ἄχη.

Π. α'.   οἴμοι, τί δράσω; ποῖ φύγω μητρὸς χέρας;
Π. β'.   οὐκ οἶδ', ἀδελφὲ φίλτατ'· ὀλλύμεσθα γάρ.

Str.

I. ᴗː ⏤⏤ᴗ|⏤⏤ᴗ|⏜∧‖
   ⁝⏤ᴗᴗᴗ|⏤,ᴗ‖ᴗᴗᴗᴗᴗ|⏤∧‖
   ᴗːᴗᴗ⏤ᴗ|⏤ᴗ,‖⏤⏤ᴗ|⏤∧‖
   ᴗː⏤⏤ᴗ|⏤.ᴗ‖⏤⏤ᴗ|⏤∧⟧

II. >ː⏤⌣ᴗ|⏤ᴗ|⏤ᴗ⏤‖   5
    ᴗː⏤⏤ᴗ|⏤>|⌣ᴗ⏤⟧

III. ᴗːᴗᴗ⏤ᴗ|⏤∧‖
     ⁝ᴗᴗ⏤ᴗ|⏤∧⟧

IV. ᴗːᴗᴗ⏤ᴗ|⏤ᴗ,‖ᴗᴗ⏤ᴗ|⏤ᴗ.‖⏤⏤ᴗ|⏤.ᴗ.‖
    ⌣⏤ᴗ|⏤.⁝.‖ᴗᴗ⏤ᴗ|⏤∧⟧

I. 3 ba.   II. amph.⎫   III. do.⎫   IV. do.⎫
{do.⎫   amph.⎭   do.⎭   do.⎬
{do.⎭   do.
{do.⎫   do.⎬
{do.⎭   do.
{do.⎫
{do.⎭

Verses 5 and 6 are amphidochmii, for which see § 23, 5, and *Eurhythmie*, § 18, 9. The resolutions and irrational syllables make any other classification of these verses impossible.

The third period fits the second and fourth periods together, and gives the singer a chance to recover after the agitated amphidochmii that precede before passing to the long dochmiac verse that follows. The parts of this period are skilfully separated by the punctuation, so that the first verse belongs closely to the foregoing period, the second to the one that follows.

κ. α'.   Χ. Ἀκούεις βοὰν ἀκούεις τέκνων;
ἰὼ τλᾶμον ὦ κακοτυχὲς γύναι.
Παρέλθω δόμους; ἀρῆξαι φόνον
δοκεῖ μοι τέκνοις.
5 Π. Ναί, πρὸς θεῶν, ἀρήξατ'· ἐν δέοντι γάρ·
ὡς ἐγγὺς ἤδη γ' ἐσμὲν ἀρκύων ξίφους.

κ. β'.   Χ. Τάλαιν', ὡς ἄρ' ἦσθα πέτρος ἢ σίδαρος, ἅτις τέκνων
ὃν ἔτεκες
ἄροτον αὐτόχειρι μοίρᾳ κτενεῖς.

κ. γ'. 10   Μίαν δὴ κλύω μίαν τῶν πάρος
γυναῖκ' ἐν φίλοις χέρα βαλεῖν τέκνοις,
Ἰνὼ μανεῖσαν ἐκ θεῶν, ὅθ' ἡ Διὸς
δάμαρ νιν ἐξέπεμψε δωμάτων ἄλῃ.
Πίτνει δ' ἁ τάλαιν' ἐς ἅλμαν φόνῳ
15   τέκνων δυσσεβεῖ,
ἀκτῆς ὑπερτείνασα ποντίας πόδα,
δυοῖν τε παίδοιν συνθανοῦσ' ἀπόλλυται.

κ. δ'.   Τί δῆτ' οὖν γένοιτ' ἂν ἔτι δεινόν; ὦ γυναικῶν λέχος
πολύπονον,
20   ὅσα βροτοῖς ἔρεξας ἤδη κακά.

Kommata.

We might assume that two trimeters of the boys had fallen out after the first period of komma α', and then unite the first two kommata into a strophe and the next two into the antistrophe. But in that case the assignment of the strophe partly to the boys and partly to the chorus, while the whole of the antistrophe would be assigned to the chorus, would be irregular. Moreover, κομμοί occur not only frequently in Euripides but also in Sophocles which begin with strophes and end with κόμματα. Cf. *Oed. Col.* I. and *Phil.* V.

Komma α'.

I. Ch. ∪ ⁞ _ _ ∪ | _, ∪ ‖ _ _ _ ∪ | _ ∧ ‖   I. {do. II. do.
       ∪ ⁞ _ _ ∪ | _, ∪ ‖ ∪ ∪ _ ∪ | _ ∧ ⟧   {do.   do.
II.   ∪ ⁞ _ _ ∪ | _, ∪ ‖ _ _ _ ∪ | _ ∧ ‖   {do.   do.
       ∪ ⁞ _ _ ∪ | _ ∧ ⟧   {do.
Boys. trim.   5
     trim.

Komma β'.

Ch. ∪ ⁞ _ _ ∪ | _ ∪, ‖ ∪ ∪ _ ∪ | _ ∪, ‖ _ _ ∪ | _ ∧ ‖   do.
    ∪ ∪ ∪ | _ ∧ ‖   do.
    ∪ ⁞ ∪ ∪ _ ∪ | _ ∪, ‖ _ _ ∪ | _ ∧ ⇑   do.
                                                         2
                                                        do.
                                                        do.

Komma γ'.

I.   ∪ ⁞ _ _ ∪ | _, ∪ ‖ _ _ _ ∪ | _ ∧ ‖   I. {do. II. do.   10
     ∪ ⁞ _ _ ∪ | _, ∪ ‖ ∪ ∪ _ ∪ | _ ∧ ⟧   {do.   do.
     trim.   {do.
     trim.   {do.
II. ∪ ⁞ _ _ ∪ | _, ∪ ‖ _ _ ∪ | _ ∧ ‖
     ∪ ⁞ _ _ ∪ | _ ∧ ⟧   15
     trim.
     trim.

Komma δ'.

                                                        do.
                                                        do.
∪ ⁞ _ _ ∪ | _, ∪ ‖ ∪ ∪ _ ∪ | _, ∪ ‖ _ _ ∪ | _ ∧ ‖   do.
∪ ∪ ∪ | _ ∧ ‖   2
∪ ⁞ ∪ ∪ _ ∪ | _ ∪, ‖ _ _ ∪ | _ ∧ ⇑   do.
                                                        do.   20

THE LYRIC PARTS OF THE ANTIGONE.

I.

THE PARODOS (vv. 100–154).

σ. ά. Ἀκτὶς ἀελίου, τὸ κάλλιστον ἑπταπύλῳ φανὲν Θήβᾳ τῶν προτέ-
ρων φάος,
ἐφάνθης ποτ', ὦ χρυσέας ἁμέρας βλέφαρον, Διρκαίων ὑπὲρ ῥεέθρων
μολοῦσα,
Τὸν λεύκασπιν Ἀπιόθεν φῶτα βάντα πανσαγίᾳ
φυγάδα πρόδρομον ὀξυτέρῳ κινήσασα χαλινῷ.

στ. ά.   Ὃς ἐφ' ἁμετέρᾳ γᾷ Πολυνείκους
ἀρθεὶς νεικέων ἐξ ἀμφιλόγων
ὀξέα κλάζων
ἀετὸς ἐς γᾶν ὑπερέπτα,
5   λευκῆς χιόνος πτέρυγι στεγανός,
πολλῶν μεθ' ὅπλων
ξύν θ' ἱπποκόμοις κορύθεσσιν.

ά. ά.   Στὰς δ' ὑπὲρ μελάθρων φονώσαισιν ἀμφιχανὼν κύκλῳ λόγχαις
ἑπτάπυλον στόμα,
ἔβα, πρίν ποθ' ἁμετέρων αἱμάτων γένυσιν πλησθῆναί τε καὶ στεφά-
νωμα πύργων
Πευκάενθ' Ἥφαιστον ἑλεῖν. τοῖος ἀμφὶ νῶτ' ἐτάθη
πάταγος Ἄρεος, ἀντιπάλῳ δυσχείρωμα δράκοντι.

στ. β'.   Ζεὺς γὰρ μεγάλης γλώσσης κόμπους
ὑπερεχθαίρει, καί σφας ἐσιδὼν
πολλῷ ῥεύματι προσνισσομένους

Str. a'.

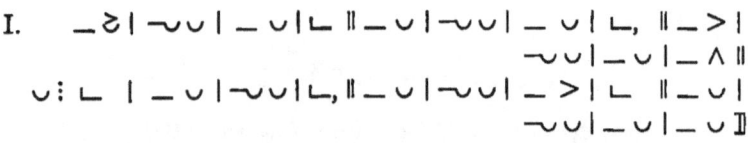

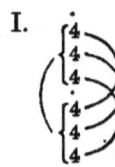   

Str. a'.

Per. I. The joy which the chorus feels on account of victory is expressed in verses that are in themselves rhythmically well-divided, but still group themselves subordinately in the greater whole of the palinodic period. The period is not to be regarded antithetic, although this is possible, as far as the close of the words is concerned, as follows:

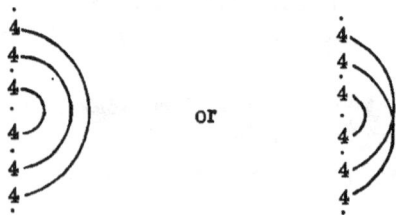

Per. II. The inverted order of the first two measures of the third verse of the strophe ($\_ > | \_ \cup |$, not $\_ \cup | \_ > |$, as was to be expected, see § 13, 2) is noteworthy. The antistrophe, however, is regular ($\_ > | \_ > |$).

χρυσοῦ καναχῇ θ᾿ ὑπερόπτας,
5 παλτῷ ῥιπτεῖ πυρὶ βαλβίδων
ἐπ᾿ ἄκρων ἤδη
νίκην ὁρμῶντ᾿ ἀλαλάξαι.

σ. β'. Ἀντίτυπος δ᾿ ἐπὶ γᾷ πέσε τανταλωθεὶς
πυρφόρος, ὃς τότε μαινομένᾳ ξὺν ὁρμᾷ
Βακχεύων ἐπέπνει ῥιπαῖς ἐχθίστων ἀνέμων.
εἶχε δ᾿ ἄλλᾳ τὰ μέν,
5 Ἄλλα δ᾿ ἐπ᾿ ἄλλοις ἐπενώμα στυφελίζων μέγας Ἄρης
δεξιόσειρος.

σα. γ'. Ἑπτὰ λοχαγοὶ γὰρ ἐφ᾿ ἑπτὰ πύλαις
ταχθέντες ἴσοι πρὸς ἴσους ἔλιπον
Ζηνὶ τροπαίῳ πάγχαλκα τέλη,
πλὴν τῶν στυγερῶν, ὦ πατρὸς ἑνὸς
5 μητρός τε μιᾶς φύντε καθ᾿ αὑτοῖν
δικρατεῖς λόγχας στήσαντ᾿ ἔχετον
κοινοῦ θανάτου μέρος ἄμφω.

ἀ. β'. Ἀλλὰ γὰρ ἁ μεγαλώνυμος ἦλθε Νίκα
τᾷ πολυαρμάτῳ ἀντιχαρεῖσα Θήβᾳ,
Ἐκ μὲν δὴ πολέμων τῶν νῦν θέσθε λησμοσύναν,
θεῶν δὲ ναοὺς χοροῖς
5 Παννυχίοις πάντας ἐπέλθωμεν, ὁ Θήβας δ᾿ ἐλελίχθων
Βάκχιος ἄρχοι.

ANTIGONE I. (100–154). 173

Str. β'.

I. ⏑⏑ | ⏑⏑ | ⏑⏑ | _⏑ | ⌴ | _ ∧ ‖
   ⏑⏑ | ⏑⏑ | ⏑⏑ | _⏑ | ⌴ | _ ∧ ⟧

II. _ > | ⏑⏑ | _ > | ⌴, ‖ _ ᷃ | ⏑⏑ | _ ∧ ‖
    _ ⏑ | ⌴ | _ ⏑ | _ ∧ ⟧

III. ⏑⏑ | ⌴ | ⏑⏑ | ⌴ ‖ ⏑⏑ | ⌴ | ⏑⏑ | _⏑ ‖
     ⏑⏑ | _ ⏑ ⟧

I. $\begin{pmatrix} \dot{6} \\ \dot{6} \end{pmatrix}$ II. $\begin{pmatrix} \dot{4} \\ 3 \\ \dot{4} \end{pmatrix}$ III. $\begin{pmatrix} \dot{4} \\ \dot{4} \end{pmatrix}$
$\dot{2} = \epsilon\pi.$

Str. β'.

Per. II. In Sophocles logaoedic periods often close in this way with a choreic sentence, becoming less vivacious toward the end.

Per. III. The so-called *versus Adonius* (§ 22, 11) as *postlude* is noteworthy.

These three periods are but little separated from one another by punctuation (see Schmidt, *Eurhythmie*, § 13, 5).

II.

First Stasimon (332–374).

σ. α'. Πολλὰ τὰ δεινά, κοὐδὲν ἀνθρώπου δεινότερον πέλει·
τοῦτο καὶ πολιοῦ πέραν πόντου χειμερίῳ νότῳ
 Χωρεῖ, περιβρυχίοισιν
περῶν ὑπ' οἴδμασιν,
5 θεῶν δὲ τὰν ὑπερτάταν, Γᾶν
 Ἄφθιτον, ἀκαμάταν ἀποτρύεται,
ἰλλομένων ἀρότρων ἔτος εἰς ἔτος,
ἱππείῳ γένει πολεύων.

ἀ. α'. Κουφονόων τε φῦλον ὀρνίθων ἀμφιβαλὼν ἄγει
καὶ θηρῶν ἀγρίων ἔθνη, πόντου τ' εἰναλίαν φύσιν
 Σπείραισι δικτυοκλώστοις
περιφραδὴς ἀνήρ·
5 κρατεῖ δὲ μηχαναῖς ἀγραύλου
 Θηρὸς ὀρεσσιβάτα, λασιαύχενά θ'
ἵππον ὀχμάζεται ἀμφιβαλὼν ζυγόν,
οὔρειόν τ' ἀκμῆτα ταῦρον.

σ. β'. Καὶ φθέγμα καὶ ἀνεμόεν
φρόνημα καὶ ἀστυνόμους ὀργὰς ἐδιδάξατο καὶ δυσαύλων
 Πάγων ἐναίθρεια καὶ δύσομβρα φεύγειν βέλη,
παντοπόρος· ἄπορος ἐπ' οὐδὲν ἔρχεται
5 τὸ μέλλον· Ἅιδα μόνον φεῦξιν οὐκ ἐπάξεται·
νόσων δ' ἀμηχάνων φυγὰς ξυμπέφρασται.

ἀ. β'. Σοφόν τι τὸ μηχανόεν
τέχνας ὑπὲρ ἐλπίδ' ἔχων ποτὲ μὲν κακόν, ἄλλοτ' ἐπ' ἐσθλὸν ἕρπει·
 Νόμους τ' ἀείρων χθονὸς θεῶν τ' ἔνορκον δίκαν,
ὑψίπολις· ἄπολις, ὅτῳ τὸ μὴ καλὸν
5 ξύνεστι, τόλμας χάριν. μήτ' ἐμοὶ παρέστιος
γένοιτο μήτ' ἴσον φρονῶν ὃς τάδ' ἔρδει.

Str. α'.

I. ⌣⌣ | _ ⌣ | _ ⌣ | ⌊ ‖ _ > | ⌣⌣ | _ ⌣ | _ ∧ ‖
   _ ⌣ | ⌣⌣ | _ ⌣ | ⌊, ‖ _ > | ⌣⌣ | _ ⌣ | _ ∧ ⟧

II. > ⁝ _ ⌣ | ⌣⌣ | ⌊ | _ ∧ ‖
    ⌣ ⁝ _ ⌣ | _ ⌣ | _ ∧ ‖
    ⌣ ⁝ _ ⌣ | _ ⌣ | _ ⌣ | _ ⌣ ⟧

$$\text{I. } \begin{Bmatrix}4\\4\end{Bmatrix} \quad \text{II. } \begin{Bmatrix}4\\3\end{Bmatrix} \quad \text{III. } \begin{Bmatrix}4\\4\end{Bmatrix}$$
$$6 = \ell\pi.$$

III. _ ω | _ ω | _ ω | _ ω ‖
     _ ω | _ ω | _ ω | _ ω ‖
     ⌊ | ⌊ | _ ⌣ | _ ⌣ | ⌊ | _ ∧ ⟧

Str. β'.

I. > ⁝ _ ω | _ ω | _ ∧ ‖
   ⌣ ⁝ _ ω | _ ω | _ ω̌ | _, ω ‖ _ ω | _ ⌣ | ⌊ | _ ∧ ⟧

II. ⌣ ⁝ _ ⌣ | ⌊ | _ ⌣ | _, ⌣ ‖ _ ⌣ | ⌊ | _ ⌣ | _ ∧ ‖
    _ ⌣ | ⌣⌣⌣ | ⌣⌣⌣ | _ ⌣ | _ ⌣ | _ ∧ ‖
    ⌣ ⁝ _ ⌣ | ⌊ | _ ⌣ | ⌊, ‖ _ ⌣ | _ ⌣ | _ ⌣ | _ ∧ ‖
    ⌣ ⁝ _ ⌣ | _ ⌣ | _ ⌣ | ⌊ | _ ⌣ | _ ⌣ ⟧

$$\text{I. } \begin{Bmatrix}3\\4\\4\end{Bmatrix} = \pi\rho. \quad \text{II. } \begin{Bmatrix}4\\4\\6\\4\\4\\6\end{Bmatrix}$$

The chorus begins with a logaoedic period; then follow choreic periods, the first of which, however, begins with a logaoedic verse, which softens the change from the one rhythm to the other. Str. α', Per. III., and Str. β', Per. I., are not logaoedic, but choreic. The apparent dactyls are, therefore, not cyclic dactyls (⌣⌣, i. e. ♩♪♪), but what may be called *choreic* dactyls (_ ω, i. e. ♩ ♫). The caesura in Str. β', verse 2, makes this clear. The apparent correspondence, therefore, in this same verse, _ ⌣⌣, is in fact _ ω̇. Concerning choreic dactyls see § 15.

III.

Second Stasimon (582 – 625).

σ. α΄. Εὐδαίμονες οἷσι κακῶν ἄγευστος αἰών.
  οἷς γὰρ ἂν σεισθῇ θεόθεν δόμος, ἄτας
    Οὐδὲν ἐλλείπει γενεᾶς ἐπὶ πλῆθος ἕρπον·
    ὅμοιον ὥστε ποντίαις οἶδμα, δυσπνόοις ὅταν
5 Θρῄσσαισιν ἔρεβος ὕφαλον ἐπιδράμῃ πνοαῖς,
    Κυλίνδει βυσσόθεν κελαινὰν θῖνα, καὶ
    δυσάνεμον στόνῳ βρέμουσιν ἀντιπλῆγες ἀκταί.

ἀ. α΄. Ἀρχαῖα τὰ Λαβδακιδᾶν οἴκων ὁρῶμαι
  πήματα φθιτῶν ἐπὶ πήμασι πίπτοντ᾽,
    Οὐδ᾽ ἀπαλλάσσει γενεὰν γένος, ἀλλ᾽ ἐρείπει
    θεῶν τις, οὐδ᾽ ἔχει λύσιν. νῦν γὰρ ἐσχάτας ὑπὲρ
5 ῥίζας ἐτέτατο φάος ἐν Οἰδίπου δόμοις —
    Κατ᾽ αὖ νιν φοινία θεῶν τῶν νερτέρων
    ἀμᾷ κοπὶς λόγου τ᾽ ἄνοια καὶ φρενῶν ἐρινύς.

σ. β΄. Τεάν, Ζεῦ, δύνασιν τίς ἀνδρῶν ὑπερβασία κατάσχοι,
  τὰν οὔθ᾽ ὕπνος αἱρεῖ ποθ᾽ ὁ παντοθήρας
    Οὔτε θεῶν ἄκματοι μῆνες, ἀγήρως δὲ χρόνῳ
    δυνάστας κατέχεις Ὀλύμπου μαρμαρόεσσαν αἴγλαν·
5   Τύ τ᾽ ἔπειτα καὶ τὸ μέλλον
    καὶ τὸ πρὶν ἐπαρκέσει
    νόμος ὅδ᾽· οὐδὲν ἕρπει
    θνατῶν βίοτον τὸν πολὺν ἐκτὸς ἄτας.

ἀ. β΄. Ἁ μὲν γὰρ πολύπλαγκτος ἐλπὶς πολλοῖς μὲν ὄνησις ἀνδρῶν,
  πολλοῖς δ᾽ ἀπάτα κουφονόων ἐρώτων·
    Εἰδότι δ᾽ οὐδὲν ἕρπει, πρὶν πυρὶ θερμῷ πόδα τις
    προσαύσῃ. σοφίᾳ γὰρ ἔκ του κλεινὸν ἔπος πέφανται·
5   "Τὸ κακὸν δοκεῖν ποτ᾽ ἐσθλὸν
    τῷδ᾽ ἔμμεν ὅτῳ φρένας
    θεὸς ἄγει πρὸς ἄταν."
    πράσσει δ᾽ ὀλιγοστὸν χρόνον ἐκτὸς ἄτας.

ANTIGONE III. (582–625).

Str. α′.

I. >ː ⌣‿⌣ | ⌣‿⌣ | _ ⸏ | _ ⌣ | ⌶ | _ ∧ ‖
   _ ⌣ | _ > | ⌣‿⌣ | ⌣‿⌣ | ⌶ | _ ∧ ⟧

II. _ ⌣ | _ > | ⌣‿⌣ | ⌣‿⌣ | _ ⌣ | _ ⌣ ‖
    ⌣ː _ ⌣ | _ ⌣ | _ ⌣ | ⌶ , ‖ _ ⌣ | _ ⌣ | _ ⌣ | _ ∧ ‖
    >ː _ ⌣ | ⌣⌣⌣ | ⌣⌣⌣ | ⌣⌣⌣ | _ ⌣ | _ ∧ ⟧   5

III. ⌣ː ⌶ | ⌶ | _ ⌣ | _ , ⌣ ‖ ⌶ | ⌶ | _ ⌣ | _ ∧ ‖
     ⌣ː _ ⌣ | _ ⌣ | _ ⌣ | _ ⌣ , ‖ _ ⌣ | _ ⌣ | ⌶ | _ ∧ ⟧

I.   II. 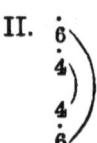 III.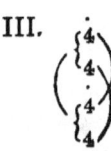

Str. β′.

I. ⸏ː ⌶ | ⌣‿⌣ | _ ⌣ | ⌶ ‖ _ ⸏ | ⌣‿⌣ | _ ⌣ | _ ⌣ ‖
   >ː ⌣‿⌣ | ⌶ | ⌣‿⌣ | _ ⌣ | ⌶ | _ ∧ ⟧

II. ⌣‿⌣ | _ ⌣ | ⌶ | ⌶ , ‖ ⌣‿⌣ | ⌶ | ⌣‿⌣ | _ ∧ ‖
    ⌣ː ⌶ | ⌣‿⌣ | _ ⌣ | _ > , ‖ ⌣‿⌣ | _ ⌣ | ⌶ | _ ∧ ⟧

III. ωː _ ⌣ | _ ⌣ | ⌶ | _ ∧ ‖   5
     >ː ⌣‿⌣ | _ ⌣ | _ ∧ ‖
     ⌣⌣⌣ | _ ⌣ | ⌶ | _ ∧ ‖
     >ː ⌣‿⌣ | ⌶ | ⌣‿⌣ | _ ⌣ | ⌶ | _ ∧ ⟧

I. 4)
   4)
   6 = ἐπ.

II.

III. 4
     4
     3
     4
     6 = ἐπ.

IV.

Third Stasimon (781 – 800).

σ. Ἔρως ἀνίκατε μάχαν, Ἔρως ὃς ἐν κτήμασι πίπτεις,
ὅτ' ἐν μαλακαῖς παρειαῖς νεάνιδος ἐννυχεύεις·
   Φοιτᾷς δ' ὑπερπόντιος ἔν τ' ἀγρονόμοις αὐλαῖς,
καί σ' οὔτ' ἀθανάτων φύξιμος οὐδεὶς
5 οὔθ' ἀμερίων ἐπ' ἀνθρώπων, ὁ δ' ἔχων μέμηνεν.

ἀ. Σὺ καὶ δικαίων ἀδίκους φρένας παρασπᾷς ἐπὶ λώβᾳ,
σὺ καὶ τόδε νεῖκος ἀνδρῶν ξύναιμον ἔχεις ταράξας·
   Νικᾷ δ' ἐνιργὴς βλεφάρων ἵμερος εὐλέκτρου
νύμφας, τῶν μεγάλων τῶνδε πάρεδρος
5 θεσμῶν. ἄμαχος γὰρ ἐμπαίζει θεὸς Ἀφροδίτα.

I. ∪ : _ ∪ | ∟ |‿∪ | _, ∪ ‖ _ ∪ | ∟ |‿∪ | _ ∪ ‖
   ∪ : ‿∪ | _ ∪ | ∟ | _, ∪ ‖ ‿∪ | _ ∪ | ∟ | _ ∧]]

II. > : _ ∪ | ∟ |‿∪ | ∟, ‖ ‿∪ | ∟ | ∟ | _ ∧ ‖
    _ > |‿∪ | ∟, ‖ ‿∪ | ∟ | _ ∧ ‖
5   > : ‿∪ | _ ∪ | ∟ | ∟ ‖ ‿∪ | _ ∪ | ∟ | _ ∧]]

 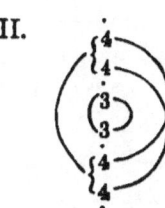

V.

Κομμος (806 – 882).

Α. Ὁρᾶτ' ἔμ', ὦ γᾶς πατρίας πολῖται, τὰν νεάταν ὁδὸν   σ. α'.
στείχουσαν, νέατον δὲ φέγγος λεύσσουσαν ἀελίου,
κοὔποτ' αὖθις· ἀλλά μ' ὁ παγκοίτας Ἅιδας ζῶσαν ἄγει
τὰν Ἀχέροντος
   Ἀκτάν, οὔθ' ὑμεναίων ἔγκληρον, οὔτ' ἐπινύμφειός   5
πώ μέ τις ὕμνος ὕμνησεν, ἀλλ' Ἀχέροντι νυμφεύσω.

Χ. Οὐκοῦν κλεινὴ καὶ ἔπαινον ἔχουσ'   συ. α'.
ἐς τόδ' ἀπέρχει κεῦθος νεκύων,
οὔτε φθινάσιν πληγεῖσα νόσοις
οὔτε ξιφέων ἐπίχειρα λαβοῦσ',
ἀλλ' αὐτόνομος ζῶσα μόνη δὴ   5
θνητῶν Ἅιδην καταβήσει.

Α. Ἤκουσα δὴ λυγροτάταν ὀλέσθαι τὰν Φρυγίαν ξέναν   ἀ. α'.
Ταντάλου Σιπύλῳ πρὸς ἄκρῳ, τὰν κισσὸς ὡς ἀτενὴς
πετραία βλάστα δάμασεν, καί νιν ὄμβροι τακομέναν
ὡς φάτις ἀνδρῶν
   Χιών τ' οὐδαμὰ λείπει, τέγγει δ' ὑπ' ὀφρύσι παγκλαύτοις   5
δειράδας· ᾇ με δαίμων ὁμοιοτάταν κατευνάζει.

Str. α'.

I. ᵈ: ‿∪| ∟ |‿∪∪|‿,∪‖‿>|‿∪∪|‿∪|‿∧‖
    ‿ᵈ|‿∪∪|‿∪|‿>,‖ ∟ |‿∪|‿∪∪|‿∧‖
    ‿∪|‿ᵈ|‿∪∪| ∟, ‖‿ᵈ|‿>|‿∪∪|‿∧‖
    ‿∪∪|‿∪]

II. ᵈ: ∟ |‿∪∪|‿>| ∟ ‖‿∪|‿∪∪|‿>|‿∧‖   5
    ‿∪∪|‿∪| ∟ |‿∪‖‿∪∪|‿∪|‿>|‿∧]

σͳ β'.   Χ. Ἀλλὰ θεός τοι καὶ θεογεννής,
         ἡμεῖς δὲ βροτοὶ καὶ θνητογενεῖς.
         καίτοι φθιμένῳ τοῖς ἰσοθέοις
         ἔγκληρα λαχεῖν μέγ' ἀκοῦσαι.

σ. β'.   Α. Οἴμοι γελῶμαι. τί με, πρὸς θεῶν πατρῴων,
         οὐκ οἰχομέναν ὑβρίζεις, ἀλλ' ἐπίφαντον;
         ὦ πόλις, ὦ πόλεως πολυκτήμονες ἄνδρες·
         Ἰὼ Διρκαῖαι κρῆναι
      5 Θήβας τ' εὐαρμάτου ἄλσος, ἔμπας ξυμμάρτυρας ὔμμ' ἐπικτῶμαι,
         Οἵα φίλων ἄκλαυτος, οἵοις νόμοις
         πρὸς ἕρμα τυμβόχωστον ἔρχομαι τάφου ποταινίου·
         ἰὼ δύστανός γ', οὔτ' ἐν [τοῖσιν ἔτ'] οὔτε [τοῖσιν]
         μέτοικος, οὐ ζῶσιν, οὐ θανοῦσιν.

σ. γ'.   Χ. Προβᾶσ' ἐπ' ἔσχατον θράσους
         ὑψηλὸν ἐς Διὸς βάθρον
         προσέπεσες, ὦ τέκνον, πολύν.
         πατρῷον δ' ἐκτίνεις τιν' ἆθλον.

ἀ. β'.   Α. Ἔψαυσας ἀλγεινοτάτας ἐμοὶ μερίμνας
         πατρὸς τριπόλιστον οἶκτον, τοῦ τε πρόπαντος
         ἁμετέρου πότμου κλεινοῖς Λαβδακίδαισιν.
         Ἰὼ ματρῷαι λέκτρων
      5 ἆται κοιμήματά τ' αὐτογέννητ' ἐμῷ πατρὶ δυσμόρῳ ματρός,
         Οἵων ἐγώ ποθ' ἁ ταλαίφρων ἔφυν·
         πρὸς οὓς ἀραῖος, ἄγαμος, ἅδ' ἐγὼ μέτοικος ἔρχομαι.
         ἰὼ δυσπότμων κασίγνητε γάμων κυρήσας,
         θανὼν ἔτ' οὖσαν κατήναρές με.

ἀ. γ'.   Χ. Σέβειν μὲν εὐσέβειά τις,
         κράτος δ' ὅτῳ κράτος μέλει
         παραβατὸν οὐδαμῇ πέλει,
         σὲ δ' αὐτόγνωτος ὤλεσ' ὀργά.

ἐπ.   Α. Ἄκλαυτος, ἄφιλος, ἀνυμέναιος ἄγημαι ταλαίφρων
         τάνδ' ἑτοίμαν ὁδόν·
         Οὐκέτι μοι τόδε λαμπάδος ἱρὸν
         ὄμμα θέμις ὁρᾶν ταλαίνᾳ·
      5 τὸν δ' ἐμὸν πότμον ἀδάκρυτον
         οὐδεὶς φίλων στενάζει.

Str. β'.

I. > ⋮ ‿ ∪ | ∟ | ⌣ ∪ | ‿ ∪ | ‿ ∪ | ‿ ∪ ||
   ㆆ ⋮ ⌣ ∪ | ‿ ∪ | ‿ > | ⌣ ∪ | ∟ | ‿ ∧ ||
   ⌣ ∪ | ‿ ∪ | ‿ ㆆ | ∟ | ⌣ ∪ | ‿ ∪]

II. > ⋮ ‿ > | ‿ > | ∟ | ‿ ∧ ||
    > ⋮ ‿ > | ⌣ ∪ | ‿ ∪ | ∟ || ‿ ㆆ | ⌣ ∪ | ‿ ∪ | ∟ | ‿ ∧] 5

III. > ⋮ ‿ ∪ | ‿ ∪ | ‿ ∪ | ∟ | ‿ ∪ | ‿ ∧ ||
     ∪ ⋮ ‿ ∪ | ‿ ∪ | ⌢ ∪ | ‿ ∪ || ‿ ∪ | ‿ ∪ | ‿ ∪ | ‿ ∧ ||
     ∪ ⋮ ∟ | ‿ ㆆ | ‿ ∪ | ∟ || ⌣ ∪ | ‿ ∪ | ∟ | ‿ ∧ ||
     ∪ ⋮ ‿ ∪ | ∟ | ‿ ∪ | ‿ ∪ | ∟ | ‿ ∧]

I. 6⎫
    6⎬
    6⎭

II. 4⎫
    4⎬
    6=ἐπ.

III. ⎛4⎫
     ⎜4⎭
     ⎜4⎫
     ⎝4⎭
      6

Str. γ'.

∪ ⋮ ‿ ∪ | ‿ ∪ | ‿ ∪ | ‿ ∧ || 4⎫
ㆆ ⋮ ‿ ∪ | ‿ ∪ | ‿ ∪ | ‿ ∧ || 4⎬
∪ ⋮ ∪ ∪ ∪ | ‿ ∪ | ‿ ∪ | ‿ ∧ || 4⎭
∪ ⋮ ∟ | ∟ | ‿ ∪ | ‿ ∪ | ∟ | ‿ ∧]   6=ἐπ.

Epod.

I. ∪ ⋮ ‿ ∪ | ∪ ∪ ∪ | ∪ ∪ ∪ | ∟ || ∪ ∪ ∪ | ‿ ∪ | ∟ | ‿ ∧ ||
   ‿ ∪ | ∟ | ‿ ∪ | ‿ ∧]

II.   ‿ ω | ‿ ω | ‿ ω | ‿ ∪ ||
       ‿ ∪ | ∪ ∪ ∪ | ‿ ∪ | ‿ ∪ ||
       ‿ ∪ | ‿ ∪ | ∪ ∪ ∪ | ‿ ∪ ||
       > ⋮ ‿ ∪ | ‿ ∪ | ∟ | ‿ ∧ ||

I. 4⎫
   4⎬
   4⎭

II. 4⎫
    4⎬
    4⎬ 5
    4⎭

This chorus begins (str. α') with sentences of like form (Glyconics), then becomes more varied by the interchange of sentences of different lengths (str. β'), and finally closes with series of like form (str. γ', epod.).

The first strophe and the beginning of the second are in logaoedic measure. After these come choreic periods, which become more lively toward the close in consequence of the occurrence of the three choreic dactyls. We have already seen, in the *First Stasimon* above, how choreic dactyls were introduced to relieve the otherwise too great repose of choreic series.

VI.

Fourth Stasimon (944-987).

σ. α'.   Ἔτλα καὶ Δανάας οὐράνιον φῶς
ἀλλάξαι δέμας ἐν χαλκοδέτοις αὐλαῖς·
  Κρυπτομένα δ' ἐν τυμβήρει θαλάμῳ κατεζεύχθη·
καίτοι μὲν γενεᾷ τίμιος, ὦ παῖ, παῖ,
5 καὶ Ζηνὸς ταμιεύεσκε γονὰς χρυσορύτους.
ἀλλ' ἁ μοιριδία τις δύνασις δεινά·
  Οὔτ' ἄν νιν ὄλβος οὔτ' Ἄρης, οὐ πύργος, οὐχ ἁλίκτυποι
κελαιναὶ νᾶες ἐκφύγοιεν.

ἀ. α'.   Ζεύχθη δ' ὀξύχολος παῖς ὁ Δρύαντος,
Ἠδωνῶν βασιλεύς, κερτομίοις ὀργαῖς,
  Ἐκ Διονύσου πετρώδει κατάφαρκτος ἐν δεσμῷ.
οὕτω τᾶς μανίας δεινὸν ἀποστάζει
5 ἀνθηρὸν τὸ μένος· κεῖνος ἐπέγνω μανίαις
ψαύων τὸν θεὸν ἐν κερτομίοις γλώσσαις.
  Παύεσκε μὲν γὰρ ἐνθέους γυναῖκας εὔιόν τε πῦρ,
φιλαύλους τ' ἠρέθιζε Μούσας.

σ. β'.   Παρὰ δὲ Κυανέων σπιλάδων διδύμας ἁλὸς
ἀκταὶ Βοσπόριαι ἴν' ὁ Θρῃκῶν ἄξενος
  Σαλμυδησσός, Ἄρης τ' ἀγχίπολις
δισσοῖσι Φινείδαις
5 εἶδεν ἀρατὸν ἕλκος
  Ἀραχθὲν ἐξ ἀγρίας δάμαρτος
ἀλαὸν ἀλαστόροισιν ὀμμάτων κύκλοις
ἄτερθ' ἐγχέων, ὑφ' αἱματηραῖς
χείρεσσι καὶ κερκίδων ἀκμαῖσιν.

ἀ. β'.   Κατὰ δὲ τακόμενοι μέλεοι μελέαν πάθαν
κλαῖον ματρὸς ἔχοντες ἀνύμφευτον γονάν·
  Ἁ δὲ σπέρμα μὲν ἀρχαιογόνων·
ἄντασ' Ἐρεχθειδᾶν,
5 τηλεπόροις ἐν ἄντροις

ANTIGONE VI. (944-987).

Τράφη θυέλλαισιν ἐν πατρῴαις
Βορεὰς ἄμιππος ὀρθόποδος ὑπὲρ πάγου
θεῶν παῖς· ἀλλὰ κἀπ᾽ ἐκείνᾳ
Μοῖραι μακραίωνες ἔσχον, ὦ παῖ.

Str. α'.

I. _ > | ⌣⌣ | ⌣, ‖ ⌣⌣ | ⌣ | _ ∧ ‖
    _ > | ⌣⌣ | ⌣, ‖ ⌣⌣ | _ > | _ ∧ ⟧

II. ⌣⌣ | _ > | _ > ‖ ⌣⌣ | _ ⌣ | _ > | _ ∧ ‖
    _ > | ⌣⌣ | ⌣, ‖ ⌣⌣ | _ > | _ ∧ ‖
    _ > | ⌣⌣ | ⌣ ‖ ⌣⌣ | ⌣ | ⌣⌣ | _ ∧ ‖   5
    _ > | ⌣̇⌣ | ⌣, ‖ ⌣⌣ | _ > | _ ∧ ⟧

III. > ⋮ _ ⌣ | _ ⌣ | _ ⌣ | _, ᷅ ‖ _ ⌣ | _ ⌣ | _ ⌣ | _ ∧ ‖
     ⌣ ⋮ ⌣ | ⌣ | _ ⌣ | _ ⌣ | ⌣ | _ ∧ ⟧

I. ⎛ ₍3₎ ⎞   II. ⎛ 3 ⎞   III. 4⎞
    ⎝ ₍3₎ ⎠   ⎜ 4 ⎟   4⎠
                       ⎜ 3 ⎟
    ⎛ ₍3₎ ⎞   ⎜ 3 ⎟   6 = ἐπ.
    ⎝ ₍3₎ ⎠   ⎜ 3 ⎟
                       ⎜ 4 ⎟
                       ⎜ 3 ⎟
                       ⎝ 3 ⎠

Str. β'.

I. ⌣ ⌣ ⌣̇ | ⌣⌣ | ⌣⌣ | ⌣⌣ | _ ⌣ | _ ∧ ‖
    _ > | ⌣⌣ | ⌣⌣ | _ > | _ ⌣ | _ ∧ ⟧

II. _ ⌣ | ⌣⌣ | ⌣ ‖ ⌣⌣ | _ ∧ ‖
    > ⋮ _ ⌣ | ⌣⌣ | _ ∧ ‖
    ⌣⌣ | _ ⌣ | ⌣ | _ ∧ ⟧

III. ⌣ ⋮ _ ⌣ | ⌣ | _ ⌣ | _ ⌣ | ⌣ | _ ∧ ‖
     ⌣ ⋮ ⌣⌣⌣ | _ ⌣ | _ ⌣ | ⌣̱ ⌣ | _ ⌣ | _ ∧ ‖
     ⌣ ⋮ ⌣ | ⌣ | _ ⌣ | _ ⌣ | ⌣ | _ ∧ ‖
     > ⋮ _ ⌣ | ⌣ | _ ⌣ | _ ⌣ | ⌣ | _ ∧ ⟧

I. 6⎞   II. 3⎞   III. 6⎞
    6⎠   2⎟   6⎟
                    3⎟   6⎟
                    4 = ἐπ.   6⎠

VII.

Hyporchema (1115-1154).

σ. α'.
Πολυώνυμε, Καδμείας νύμφας άγαλμα
καὶ Διὸς βαρυβρεμέτα
γένος, κλυτὰν ὃς ἀμφέπεις
Ἰταλίαν, μέδεις τε
5   παγκοίνοις Ἐλευσινίας
Δῃοῦς ἐν κόλποις, Βακχεῦ, Βακχᾶν
Ὁ ματρόπολιν Θήβαν
ναιετῶν παρ' ὑγρῶν
Ἰσμηνοῦ ῥείθρων, ἀγρίου τ' ἐπὶ σπορᾷ δράκοντος·

ἀ. α'.
Σὲ δ' ὑπὲρ διλόφου πέτρας στέροψ ὄπωπε
λιγνύς, ἔνθα Κωρύκιαι
Νύμφαι στίχουσι Βακχίδες,
Κασταλίας τε νᾶμα.
5   καί σε Νυσαίων ὀρέων
κισσήρεις ὄχθαι χλωρά τ' ἀκτὰ
Πολυστάφυλος πέμπει,
ἀβρότων ἐπέων
Εὐαζόντων, Θηβαίας ἐπισκοποῦντ' ἀγυιάς·

σ. β'.
Τὰν ἐκ πασᾶν τιμᾷς ὑπερτάταν πόλεων
ματρὶ σὺν κεραυνίᾳ·
καὶ νῦν, ὡς βιαίας ἔχεται
πάνδαμος πόλις ἐπὶ νόσου,
5   μολεῖν καθαρσίῳ ποδὶ Παρνασίαν ὑπὲρ κλιτὺν
ἢ στονόεντα πορθμόν.

ἀ. β'.
Ἰὼ πῦρ πνειόντων χοράγ' ἄστρων, νυχίων
φθεγμάτων ἐπίσκοπε,
παῖ Διὸς γένεθλον, προφάνηθ',
ὦναξ σαῖς ἄμα περιπόλοις
5   Θυίαισιν, αἵ σε μαινόμεναι πάννυχοι χορεύουσι
τὸν ταμίαν Ἴακχον.

Str. α'.

I. ω: ⏑⏑ | ‒⏓ | ‒⏓ | ‒⏑ | ⌊ | ‒ ∧ ‖
    ‒ ⏑ | ‒ ⏑ | ⏑⏑ | ‒ ∧ ‖
  ⏓: ‒ ⏑ | ‒ ⏑ | ‒ ⏑ | ‒ ∧ ‖
    ⏑⏑ | ‒ ⏑ | ⌊ | ‒ ∧ ‖
    ‒ ⏓ | ‒ ⏑ | ⏑⏑ | ‒ ∧ ‖
  >: ⌊ | ⌊ | ‒> | ‒> | ⌊ | ‒ ∧ ⟧

II. ⏑: ⏑⏑ | ‒> | ‒ ∧ ‖
    ‒ ⏑ | ⏑⏑ | ‒ ∧ ⟧

III.   ‒> | ‒> | ⏑⏑ | ‒,⏑‖ ‒ ⏑ | ‒ ⏑ | ⌊ | ‒ ∧ ⟧

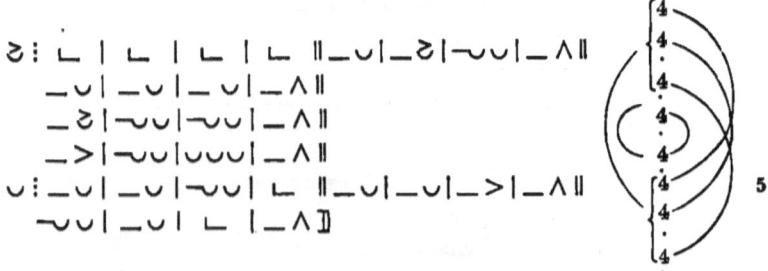

Str. β'.

⏓: ⌊ | ⌊ | ⌊ | ⌊ ‖ ‒ ⏑ | ‒ ⏓ | ⏑⏑ | ‒ ∧ ‖
    ‒ ⏑ | ‒ ⏑ | ‒ ⏑ | ‒ ∧ ‖
    ‒ ⏓ | ⏑⏑ | ⏑⏑ | ‒ ∧ ‖
    ‒> | ⏑⏑ | ⏑⏑⏑ | ‒ ∧ ‖
⏑: ‒ ⏑ | ‒ ⏑ | ⏑⏑ | ⌊ ‖ ‒ ⏑ | ‒ ⏑ | ‒> | ‒ ∧ ‖
    ⏑⏑ | ‒ ⏑ | ⌊ | ‒ ∧ ⟧

The antithetic construction of the period is especially adapted to hyporchemata. In Sophocles the majority of the hypo̓rchemata consist of antithetic periods, which it is not possible to suppose could have come about by mere chance.

In arranging the periods above, compare carefully § 37. In Str. α', Per. I., the exact correspondence of vv. 2 and 5 shows that the period is purely antithetic. In Str. β', v. 6 cannot be regarded a postlude, since the almost exact metrical agreement of vv. 3 and 4 shows their correspondence.

VIII.

The Exodos (1261-1347).

σ. α΄.

    Κ. Ἰώ·
φρενῶν δυσφρόνων ἁμαρτήματα
στερεὰ θανατόεντ'.
ὢ κτανόντας τε καὶ
5   θανόντας βλέποντες ἐμφυλίους.
    Ὤμοι ἐμῶν ἄνολβα βουλευμάτων.
ἰὼ παῖ, νέος νέῳ ξὺν μόρῳ,
αἰαῖ αἰαῖ,
Ἔθανες, ἀπελύθης,
10   ἐμαῖς οὐδὲ σαῖσι δυσβουλίαις.

    Χ. Οἴμ' ὡς ἔοικας ὀψὲ τὴν δίκην ἰδεῖν.

σ. β΄.

    Κ. Οἴμοι,
ἔχω μαθὼν δείλαιος· ἐν δ' ἐμῷ κάρᾳ
    θεὸς τότ' ἄρα τότε μέγα βάρος μ' ἔχων
ἔπαισεν, ἐν δ' ἔσεισεν ἀγρίαις ὁδοῖς,
5   οἴμοι λακπάτητον ἀντρέπων χαράν.
φεῦ φεῦ, ὦ πόνοι βροτῶν δύσπονοι.

    Ε. Ὦ δέσποθ', ὡς ἔχων τε καὶ κεκτημένος,
τὰ μὲν πρὸ χειρῶν τάδε φέρων, τὰ δ' ἐν δόμοις
ἔοικας ἥκειν καὶ τάχ' ὄψεσθαι κακά.
    Κ. τί δ' ἔστιν; ἢ κάκιον αὖ κακῶν ἔτι;
    Ε. γυνὴ τέθνηκε τοῦδε παμμήτωρ νεκροῦ,
δύστηνος, ἄρτι νεοτόμοισι πλήγμασιν.

ἀ. α΄.

    Κ. Ἰώ,
ἰὼ δυσκάθαρτος Ἅιδου λιμήν,
τί μ' ἄρα τί μ' ὀλέκεις;
ὦ κακάγγελτά μοι
5   προπέμψας ἄχη, τίνα θροεῖς λόγον;

ANTIGONE VIII. (1261–1347). 187

Αἰαῖ, ὀλωλότ' ἄνδρ' ἐπεξειργάσω.
τί φής, ὦ παῖ, τίνα λέγεις μοι νέον,
αἰαῖ αἰαῖ,
Σφάγιον ἐπ' ὀλέθρῳ
γυναικεῖον ἀμφικεῖσθαι μόρον; 10

Χ. Ὁρᾶν πάρεστιν· οὐ γὰρ ἐν μυχοῖς ἔτι.

Κ. Οἴμοι,   ἀ. β'.
κακὸν τόδ' ἄλλο δεύτερον βλέπω τάλας.
τίς ἄρα, τίς με πότμος ἔτι περιμένει;
ἔχω μὲν ἐν χείρεσσιν ἀρτίως τέκνον,
τάλας, τὸν δ' ἔναντα προσβλέπω νεκρόν. 5
φεῦ φεῦ μᾶτερ ἀθλία, φεῦ τέκνον.

Str. α'.

I. ⏗ ː ‿
  ᴗ ː ‿‿⏑ | ‿⏑ ‖ ‿‿⏑ | ‿∧ ‖
  ᴗ ː ⏑⏑⏑⏑⏑ | ‿⏘ ‖
  ‿⏑‿ | ‿⏑‿ ‖
  ᴗ ː ‿‿⏑ | ‿⏑ ‖⏝‿⏑ | ‿∧ ⟧   5
II. > ː ⏑⏑‿⏑ | ‿⏑ ‖ ‿‿⏑ | ‿∧ ‖
  ᴗ ː ‿‿⏗ |⏝⏑ ‖ ‿‿⏑ | ‿∧ ⟧
  ‿‿‿‿
III. ᴗ ː ⏑⏑⏑⏑⏑ | ‿∧ ‖
  ᴗ ː ‿‿⏑ | ‿⏑ ‖ ‿‿⏑ | ‿∧ ⟧

I. {do.
    {do.
   (2 ba.
    2 pac.)
    {do.
    {do.   5
II. {do.
    {do.   III. do.
    {do.   do.
    {do.   10

Str. β'.

‿‿
trim.
ᴗ ː ⏝⏝⏑ |⏝⏑ ‖ ⏑⏑⏝⏑ | ‿∧ ‖
trim.
⏗ ː ⌐ | ‿⏑ | ‿⏑ | ‿⏑ | ‿⏑ | ‿∧ ‖
> ː ‿‿⏑ | ‿⏑ ‖ ‿‿⏑ | ‿∧ ⟧

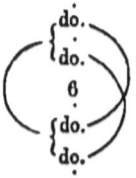

Ε. Πᾶ' ὀξυθήκτῳ βωμία περὶ ξίφει ·
λύει κελαινὰ βλέφαρα, κωκύσασα μὲν
τοῦ πρὶν θανόντος Μεγαρέως κλεινὸν λάχος,
αὖθις δὲ τοῦδε, λοίσθιον δὲ σοὶ κακὰς
πράξεις ἐφυμνήσασα τῷ παιδοκτόνῳ.

σ. γ'.   Κ. Αἰαῖ αἰαῖ,
ἀνέπταν φόβῳ. τί μ' οὐκ ἀνταίαν
ἔπαισέν τις ἀμφιθήκτῳ ξίφει;
Δείλαιος ἐγὼ ἐγώ,
5   δειλαίᾳ δὲ συγκέκραμαι δύᾳ.

Ε. Ὡς αἰτίαν γε τῶνδε κἀκείνων ἔχων
πρὸς τῆς θανούσης τῆσδ' ἐπεσκήπτου μόρων.
Κ. ποίῳ δὲ κἀπελύσατ' ἐν φοναῖς τρόπῳ;
Ε. παίσασ' ὑφ' ἧπαρ αὐτόχειρ αὑτήν, ὅπως
παιδὸς τόδ' ἤσθετ' ὀξυκώκυτον πάθος.

σ. δ'.   Κ. Ὤμοι μοι, τάδ' οὐκ ἐπ' ἄλλον βροτῶν
ἐμᾶς ἁρμόσει ποτ' ἐξ αἰτίας.
ἐγὼ γάρ σ' ἐγὼ ἔκανον, ὦ μέλεος,
ἐγώ, φάμ' ἔτυμον, ἰὼ πρόσπολοι,
5   ἀπάγετέ μ' ὅτι τάχος, ἄγετέ μ' ἐκποδών
τὸν οὐκ ὄντα μᾶλλον ἢ μηδένα.

Χ. Κέρδη παραινεῖς, εἴ τι κέρδος ἐν κακοῖς·
βράχιστα γὰρ κράτιστα τἀν ποσὶν κακά.

ἀ. γ'.   Κ. Ἴτω ἴτω,
φανήτω μόρων ὁ κάλλιστ' ἐμῶν
ἐμοὶ τερμίαν ἄγων ἀμέραν
Ὕπατος· ἴτω ἴτω,
5   ὅπως μηκέτ' ἦμαρ ἄλλ' εἰσίδω.

Χ. Μέλλοντα ταῦτα. τῶν προκειμένων τι χρὴ
πράσσειν. μέλει γὰρ τῶνδ' ὅτοισι χρὴ μέλειν.
Κ. ἀλλ' ὧν ἐρῶμαι, ταῦτα συγκατηυξάμην.
Χ. μή νυν προσεύχου μηδέν· ὡς πεπρωμένης
οὐκ ἔστι θνητοῖς συμφορᾶς ἀπαλλαγή.

ANTIGONE VIII. (1261-1347).   189

K. Ἄγοιτ' ἂν μάταιον ἄνδρ' ἐκποδών,   ἀ. δ'.
ὅς, ὦ παῖ, σέ τ' οὐχ ἑκὼν κατέκανον,
σέ τ' αὖ τάνδ'. ὤμοι μέλεος, οὐδ' ἔχω
πρὸς πότερον πρότερον ἴδω, πᾷ κλιθῶ.
λέχρια τὰν χεροῖν, τὰ δ' ἐπὶ κρατί μοι   5
πότμος δυσκόμιστος εἰσήλατο.

Str. γ'.

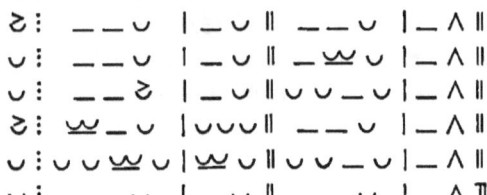

Str. δ'.

Exodos.

Throughout this entire chorus the dochmii are distinguished by the absence of the regular caesura. Where, therefore, the caesura does happen to occur, it has not been marked.

Str. α'.

In consequence of the correspondence of vv. 3 and 4, v. 3 must be regarded a catalectic bacchic dipody. These syllables have not infrequently such value.

Str. β'.

We must not regard v. 5 a dochmius with following choreic tripody:

$$\overset{\circ}{\varsigma} : \_\_\_ \cup | \_, \cup \| \_ \cup | \_ \cup | \_ \wedge \|$$

Such a verse would be altogether unrhythmical. It is equally impossible to suppose it consists of two dochmii, the second of an unheard-of form:

$$\overset{\circ}{\varsigma} : \_\_ \cup | \_ \cup \| \smile \_ \cup | \_ \wedge \|$$

Cf. *Eurhythmie*, § 18, 5. It is simply a melic iambic trimeter, which probably was not sung but recited:

$$\overset{\circ}{\varsigma} | \sqcup | \_ \cup | \_ \cup | \_ \cup | \_ \cup | \_ \wedge \|$$

Str. γ'.

Str. γ' and str. α' close with exactly the same period.

INDEX OF METRICAL AND MUSICAL CHARACTERS.

Note. — The references are to pages.

︶	♪	7; 36.	︶		3.
‒	♩	7; 36.	‒		3.
⌊‑	♩.	36.	>		24; 43.
⌊	♩	36.	_>		41; 43 *bis*.
⊔	♩ ♪	36.	_ᔒ		43; 52.
∧	𝄾	27.	ᔒ		52.
⊼	𝄾	27.	ᔒ ︶ ︶		53.
⊼	𝄾.	27.	♫		23.
⊼	―	27.	♪		44.
. : :	>―	11 *sq*.			
ᗺ	♪♪	23.			
ʢ	♫	23.			
⋮	⋮ ♪	24.			
⌊ ︶	♩. ♪	41.			
︶ ︶ >	♫ ♩	42; 51.			
︵	♫	44; 48.			
︵ ︶	♫ ♩	44.			
ω	♫	49.			

‖ marks the end of a sentence or verse.
𝄂 marks the end of a period.
𝄐 marks the end of a system (sometimes of a period) with a hold.
συ. (σύστημα) always signifies in this book an anapaestic system.
ἐπ. and πρ., see page 134.

In the *text*, a black letter signifies the beginning of a new sentence within a verse.

INDEX TO THE METRES OF HORACE.

METRES.

NOTE.—The reference is to paragraphs. The page is added in parentheses.

I.	Iambic Trimeter	§ 26, 3, III. (84).
II.	Iambic Group	§ 28, 3, I. (94).
III.	First Pythiambic Group	§ 28, 3, II. (94).
IV.	Second Pythiambic Group	§ 28, 3, III. (94).
V.	Alcmanian Group	§ 28, 3, IV. (95).
VI.	First Archilochian Group	§ 28, 4, I. (95).
VII.	Second Archilochian Group	§ 28, 4, II. (95).
VIII.	Lesser Asclepiadean Group	§ 29, 2, I. (97).
IX.	Greater Asclepiadean Group	§ 29, 2, II. (98).
X.	Dactylic Archilochian Group	§ 29, 3, I. (99).
XI.	Greater Sapphic Group	§ 29, 3, II. (100).
XII.	Logaoedic Archilochian Group	§ 29, 3, III. (100).
XIII.	Four-lined Alcmanian Group	§ 29, 3, IV. (101).
XIV.	Interchanging Asclepiadean Group	§ 29, 3, V. (101).
XV.	Contrasted Asclepiadean Group	§ 29, 4, I. (102).
XVI.	Alcaic Group	§ 29, 4, II. (102).
XVII.	Ionic Group	§ 29, 4, III. (103).
XVIII.	Asclepiadean Glyconic Group	§ 29, 5, I. (103).
XIX.	Common Sapphic Group	§ 29, 5, II. (104).
XX.	Four-lined Trochaic Group	*

* Consists of a catalectic trochaic tetrapody and a catalectic iambic hexapody, repeated.

Book.	Ode.	Metre.	Book.	Ode.	Metre.	Book.	Ode.	Metre.
I.	1	VIII.	II.	1	XVI.	III.	18	XIX.
	2	XIX.		2	XIX.		19	XIV.
	3	XIV.		3	XVI.		20	XIX.
	4	XII.		4	XIX.		21	XVI.
	5	XV.		5	XVI.		22	XIX.
	6	XVIII.		6	XIX.		23	XVI.
	7	XIII.		7	XVI.		24	XIV.
	8	XI.		8	XIX.		25	XIV.
	9	XVI.		9	XVI.		26	XVI.
	10	XIX.		10	XIX.		27	XIX.
	11	IX.		11	XVI.		28	XIV.
	12	XIX.		12	XVIII.		29	XVI.
	13	XIV.		13	XVI.		30	VIII.
	14	XV.		14	XVI.			
	15	XVIII.		15	XVI.	IV.	1	XIV.
	16	XVI.		16	XIX.		2	XIX.
	17	XVI.		17	XVI.		3	XIV.
	18	IX.		18	XX.		4	XVI.
	19	XIV.		19	XVI.		5	XVIII.
	20	XIX.		20	XVI.		6	XIX.
	21	XV.					7	X.
	22	XIX.	III.	1	XVI.		8	VIII.
	23	XV.		2	XVI.		9	XVI.
	24	XVIII.		3	XVI.		10	IX.
	25	XIX.		4	XVI.		11	XIX.
	26	XVI.		5	XVI.		12	XVIII.
	27	XVI.		6	XVI.		13	XV.
	28	XIII.		7	XV.		14	XVI.
	29	XVI.		8	XIX.		15	XVI.
	30	XIX.		9	XIV.	Carmen Saeculare		XIX.
	31	XVI.		10	XVIII.	Epod. 1–10		II.
	32	XIX.		11	XIX.		11	VII.
	33	XVIII.		12	XVII.		12	V.
	34	XVI.		13	XV.		13	VI.
	35	XVI.		14	XIX.		14	III.
	36	XIV.		15	XIV.		15	III.
	37	XVI.		16	XVIII.		16	IV.
	38	XIX.		17	XVI.		17	I.

GENERAL INDEX.

NOTE. — The references are to pages. The letters *sq.* or *sqq.*, placed after the number of a page, show that the subject referred to extends into the following page or pages. The important word is in black letter, and is often represented in the body of the reference by a dash (—). The heavy-faced numeral marks the more important reference.

Acatalectic verse, 27.
Accent, basis of English poetry, 10; not to be confounded with quantity, 11; in late Greek coincides with ictus, 14; not affected by quantity of final syllable, 18.
Accents, not marks of protraction or sharpening of vowels, 4; nor of quantity, 11; nor of intonation, 13; but of pitch, 16; derivation of name of, 16; no conflict between, and quantity or ictus, 16.
Accentuation, 15 sqq.; not to be confounded with intonation, 18.
Acute accent, 16.
Adonius, 70.
Agreement, metrical, of Corresponding Members, 144 sqq.
Alcaic group, 102 sq.
Alcaicum dodecasyllabum and hendecasyllabum, 72.
Alcaicus enneasyllabus and decasyllabus, 71.
Alcmanian group, 95; four-lined, 101.
Amphidochmius, 78.
Amphimacer, 27.
Anacreontics, 107.
Anacrusis, 24 sq.
ἀνάκλασις, 74.
'Ανακρεόντειον ὀκτωσύλλαβον, 70.
Anapaest, 26 and 28; as used in march melodies, 113 sqq.

Anapaestic tetrameter, 88 and 114 sq.
ἀντεπίρρημα, 123.
Antistrophe, 120 and 123.
Antithetic period, 126 sq.; palinodic
— period, 128 sqq.; verse-pause in
— period, 139 sq.; verse-pause in palinodic — period, 140 sq.
ἀντῳδή, 123.
Archilochian groups, 95 sq.; dactylic
— group, 99 sq.; logaoedic — group, 100 sq.
'**Αριστοφάνειον**, 70.
Arsis (ἄρσις), 22.
Asclepiadean group, lesser, 97 sq.; greater, 98 sq.; verse, lesser, 97 sq.; greater, 98 sq.; interchanging — group, 101 sq.; contrasted — group, 102; — Glyconic group, 103 sq.
Asynartete verses, 60 sq.
Attica correptio, 8.

Bacchius, 27 and 34; 69; interchange of, with paeon, 75 sq.
βαρεῖα, προσῳδία, 16.
Basis, 90 sqq.
Break, defined, 60.

C, pronunciation of, in Latin, 10.
Caesura, 59.
Catalectic verse, 27.
Catalexis, 27.
Choliambus, 37 sq. and 86.

GENERAL INDEX.

Choree, 26 and 30 ; recitative, 50 sq.; inverted, 92 sq.
Choreic sentences, 68 sq.
Choriambic sentences, 69.
Choriambus, 26 and 31 ; admitted into ionic verse, 74.
Choric type, 116 sqq.; strophes, 120 sqq.; chief laws of, 119 sq.
Chorus, highly developed, 119 ; different names of, 122 sq.
Circumflex accent, 16 ; only on contracted syllables, 17 ; not mark of protraction, 18.
Consonants, apparent doubling of, in Homer, 9.
Contraction, 22 sqq.
Correspondence, metrical, 52 sqq.
Cratineum, metrum, 87.
Cretic, 27.
Cyclic dactyl, 44; in the trimeter, 51; — proceleusmatic, 49.

Dactyl, 26 and 28 ; light and heavy, 10 sq. and 26 ; cyclic, 44 ; choreic, 49 sq.
Dactylic sentences, 67 ; hexameter, 83 sq.
Dance melodies wherein different from march melodies, 120.
Declamation, 81 ; facts which show the odes of Horace intended for, 105.
Diaeresis, 58 sq.
Dichoree, 26 and 32; interchange with ionic, 74.
Dichoreic sentences, 69.
Diphthongs, regarded as protracted vowels, 4.
Dipody, 63.
Distichon, 93 sq.
Division, of measures, 25.
Dochmius, 76 sqq.
Doric melodies, 41 sqq.; sentences, 67 sq.

Elegiac verse, 39 sq.; 93.
Elision, in Latin poetry, 5 sq.
ἐμβατήριον, 114.

ἡμίαμβος, 68.
Encomiologicum, 67.
ἐνόπλιος, 116.
ἐπίρρημα, 123.
ἐπίτριτος δεύτερος, 41 ; 43.
Epode (ἡ ἐπῳδός), 120 sq.
Epodes (οἱ ἐπῳδοί), 93 sqq.
ἐπῳδικόν, 118 ; 134 sqq.
ἡρῷον ηὐξημένον, 86.
Eupolideum, metrum, 87.
Eurhythmy, 124 sqq.
ἑξάμετρον περιττοσυλλαβές, 86.
Exodos, anapaests in the, of Attic tragedy, 115 ; 122.
Extension, of measures, 25.

Falling sentences or verses, 37.
Four-lined Groups, 96 sqq.
Free Metrical Forms, 89 sqq.
French, misuse of accents of, 18.

Galliambic, 88 sq.
Glyconics, 70.
Grave accent, 16.
Greek, rich in short syllables, 7 ; pronounced rapidly, 8 sqq.
Group, distinguished from system, 106.

Halting iambi, 37.
Hemiambics, 107.
Hexameter, contraction in, 23.
Hexapody, 64 sq.
Hiatus, where allowed, 58.
Hyporchema, 122 ; 132 sq.

Iambelegus, 68.
Iambic trimeter, why so called, 32 ; 84 sqq.; group, 94.
Iambus, identity of with trochee, 25 ; equal to choree with anacrusis, 26 and 30.
Ictus, 11 sqq.; in prose, 13 sq.; on first part of measure, 20 ; secondary, 23 ; doctrine of belongs to rhythmic, 55.
Interchange of Measures, 73 sqq.
Interlude, 118.

Intonation, 11 sqq.; of measures, 25; of sentences, 61 sq.
Inverted dochmius, 78; choree, 92 sq.
Ionic, 26 and 31; interchange of with dichoree, 74; forms of, 74.
Ionic sentences, 69; groups, 103.
Ionicus anaclomenus, 75.
Irrational syllable, 24; choree, 43 sq.; — measures where allowed in recitative verse, 50; — choree resolved in comedy, 51; correspondence of — and rational syllables in arsis, 52 sq.

κατάληξις, 27.
κομμάτιον, 122.
κομμοί, 122.
κορυφαῖος, 123.
κῶλον, 55 sqq.

Λίνος, 19; 117.
Logaoedic sentences, 70 sqq.
Logaoedics, 43 sqq.; forms of, 44; proofs of correctness of Schmidt's theory of, 45 sqq.
Lyric type, 89 sqq.; systems, 105 sqq.

μακρόν, 115; 122.
March type, characteristics of, 113; different — melodies, 114 sqq.; — melodies wherein different from dance melodies, 120.
Measures, defined, 20; equal, unequal, and quinquepartite, 20 and 26 sq.; beginning of, has an ictus, 20 and 22; preliminary statements concerning, 22 sqq.; fundamental forms of, 25 sqq.; shortened final, 27 sq.; examples of, 28 sqq.; final remarks concerning forms of, 54; rhythmical value of, 55; interchange of, 73 sqq.; forms of ionic, 74.
Mesode, 121.
Mesodic period, 127 sq.; palinodic — period, 133 sq.; verse-pause in — period, 141 sqq.; verse-pause in palinodic — period, 143.
μεσῳδικόν, 113.

Metric, defined, 3; 19 sqq.; 55.
Metrical correspondence, 52 sqq.; agreement of corresponding members, 144 sqq.
Molossus, 26 and 33.
Monody, 81; 122.
Mora, 65.
Music, origin of the forms of, 19 sqq.; instrumental, 21; limitations of vocal, 21; development of, 80 sqq.

Notes of Greek vocal music, 36; use of the longer, 37 sqq.; sixteenth, 49 sq.

ᾠδή, 123.
ὀξεῖα, προσῳδία, 16.

Paeon, 27 and 33; interchange of with bacchius, 75.
Paeonic verse, final measure of, 40; sentences, 69; dochmius, 78.
Palinodic period, 125; repeated — period, 126; — antithetic period, 128 sqq.; — mesodic period, 133 sq.; verse-pause in — period, 138; verse-pause in repeated — period, 138 sq.; verse-pause in — antithetic period, 140 sq.; verse-pause in — mesodic period, 143.
Parabasis, 122.
Parodos, anapaests in the, of Attic tragedy, 115; 122.
Paroemiac, 38 sq.; 114.
Pauses, marks of, 27; never in the middle of a verse, 40; position of, 136 sqq.
Pedes, 20.
Pentameter, elegiac so-called, 93.
Pentapody, 64.
Period, 79; according to grouping, 124 sqq.; last group in repeated — never incomplete, 139.
Periodology, 79.
περισπωμένη, προσῳδία, 16.
Phalaeceum hendecasyllabum, 72.
Pherecratean, first and second, 70.

Phonology, 3 sqq.
πνῖγος, 115 ; 122.
πόδες, 20.
Poetry, origin of the forms of, 19 sqq.; development of, 80 sqq.; genesis of types of, 82.
Position, rules for, 8.
Postlude, 118 ; 134 sqq.; pauses before, 143 sq.
Πραξίλλειον, μέτρον, 71.
Prelude, 118 ; 134 sqq.; pauses after, 143 sq.
Priapeus, first, 87 ; second and third, 88.
Prolongation of long syllables, 34 sqq.; in ionics and dochmii, 40.
Pronunciation, of the vowels, 4 ; of the elided vowels and syllables of Latin poetry, 5 sq.
Proöde, 121.
προῳδικόν, 118 ; 134 sqq.
προσοδιακός, 116.
προσῳδίαι, Greek equivalent of Latin *accentus*, 16.
Prosody, 18.
Protraction of vowels, 3 sqq.
Pyrrhic, 91 sq.
Pythiambic group, first and second, 94.

Quantity, defined, 7 ; marks of, 7 ; independent of vowel-articulation, 7 sq.; rules of, 8 ; relative, of long and short syllables, 10.

Recitative poetry, 80 ; type, 83 sqq.; characteristics of, 83.
Resolution, 22 sqq.
Rhythm, 3.
Rhythmic, defined, 3 ; 55 sqq.
Rhythmical sentence, 55 sqq.; period, 79.

Sapphic group, greater, 100 ; common — group, 104.
Sapphicum hendecasyllabum, 72.
Scazon, tetrameter, 86 ; trimeter, 86.

Sentence, rhythmical, 55 sqq.; grammatical defined, 56 sq.; rhythmical defined, 57 ; close of, 57 sqq.; intonation of, 61 sq.; division of, 61 ; ictuses of, 61 sq.; length of, 63 sqq.; rules for length of, 65 sq.; most frequent varieties of, 67 sqq.; highest rhythmical unit in lyric system, 106.
Sharpening of vowels, 3 sqq.
Sotadeum, 88.
Spondaic sentences, 68.
Spondees, 26 and 29.
Stasima, 122.
Stichic period, 124 ; repeated — period, 124 sq.; verse-pause in — period, 137 ; verse-pause in repeated — period, 138.
Strophe, 52 ; choric, 120 sqq.; in encomiastic poetry, 120 sq.; 123.
Syllaba anceps, 58.
Syllables, long and short, 7 ; natura, positione longae, 8 ; relative value of long and short, 10 ; mark of irrational, 24 ; prolongation of long, 34 sqq.; laws for determining value of long, 36 sq.; short as long arsis, 42 sq.; "half-shorts," 49.
Syncope, 35 ; 37 sqq.
Synizesis as proof of rapid pronunciation in Greek, 9.
Systems, lyric, 105 sqq.

T, pronunciation of in Latin, 10.
Tetrapody, 64.
Thesis (θέσις), 22 ; primary and secondary in paeons and choriambi, 25.
Τιμοκρεόντειον, 75.
Τονή, 34 sqq.
Tone, duration, strength, and elevation of, 11 ; five to be distinguished, 15 sqq.; names of in Greek, 16.
Tribrach, 26 ; in comedy, 51.
Tripody, 64.
Trochaic tetrameter, why so called, 32 ; 84.
τροχαῖος δίσημος, 44, 48.
Trochee, identity of with iambus, 25 ;

equal to choree without anacrusis, 26 and 30; "two-timed" trochee, 48.
Type, recitative, 83 sqq.; lyric, 89 sqq.; march, 113 sqq.; choric, 116 sqq.
Typology, 80 sqq.

ὑπορχήματα, 122; 132 sq.

Verse, defined, 58; asynartete, 60 sq.; different from sentence, 63; recitative, 83 sqq.
Vowel-articulation, 3 sqq.
Vowels, protracted, 3; sharp, 3; proper pronunciation of, 3 sqq.; doubtful, 5.

THE END.

www.ingramcontent.com/pod-product-compliance
Lightning Source LLC
Chambersburg PA
CBHW020907230426
43666CB00008B/1349